# McIlroys & Their Kin

# McIlroys & Their Kin

## McElroy, Lewis, Hyde, Hooker, McLean

James Roland McIlroy

iUniverse, Inc.
New York  Lincoln  Shanghai

## McIlroys & Their Kin
### McElroy, Lewis, Hyde, Hooker, McLean

iUniverse books may be ordered through booksellers or by contacting:

iUniverse
2021 Pine Lake Road, Suite 100
Lincoln, NE 68512
www.iuniverse.com
1-800-Authors (1-800-288-4677)

ISBN: 978-0-595-46736-5 (pbk)
ISBN: 978-0-595-91031-1 (ebk)

Printed in the United States of America

# Some Helpful Contributors[*]

Mrs. William Carlton Apperson

Sarah Birge

Helen Bly

Marie Burrows

Mary Chesney

Rachel Chesney

Pat Crouse

Betty Joann McIlroy Erickson

Blanch Everett

W.L. Farmer

Marjerie Fischer

Vivian Boyd Goodman

Herma Lewis Hawley

Jodie Sneed Helsley

Alma Taylor Jackson

Alene Jordan

Maxine Kindle

R.E. Lang

Byron R. Lewis

Nancy Jane McIlroy Maurey

Ann McElroy

Bert McElroy

Billy Cowan McElroy

Charles W. McElroy

Gaither W. McElroy

Mrs. James Marguerite McElroy

Paul McElroy

Sylvan McElroy Jr.

Mrs. W.J. McElroy

Charles R. McIlroy

Doug McIlroy

J. Craig McIlroy

James A. McIlroy

Raymond McIlroy

C.E. McLain

Mrs. W. W. McMullen

Ruth Millon

Galene Morris

Vera Belle Neal

Neena A. Newman

Georgia Stewart

Sandra Taylor

Clinton Wagner

Ruth Wiggins

Diana Yancey

---

[*] Some of the above I have had no communication with, but they all helped in one way or another. I had several hundred letters of correspondence and am sure I have left off a few of those that helped. I couldn't use all of the information, and I apologize to anyone that was overlooked. I really appreciate all of the help.

# Some Helpful Sources

<u>Bishop Family</u> (unpublished)

County publications

<u>Goodspeed's Biographies</u> published in several states

<u>McIlroys</u> by Jessie McIlroy Smith

<u>The Irvines and Their Kin</u> by L. Boyd

The McElroy Family Newsletter Edited and Published by Kenneth Graves

<u>The Scotch-Irish McElroys in America</u> by Reverend John M. McElroy

United States Census

# Table of Contents

# Introduction

Most of this research was done about twenty-five years ago, and I have not brought much of it up to date. The census is out now for 1930 and this can connect with the information I have found. This account of the McIlroys is not complete—I have worked on this for many years and have almost run out of time, so I am putting it in some kind of order while I can. For sake of time, I am not putting in the documentation, but I think that this is ninety-five percent correct. If I do make any assumption, I will note that.

As a boy, I listened to my grandmother talk about Randolph County, Arkansas and the kin she and her family left there. I was always interested in history, so it was natural for me to seek more.

About twenty-five years ago, I was at a standstill on my research, so with the help of my family, we wrote eight thousand letters to all of the McIlroys that we could find with a good address. The results were great I wish I had time and space to include all of the information we gathered. Most of what I have gotten comes from old family bibles, U.S. Censuses, history of counties, cemeteries, and from interviews with older kin. You would be surprised at what I have gathered by word of mouth. I have talked to people that were born one hundred and forty years ago, and they told me what their grandparents told them.

One reason that I have taken so long in writing this is that I wanted to know what these people looked like and what they did and to try to make more than just a name. You will note that at the bottom of some of the pages, I will add interesting information about the individual mentioned.

Another reason I have taken so long is that I have been disappointed in my research. I have not been able to find and document some of the people that I consider key to this book. I have tried to find the McIlroys not included in Reverend John McIlroy's book written over a hundred years ago. I have not been able to find Daniel McIlroy's parents or John and Archibald's children and have had trouble proving the parents of John McIlroy of Caldwell County.

This year (2007), I realized that I had information that was going to disappear if I did not record it. This story is not complete, and some mistakes have been made. After many years of travel, research, and sending out letters, this is the best I can do. I apologize to the ones who sent me information that I cannot use. I have a file of about eighteen thousand pages of McIlroy information and will give it the Mormon library if they would like to have it.

Because of my limited knowledge, I have tried to keep this story of the McIlroy's descendants to the ones that came from County Down or nearby counties in Ulster, particularly the ones not covered by Reverend John McIlroy in his book written about 1900.

We can not assume that there were no McIlroys in America before 1700. I have records that show that in 1685, Gilbert McIlroy and William McIlroy were banned and transported from England to the American plantations. They had fought with the Argyles and would not pledge allegiance to England.

Also, there was a John Mackleroy in Maryland. He had at least three boys: John Jr. born in 1715, William on December 23, 1717, and Archibald in 1719. William had at least seven children; many of the Muckleroys and McLeroys of the south came from this branch. In Bucks County, Pennsylvania, there were McIlroys by 1717. This group was headed by William; they came from County Down and were related to most of the McIlroys that came in 1729 and the 1730s.

I hope you enjoy this information that I have compiled over many years. Good luck to all of the McIlroy genealogists who I hope will continue this work.

James Roland McIlroy

# Reminiscence of Early Farm Lifestyle

Most of the population in the United States during the early years of settlement lived in rural areas. Their lifestyle changed very little over two hundred years. My generation can relate to the lifestyle of my ancestors better than those who were born later.

My grandparents still lived about like their families had for generations. In the late 1920s, they had few modern conveniences. In fact, my grandmother Amanda Lewis McIlroy still cooked on a wood stove. There was no electricity and the family used coal oil lamps. She kept her butter and milk in deep wells (she would have kept them in a spring like she did in Arkansas, but there were no springs in Hill County, Texas). They went to bed soon after dark and rose at daylight.

Very little money was needed they milked their cows, churned their butter, kept chickens, and raised a large garden from which they canned food for winter. They had a smokehouse where they kept their pork, sausage, ham, and bacon. They ate very little beef because it would not keep. When they needed salt or flour, they would take the surplus of butter and eggs to town and swap for them. What money they had went for clothes and shoes or to pay taxes. A lot of clothes were made at home; printed flour sacks made many of their garments. Most all homes had a quilt on frames in the process of being quilted.

Hog killing was a big event. When the weather turned cool, the kin would help each other. After killing the hogs, they would hang them on a block and tackle and lower them into a pot of boiling water. They would then take them out and scrape their hair off. They quartered them for ham and bacon, and the remaining pieces were hung in sacks to make sausage. There was no waste; even the liver, feet, brains, and tail were used. They fattened the hogs to a large weight because at that time, lard was needed to cook with. Soap was also made in the same large pot by heating some of the fat and adding ashes and lye. It was a pretty harsh soap, but that was what they used for wash day, which was Monday. Before going to the fields, men would build a fire under the big kettle and heat the water. The women of the house would then throw the clothes and soap in with the boiling water. They rinsed the clothes in wash tubs and then scrubbed them on wash boards. When clean, the clothes were hung on a clothesline or fence to dry. The same wash tubs were also used for bathing.

Some of the chores that children did after school were bringing in the firewood, gathering eggs, feeding the hogs, and milking the cows. Children were expected to go to the fields to work by the time they were five or six years old. Picking cotton, chopping, hoeing, gathering corn, and shucking grain were part of the work. Schools started late and turned out during the rush of farm work. Most of the children raised on the farm walked to school, no matter how far or how bad the weather was. The schools usually had several grades to each room.

Unless the farmer had slaves or several boys or was able to hire help, he could not farm many acres with single planters and cultivators, not much ground could be covered. Their farm equipment was pulled by mules or horses and it wasn't until the early 1930s that tractors became available. Samuel McIlroy in 1813 could have had all the good flat land in east Randolph County that he wanted, but he didn't think that he had the plows or man-power to farm this type of land. They were also looking for springs for water and trees to cut for log houses and split rail fences.

Reflecting on this way of life makes us look back on our ancestors with respect. They worked hard to enable us to have the lives we have today.

# The McIlroy Name & Early History

Listed in the 1790 Federal Census were fifty-six McIlroys (of various spellings) as head of household. Twenty-five of them were in Pennsylvania, nineteen in North Carolina and South Carolina, and only one in Virginia. There probably were another thirty of forty not found due to remote locations and the fact that many dodged the taker (thinking it could put them on tax rolls). George Washington was dismayed at this 1790 Census. He said that he personally knew more people in Westmoreland County, Virginia than the amount that appeared on the census.

About one out of forty thousand people in the United States are named McIlroy. Never a common name, it was first used in Ireland and when some of them migrated to Scotland about the year one thousand, it became used by both. The ones in Ireland (with the exception of Northern Ireland) became Catholics; the ones in Scotland were and are today mostly Protestants. No matter the spelling *McGilvre, McElroy, McGillroy, McKilroy, McIlroy, McCulroy, McHilroy, McElroy, McRoy, McLcroy, McLroy, Muckleroy* they all have a common background and ancestry. The most common spelling in the United States is McElroy while in Scotland and Northern Ireland McIlroy is widely used. Those that are Irish usually use the spelling McElroy. After much research, I found about nine thousand families in the United States—there are eight thousand McElroys, four hundred McIlroys, and a remaining six hundred of various spellings.

This name of many spellings is said to have been of ancient Celtic origin. About the year one thousand, part of this group removed from Ireland to the Highlands of Scotland. Never large enough in numbers to become a separate clan, their group affiliated with the clan McGillivray. Some think they were in fact of the same stock. On one side of the River Ness they became under the protection of the McGillivray; on the other side they affiliated with the clan Grant.

For hundreds of years this group settled in the Highlands—they merged into this group and soon became very different from the group that remained in Ireland. Their language was Gaelic and some still use the language today.

In time this locality in the Highlands became overpopulated and the McIlroys began to move to the Lowlands of Scotland. This group became English—speaking and soon became Presbyterian. With the Presbyterian teaching that encouraged education and individual rights, they were not happy with the Church of England. A lot of the Lowland McIlroys lived in or near Slago (Lanark County) and it was this group that welcomed the chance to move on to something that promised a better life.

Soon after 1600, the chance to migrate did happen. England confiscated three million eight hundred thousand acres of land in Western Ireland. This land was given to the followers of King James. Most of this was given to the English followers in lots of one thousand acres or more and these became private plantations. To work these plantations, large numbers of Scots moved to Northern Ireland and became renters or long-term leasers. At first, the rents were set low to attract renters, but as the thrifty Scots improved their positions, the landlord increased the rents.

It only took a generation or so for this group to become unhappy. They could not vote, register their marriages, or participate in any way in community life as long as they did not belong to the Church of England, though all were required to pay tithes to the Church of England. This dissatisfaction caused this group of Scots-Irish to migrate to America almost in mass.

# The Story of John Lewis

An interesting example of the problems in Ulster was the case of John Lewis. This story has been told in many ways but the following seems correct. John Lewis was closely connected by marriage and otherwise to the early Scotch settlers in County Down. John Lewis's and Ephram McDowell's mothers were sisters—their last name was Calhoun. John's mother's sister was married to a McDowell, and James McIlroy's mother was a McDowell. In fact, all of the early group that came around 1730 were related.

As Scotsmen tended to do, those in Northern Ireland seemed to clan together and have a leader and marry into this group. John Lewis appeared to be the leader of a collection of Ulster men that included the McDowells, McIlroys, Mitchells, Irvins, McCues, and several others. It seems that they had a good lease on a plantation in County Down, but the lease holder died and his son had to take over. He was very hard to get along with, demanding more rents and other considerations. One day he came to the home of John Lewis and demanded that they leave. He shot several shots and killed John's younger brother and wounded John's wife Margaret Lynn Lewis.

John Lewis then picked up his scythe and cut the man's head off, or some say that he shot him. The kin and neighbors had no say in government matters, so they knew that they had to get John out of the county fast. The rest of the group realized that they needed to move also and preparations were soon made. This incident may have accelerated the migration to America by several years.

To continue the story of John Lewis after fleeing Ireland as a fugitive, he arrived in Portugal where he had a brother. The family thought his best chance for safety was to move to America. This was arranged and he received a conditional pardon providing that he move west to where no white man lived. He arrived in America a few months before his wife Margaret and three sons Thomas, Samuel, and Andrew arrived. Leaving his family in Pennsylvania, he went to Williamsburg (the seat of government in Virginia). Soon after, he moved over the Blue Ridge Mountains to a valley between the Blue Ridge and Alleghenies near where the present city of Staunton, Virginia sits. This location was on a stream which still bears his name. The valley land was very fertile and John Lewis built a fort and was very happy in that location. After his family joined him, they did not have much trouble with the Indians for several years. In time, a pardon was granted to John and also a large portion of land.

John Lewis became successful and some of his boys became leaders. One of his boys, Andrew, became a major in the local militia in a position equal to George Washington and when the time came to elect a leader to head the Revolutionary Army, he was one of those considered.

John's cousin, James McDowell, had planted corn and made a crop near John by 1737. By this time, many of the kin began to move to this Virginia location. Ephram and John McDowell, James and Mary Greenlee, plus a few more had almost reached Fort Lewis, which John Lewis had built. When a stranger came to the camp and introduced himself as Benjamin Burden, he asked if he could spend the night with them. That night he told them that he had been granted a patent for five hundred thousand acres of land, as long as the land did not interfere with other grants and at least one hundred families settled on it within ten years). The only problem was that he could not locate this acreage. John McDowell, who was an educated man and skillful surveyor, agreed to locate this land and receive one thousand acres of it in pay. This was done and many more kin moved down to this location, which is near the present city of Lexington. Among this group were some of the McClungs, McCues, McCowens, McIlroys, McKees, McCampbells, Stewarts, Paxtons, Lyles, Mitchels, Irvines, Caldwells, Calhouns, and Alexanders. In a few years, the Pattons and Prestons, Woods and Greenlee families were there. This location became known as the Burden Grant or Beverly Manor.

The John Irvine and James McLroy families did not follow their kin quickly. They waited in Cumberland County, Pennsylvania probably another fifteen years before moving to this area of Prince Edward County, Virginia. In the first group that moved down early, there was an Alexander McIlroy and wife Agnes. I have never been able to find anything about them except for several land transactions and a copy of a will naming their daughter Rachel. There also was a document witnessed in Beverly Manor by Daniel McIlroy on a property sale by Mary Greenlee. It is possible that this Daniel could have been a brother of the above Alexander.

After these two locations became quite a formidable colony, a war with the Indians broke out. It was fought with great necessity by the whites, and ferocity, cunning, and barbarity on the part of the Indians. John Lewis was quite old by this time, but his four sons, who were now grown up, were well qualified to fill his place and lead the battle to protect their homes and families. I won't go into the details of the war, during which scarcely a settlement was exempt from monthly attacks of the Indians, and during which Charles Lewis, the youngest son of John, is said never to have spent one month at a time out of active service. Charles was the hero of many of the battles, and there are few families among the locations where the name and deeds of Charles Lewis are not familiar. On one occasion, Charles was captured by the Indians while on a hunting excursion, but after he had traveled some two hundred miles barefoot, he managed to escape.

During this war, an attack was made upon the settlement of Fort Lewis at a time when the whole force of the settlement was out on active duty. So great was the surprise that many of the women and children were captured in sight of the fort, though most of them escaped and found hiding places in the woods. The fort was occupied by the elderly John Lewis, his wife, and two young men who were so afraid that they hardly moved from their seats on the ground floor of the fort. John Lewis, however, opened a port-hole where he stationed himself and fired at the savages while Margaret reloaded their guns. In this manner he was able to protect the fort for six hours, during which he killed more than a score of Indians before he was relieved by the rest of his party.

Thomas Lewis, the eldest son of John Lewis and Margaret Lynn, had a defect of vision that affected his ability to shoot and caused him to be less effective during the Indian wars than his brethren. He was, however, a man of learning and sound judgment, and represented the county of Augusta for many years in the House of Burgesses; was a member of the convention that ratified the Constitution of the United States, helped formed the constitution of Virginia, and afterwards sat for the precinct of Rockingham in the House of Delegates of Virginia. In 1765, he was in the House of Burgesses and voted for Patrick Henry's celebrated resolutions. Thomas Lewis had four sons actively participating in the war of the revolution; the youngest, Thomas, bore an ensign's commission when he was only fourteen years of age.

Andrew, the second son of John Lewis and Margaret Lynn, is the General Lewis who surrendered at the battle of Point Pleasant.

William, the third son, fought in the border war and was an officer in the Revolutionary army, in which one his sons was killed and another maimed. When the British force under Tarleton drove the legislature from Charlottesville to Staunton, volunteers were called for to prevent the passage of the British through the mountains at Rockfish Gap. The older sons of William Lewis, who then were at the old fort, were absent with the northern army. Three sons, however, were at home, whose ages were 17, 15, and 13 years. William Lewis was confined to his room by his wounds but his wife called upon their sons to go fight the English.

Charles Lewis, the youngest of the sons of John Lewis and Margaret Lynn, was the head of his regiment when leading on the attack at Point Pleasant. Charles was the most capable of all the leaders of the border warfare, and was as much beloved for his bravery as he was admired for his military talents.[*]

---

[*]   John Lewis was the son of Andrew Lewis and Mary Calhoun and was born in Donegal County, Ireland in 1687. He died at the age of eighty-four. He was a brave man, true patriot, and friend of liberty throughout the world.

# The Story of Daniel McIlroy & Kin from County Down, Ireland

Daniel McIlroy was Scotch-Irish and most of the group that I researched was of the same persuasion. That means they were Scotsmen born in Northern Ireland. The British land owners in Ireland in the 1600s had became dissatisfied with the Irish tenant farmers and replaced them with Scotsmen. These men were hard workers and thrifty and they soon became successful. Most of the land they worked was in Ulster or what is now Northern Ireland.

By tradition, a lot of the McIlroys settled in County Down and other nearby counties. Some think that many of the Scots-Irish that came to America between 1700 and 1800 came from this County Down group. I found in research that in fact there were two groups of McIlroys in County Down. One was from the original settlement of McIlroys from the Highlands near Inverness. Charles McIlroy was a soldier stationed at Carrikfergus Castle who was sent to Ulster in the wars of 1641. There was a great battle fought near Larne on a hill called Shinier-Roe. General Monroe, who was in charge of the British, was slain, but Charles distinguished himself and was part of the party who chased Phelin Roe O'Neill off the battlefield. He was awarded with some fine land near Bally Claire. Some of his line still lives there today. One of his descendants was William McIlroy. He also was a soldier with five medals and was the first man to step foot on the heights of Alma. Charles McIlroy had fought bravely for England and was rewarded a large plantation. Most of this group did not migrate to America.

The McIlroy group was not large enough for a clan, and they affiliated with the Grants on one side of the River Ness and with the McGillivrays on the other side. This Highland group had been awarded land for bravery while fighting with the British army. The other, a group from Lanark County (Glasgow) came to Northern Ireland as tenant farmers. Due to the lack of tillable land in the Highlands and overpopulation, they had moved many years before this to the Lowlands (near Glasgow).

As the British land owners became greedier on rents and the government would not allow the group's marriages to be recorded unless they belonged to the Church of England, dissatisfaction rose among their group of Scotsmen and they began to migrate to the United States almost in mass.

The first group of McIlroys that I have record of came soon after 1715 and settled in Bucks County, Pennsylvania. Records prove that in 1729 the McIlroys and their kin (Campbells, Irvins, McDowells, Lewises, Mitchells, and others) came to Bucks County, stayed awhile, moved west, and a generation later moved further south. Others came soon after this date and a large percentage settled at first in Pennsylvania because William Penn of Pennsylvania was not hard on their being Presbyterian.

Daniel McIlroy was probably born in the United States about 1752 to parents not proven. Hammet McIlroy, his grandson, said that Daniel was born in Culpepper County, Virginia and that he fought in the Revolutionary War with the Marylanders and was captured in the battle of Long Island.

Another grandson, who was well-acquainted with his grandfather, said that he came to America as a boy. This has been a great problem in my research. In fact, this his caused years of delay in this project. Due to my age, I am going to make this statement. I am not sure who Daniel McIlroy's parents were or where he was born. I have a strong feeling that he was related to the McIlroys that moved down the Valley to North Carolina and Kentucky. Samuel McIlroy, the second son of Daniel, moved to Caldwell County, Kentucky about 1806 and bought a small farm next to John McIlroy. A few years later, Samuel McIlroy married Elizabeth McLain and Isaiah McIlroy, son of the above John, married Amy Sullivant in a double wedding. These were the first marriages recorded in western Kentucky in 1808. This is probably more than a coincidence—it seems as if they were surely related.

Soon after a prisoner exchange, Daniel married Rebecca Pyott (daughter of John Pyott) and lived in northern Virginia near Maryland. He lived for a long time in Chester and near Washington City (now Washington D.C.). Much later, with his younger son Daniel Jr. and his daughters, he moved to Ohio where the government was giving land grants. This place was Ross County and it was also the place that he died. Soon after Daniel's death, his son Daniel Jr. and his daughters moved to Green County, Ohio near Cedarville, Ohio. I will follow with his descendants and with some of the families they married into.

Of his three sons Thomas, Samuel, and Daniel Jr., I know little of Thomas it is thought that he moved to Kentucky at an early time. He was born July 13, 1779 and died May 21, 1813. He never married.

Samuel, about the time his father moved to Ohio, moved south to North Carolina where he had kin. Then about 1804, he moved to Kentucky (Caldwell County) where other McIlroys lived. After his marriage to Elizabeth McLean, daughter of Alexander Jr. and Anna Haas, they moved to what is now Madison County, Missouri (then in the Louisiana Territory) where they lived only a short time before moving to what is now Randolph County, Arkansas. During this time, he went back to Kentucky and joined the army in War of 1812.

The family was looking for a place with springs for water, some bottom land, and trees for housing. Samuel was one of the first settlers of Arkansas (1813) and could have had almost any land that he wanted, but he settled on the west side of the Eleven Point River. The trails turned to roads and the McIlroy ford turned into a bridge at a later time. At this time, the original settlement was just north of where the McIlroy church and cemetery are now located. Samuel was a hatter by trade and followed his trade, but he also raised hogs and some cattle. There was no local market at that time, so each year he built a raft and floated down to New Orleans, sold his produce, then rode his horse back to what was then called the McIlroy community.

On one such trip, one of his sons died and was buried. When he returned, Samuel had his body moved to where the present cemetery is located and where he (Samuel) is also buried.

The McIlroy church which stands by the cemetery was at one time the McIlroy School and was located about a mile north of its present location. The first McIlroy school was only a one-room log cabin built around 1818-1820 and was one of the first schools in Arkansas (this picture is on the front cover of the book).

Elizabeth and Samuel lived the remaining parts of their lives in the McIlroy community. Elizabeth died a year or two before Samuel. Samuel lived by himself in the old home place. A few weeks before he died, he was not feeling well, so his sons Daniel and Hammet, who lived nearby, rotated every other night checking on him. The night that he died, Hammet got home late from court and thought his father was feeling better and didn't bother to go by the house until the next morning. When he went, his father was dead.

From tradition, family bibles records, and Hammet "Hamp" McIlroy's deposition, it seems that Samuel and Elizabeth had ten boys. Six of these reached maturity and five married and raised large families. There is some speculation that Elizabeth and Sam had a girl and she married Solomon Davis. Even though Hammet's first wife was a Davis, he makes no mention of having a sister. Some elderly relatives thought that this girl that married Solomon Davis might have been adopted or at least raised by Hammet and could have called herself a McIlroy. Many of the descendants of Solomon Davis think that she

was a sister to the boys of Samuel—so I will include her children with an *
(asterisk) because this is not proven and I have some doubts.

By 1860, the family of Samuel McIlroy had grown to a large number. It is said
they lived from Dalton (near Ripley County, Missouri border) for miles down
and on each side of the Eleven Point River. Daniel, Hammet, and Samuel Jr.
lived on the west side of the river, John and Andrew on the east side. Alexander
had moved to Green County (adjoining county) to the east.

This overpopulation and desire for cheaper land and new adventures started
the mass movement of many of them to Texas and later to Oklahoma and
other states.

The first to leave Randolph County were some of the sons of Daniel, who
was the first son of Samuel. Their mother was Elizabeth Lynch, so when part of
the Lynch family moved to Texas in the late 1860s, several of these boys went
with them to Hunt County (now Rains). A few years later, after the death of
their father, their mother and the rest of the children followed them to Hunt
County. A short time later, Alexander McIlroy's widow, Frances Kennedy,
moved to Hunt County with her children.

About ten years later, William (son of Hammet) and his brother A.Y. moved
to Tolar County, Texas. After several years of drought, they moved back to
Randolph Country for a short time before returning to Tolar. In 1900, Samuel
B. McIlroy moved to Hill County, Texas—also with him were his brothers-
in-law (Lewises) and Martha Lewis, his mother-in-law. About this same time,
John Thomas Vandergriff (cousin of Sam), moved to Carrolton, Texas. This
was the start of much migration from Randolph County, Arkansas.

The travel was not easy at that time—the first ones came by covered wagon.
They had to pole their way through some of the lowlands in Arkansas. That
meant cutting small logs and driving over them, then picking them up as they
crossed and moving them in front again. By 1900, traveling became easier.
When Sam McIlroy moved to Hill County, Texas, they rented a box car and
stored their tools, furniture, etc. and came by train. One thing that helped in
moving was that people at that time did not have the possessions that they
have now. The household was mostly a few chairs, a table, a wood-burning
cook stove, pots and pans, a few dishes, crocks, and jars for preserving food, a
few changes of clothing, a trunk or two, quilts and quilting materials, a rifle,
hats for the men and boys, bonnets for girls, and a few pictures (maybe tin
types). The ones that came by train did have a bigger problem—moving their
livestock and farming equipment, including buggies and wagons.

In 1813, Samuel McIlroy moved from what is now Madison County,
Missouri to what is now Randolph County, Arkansas. Actually, he was chang-

ing locations in the Louisiana Territory. It soon became the Missouri Territory and then the Arkansas Territory twenty-two years later when Arkansas became a state. This location was first a part of Lawrence County and later split off to become Randolph County. At the time of 1813, there were no roads, only trails. These trails, which were made by Indians and by wild animals, were formed on high ground and followed the terrain as much as possible. They followed the stream to where they could be crossed by wading or walking over logs. Most likely, Samuel came from Missouri and crossed into this location by a road called the Military Road. William Hix had opened a ferry on the northeast corner of Randolph County in 1803, which made this road possible. By 1813, this ferry was owned by Pittmans and later by Daniel McIlroy, Samuel's grandson. By 1813, this road had been widened so that wagons could travel this trail.

At this time, there were no towns anywhere near this place that became Randolph County, but as the newcomers arrived, there became a settlement called Columbia in the northeast and the town of Lawrence (soon called Davidsonville) in the southern part. A few years later, Jackson in the western part was established. Columbia and Jackson were on the Military Road. Settlers thought that Davidsonville would become a large city and probably the county seat, but soon after selling lots and some building, there was an outbreak of cholera. The plans for the road were abandoned and the Military Road was diverted further west due to easier crossing on the Eleven Point River and then the Spring River. Samuel McIlroy suffered major financial loss on the failure of Davidsonville. He had invested in a lot and was going to operate his hat shop there. (I have a copy of this transaction and also his plot location).

All the above was my trying to locate Sam's first settlement. We know that he located on or near the Military Road and most likely on the west side of the Eleven Point River. At the time of his first arrival, it was not necessary to buy land, so he could have located most anywhere he wanted. His land was not even filed on any record until after his death in 1853. We do know that he was a "hatter" and he had to live near the main road to sell his product, and there is no doubt his permanent home was just north of the present day McIlroy church. His sons owned land both south and north of this church location.

Daniel, Hammet, and Samuel Jr. all lived and died west of the Eleven Point River. Three other boys raised families east of the river—John just a short distance east, Andrew a mile or two further east, and Alexander to the next county east (Green County, Bradshaw community) where he had a store.

This location in Randolph County became the home for many of Samuel and Elizabeth McIlroy's descendants. By 1850, almost all the land from Dalton near the Missouri Line and Byrdell to the south was owned by the McIlroys or their kin. One of the first schools in Arkansas was organized by the McIlroys about 1817 and a school named McIlroy continued for many years just two miles north of the McIlroy church. In fact, the McIlroy church was made from the last McIlroy school—it was moved to its present location.

As stated before, about 1860 the urge for more land began to enter the minds of this large family just like it had their kin for many ages.

The first to leave were the widow and children of Daniel and most of them moved to Hunt County, Texas (now Rains County). A few years later, Francis Kennedy (widow of Alexander) joined them in Rains County. About 20 years later, William C. McIlroy (Hammet's older son) and his brother A.Y. moved to Hood County, Texas. They returned after a bad drought there but soon went back to Texas. In 1900, Sam McIlroy (John's son and my grandfather) moved to Hill County, Texas.

This was only the start. Today, there are McIlroys from this Randolph County beginning in Texas, New Mexico, Arizona, California, Missouri, the state of Washington, and probably several others. Thirty years ago (about 1970), I began to visit my McIlroy kin in Randolph County and there was always a large crowd at the McIlroy reunion, but today (2007), there are none remaining in Randolph County that carry the McIlroy name. I visited Charles, Hite, E.M., and John McIlroy, Guy Amos, Marie Barrow, Ruth Wiggins, and Helen Bly, (who were all still living in Randolph County at the time) just to name a few. I also visited many of the older ones that came to Texas. How many of these have the McIlroy name? Probably one hundred today. How many descend from Samuel and Elizabeth? I would say at least one thousand, probably several thousand. I have tried to find them all, but it is impossible.

# Samuel McIlroy, Son of Daniel McIlroy and Rebecca Pyott

Daniel McIlroy

Married Rebecca Pyott (daughter of John Pyott[2] and Elizabeth Brunson) in Laudoun County, Virginia in 1776

1. Thomas McIlroy b. 7-13-1779 d. 5-21-1813 (not traced)
2. Samuel McIlroy b. 1780 in Culpepper County, Virginia d. 4-8-1853 in Randolph County, Arkansas

Married Elizabeth McLean (daughter of Alexander McLean, Jr. and Anna Haas, b. 1792 d. 1851) on 2-20-1808 in Caldwell County, Kentucky

    1. Daniel McIlroy[3] b. 1809 in Kentucky d. 4-22-1853 in Randolph County, Arkansas

    1st M. Elizabeth Lynch (mother of first 10 children)

    2nd M. Mary Susan ___

        1. Samuel D. McIlroy b. 1833 in Arkansas

---

2    John Pyott was born about 1730 in Pennsylvania and died in 1787 in Loudoun County, Virginia. His wife was Elizabeth Brunson and their children were John (born about 1751), Susanna, (born about 1753), Rebecca (born about 1755), and Amos (born about 1757). John's father was Daniel Pyott, born about 1706 in New Jersey, and his mother was Alice Perigo.

3    Daniel McIlroy, the first son of Samuel and Elizabeth McLean, and his children have been hard to trace. Several children died young, some never married, and one or two were killed in the Civil War. This son of Samuel lived on the west side of the 11 Point River, maybe a mile north of the home place of his father. He was a farmer and cattle raiser. After he died in 1866, his second wife, as stated above, moved to Rains County, Texas (or what is now Rains County) where a large part of her children lived. They were related to and married into the Lynch family (their mother was a Lynch) and when many of the Lynches moved to Texas around 1860, some of the older McIlroys went with them. I have tried to find someone of either family that could give me some information, but one of the few of this group was Lora Armstrong and at that time (about 1985), she was not well and her memory was not good. She did mention that Benjamin was a peddler and lived with his brother A.G. Many McIlroys were buried at the Hooker Ridge Cemetery and the McIlroy farm is now under Lake Tawakoni.

Married Nancy Neals (b. 1834)
1. Shalley Ann McIlroy b. 1859
2. John McIlroy b. 1860
3. Samuel Sidney McIlroy b. 10-29-1861 d. 3-9-1941 in Childress County, Texas
Married Lydia Ann Sullivan on 11-24-1888
   1. William Edward McIlroy b. 11-26-1889 d. 4-2-1946
   2. Carrie Bell McIlroy b. 7-2-1891 d. 8-15-1948
   Married James R. Austin
   3. Grace Ester McIlroy b. 4-21-1894 d. 7-22-1982
   4. Jerome Kerby McIlroy b. 7-24-1896 in Indian Territory d. 7-1-1965
   5. Katie Ophelia McIlroy b. 6-9-1898 in Cooke County, TX d. 7-23-1979 in Pampa, TX
2. William McIlroy b.1834
3. Absolem (A.G.) McIlroy b. 1836
1st Married Mary E. Lynch on 9-6-1860
   1. (Daughter) b.1868
   2. (Daughter) b. 1874
   3. (Daughter) b. 1878
2nd Married C. J. _____
4. James McIlroy
5. Jesse McIlroy b. 1840
Married ____
   1. Aloe B. McIlroy b. 7-1887
   2. Albert S. McIlroy b. 2-1892
6. David McIlroy b. 1842
1st Married Letha K. Wyatt
   1. Emma Jane McIlroy b. 1875
   Married Wheeler
   2. Child
7. Benjamin F. McIlroy b. 4-3-1845 d. 6-20-1885 in Rains County, TX (Never married)
8. Edwin McIlroy b. 1847 d. 2-1-1890
9. Daniel R. McIlroy b. 1848 D.Y.
10. Elizabeth McIlroy b. 1851
Married _____ Fry on 9-7-1871
11. Christian "Hemp" McIlroy b. 1858 d. 1917
Married Mollie J. Thornton b. 9-77-1874
   1. James Thomas McIlroy b. 1896 d. 8-21-1954

Married Lora Armstrong
1. Ola Mae McIlroy
Married Humphries
2. James W. McIlroy
12. Mary McIlroy b. 3-31-1860 d. 5-1-1892
Married James L. McDaniel
  1. George C. McDaniel b. 9-1886 d. 5-24-1952
  2. Ida Bell McDaniel b. 10-1888
  Married Dalton Clemmers on 11-3-1907
    1. Mara Ida Clemmers b. 10-8-1912 d. 1983
    Married Hubert Ellis
    2. Althea Mae Clemmers
    3. Minnie A. Clemmers
    Married Ralph Williams
    4. Marvie L. Clemmers b. 7-26-1915 d. 11-5-1918
    5. James Clemmers
    Married Essie Keese
    6. Dalton Clemmers b. 9-12-1920
    Married Mamie Looney
    7. Geneva Clemmers b. 11-27-1922
    Married D.O. Norvell
    8. Ernest Clemmers b. 4-19-1926 d. 2-12-1990
      1. Ernest Clemmers, Jr.
    9. Marie Clemmers
    Married Otis Johnson
  3. Alvin Ross McDaniel b. 11-1890 d. 2-1939
  Married _____
    1. Mary McDaniel
    2. Joyce McDaniel
    3. Son
13. John F. McIlroy b. 1-1864
2. Hammet Francis McIlroy[4] b. 3-9-1811 in Missouri Territory d. 8-12-1890 in Randolph County, Arkansas
1st Married Elizabeth Davis b. 5-14-1815 on 7-11-1833

---

4  Hammet McIlroy was well-known in northeastern Arkansas. He was state representative for two terms, but voted against secession and was never elected again. His descendants say he was not actually against secession, but he did not think that they could win. Two of his boys fought with the south. Hammet followed his father's trade (hatter) for several years, but soon devoted his full time to farming and ranching, in which he was successful.

2nd Married Maria Cooper Inman in 1871 (no children by this marriage)

1. William C. McIlroy b. 1-4-1836 in Arkansas d. 7-22-1899 in Tolar, Texas

1st Married Francis Stubblefield (b. 2-6-1846 d. 8-15-1859)

2nd Married Mary C. White b. 8-13-1842 on 10-9-1860 (all children by 2nd marriage)

   1. Francis Lentia McIlroy (twin) b. 10-4-1861 d. 10-28-1861

   2. Joe McIlroy (twin) b. 10-4-1861 D.Y.

   3. Willie Ann McIlroy

Married Sam Hufstedler on 2-12-1855

     1. Nettie Hufstedler b. 1866

   Married John Neely 3-6-1905

       1. Willie Mae Neely b. 12-13-1904

       2. Horace Neely b. 6-7-1906 d. 3-3-1930

       3. Mapel Neely b. 1908

       4. Jenny Neely b. 5-13-1909

       5. Kay Neely b. 1-11-1911

       6. Christine Neely b. 3-7-1914

       7. Dwight Neely b. 2-26-1915

       8. John C. Neely b. 12-22-1922

       9. Eldon Neely b. 3-25-1925

       10. Quinton b. 6-28-1926

     2. Emmet K. Hufstedler b. ____

   Married Dottie _____ on 11-5-1905

       1. Aurina Hufstedler b. 4-22-1907

       2. Pauline Hufstedler b. 6-29-1909

   Married Edward Snelson

       3. E.K. Hufstedler b. 9-11-1911 d. 6-26-1976

       4. J.D. Hufstedler b. 9-12-1913

       5. Mary R. Hufstedler b. 4-19-1921

       6. Oneta Bell Hufstedler b. 1928

   Married K.L. Allen

       1. Kenneth L. Allen b. 1-14-1946

       1st Married Sherilyn McKiver

       2nd Married Peggy Boone

       2. Karen Lou Allen b. 7-28-47

       1st Married McGuyer

       2nd Married Cecil Emerson

       3. Kelia Lynn Allen b. 2-20-1949

Married T.L. Ballou on 3-1-1975
   1. Kennon L. Ballou b. 10-7-1878
   4. Kendra Laurel Allen b. 11-9-1952
Married Robert Sims on 5-18-1873
4. Elizabeth Idaho McIlroy b. 11-22-1864 d. 8-14-1886
Married John W. Campbell on 11-5-1885 (no children)
5. Alexander H. McIlroy b. 1-18-1867 (twin) d. 6-22-1896
6. Unnamed Twin b. 1-18-867 d. 1-18-1867
7. Elmo Murray McIlroy b. 3-7-1869 d. 10-20-1966
Married Eula Lee Hudseth b. 4-8-1872 d. 4-1946
   1. E.W. McIlroy b. 3-19-1895
   2. Mary Lorene McIlroy b. 10-10-1896
   Married Pat Jackson on 4-21-1915
      1. Harold D. Jackson b. 9-27-1917
      Married Dorothy Perry 6-27-1948
         1. Patricia Jackson b. 12-5-1952
   3. Jewel McIlroy b. 6-5-1899 d. 6-24-1924
   Married Victor Lackey
      1. Charles V. Lackey b. 9-13-1926
      Married Jimmie Lackey on 8-30-1947
      2. Thelma Jeanine Lackey b. 1-26-1928
   4. Drusilla Ora McIlroy b. 2-7-1904
   1st Married David Pirkle
   2nd Married Albert Ashley
      1. Rex O'Dell Pirkle b. 6-21-1924
      1st Married Margaret Petree 8-3-1946
         1. Dennie O'Dell Pirkle b. 10-16-1947
8. Sherman Douglas McIlroy[5] b. 2-5-1874 d. 8-25-1945
Married Kate Byrd on 3-1901
   1. Hazel McIlroy b. 1902
Married Jack Nichols

---

5   While Sherman Douglas McIlroy was in the Klondike (Alaska), he sometimes partnered with Tex Rickards. Tex was a gambler, went broke several times, but always came back. After Tex left the Klondike, he operated Madison Square Garden in New York and promoted many of the prize fights. He also owned the New York Ranger hockey team. Sherman, who was also called Tex, went broke two times with Rickards, but after that, he sent money home to his brother Henry when he made money. Henry bought much land for Sherman, and oil was brought in on practically all of it. After Sherman went into the oil business, he was a partner with Kerr McGee Oil Group, but they wanted to open service stations. Sherman sold out to them he wanted to find and refine oil.

1. Nancy Nichols b. 1931
2. Dawn Nichols b. 1935
Married Thomas Henry Thompson
    1. Leigh Thompson b. 11-4-1961
    2. Margot Thompson b. 3-21-1963
    3. Jennifer Ann Thompson b. 4-26-1967
    4. Thomas Henry Thompson Jr. b. 7-26-1968
2. Katheryn McIlroy b. 1907
Married A. Antonio in 1931
9. Henry Samuel McIlroy b. 10-2-1872 d. 6-25-1966
Married Ellen Hightower on 3-19-1895
    1. Waldo E. McIlroy b. 3-10-1896 d. 3-28-1906
    2. Willie J. McIlroy b. _____
    Married Ocile Hakins (no children)
    3. Blanch McIlroy b. _____
    Married O.C. Curl
        1. Jean Curl
    4. Bernice (twin) b. 4-2-02
    Married Guy Lackey
        1. Guy Lackey
        2. Roy Lackey
    5. Gladys (twin) McIlroy b. 4-2-02 d. 6-7-1903
    6. Edith McIlroy
    Married Harris
    7. Horace McIlroy d. 1973
    8. Winfield W. McIlroy[6] d. 2005
    Married Ruby Cruce
        1. Winfred "Winnie" Ann McIlroy
        Married Charles S. Taylor
            1. Charles Lee Taylor
            2. Winfred McIlroy Taylor
        2. Sandra McIlroy
        Married Lynn Scott
            1. Shannon Scott
            2. John David Scott

---

6    Winfield McIlroy graduated from Texas A&M University around 1935 and taught Agriculture in Caldwell, Texas. He later became a professor at Texas A&M and like many of his brothers lived until his early 90s.

3. Kirstan Scott

10. Rufus Black McIlroy b. 1-12-1875 d. 4-28-1942
Married Sallie Meeker
  1. Marvin Madison McIlroy b. 12-16-1897
  Married Elnora Johnson on 12-15-1924
  2. Julian Douglas McIlroy b. 1-8-1900
  Married Anna Repene on 1-26-1922
    1. Dorothy Marie McIlroy b. 6-20-1924
    Married William Dellessi
    2. Mildred McIlroy b. 6-4-1926
  3. Rufus Jr. McIlroy b. 12-16-1905
  Married Flora Cunningham on 12-1-1931
    1. Barbara Joy McIlroy b. 9-14-1934
    2. Richard McIlroy b. 1-13-1937
  4. Harold Grant McIlroy b. 6-29-1911
  Married Helen Jeffries (b. 8-14-1914) on 9-20-1930
    1. Patricia Rose McIlroy b. 5-16-1933

11. George Washington "Wash" McIlroy b. 12-21-1877
Married Grace Estelle Adams d. 1-1-1938 on 11-18-1903
  1. H. Douglas McIlroy b. 2-3-1905 d. 7-5-1921
  2. Mary Jane McIlroy b. 8-16-1908 d. 2-23-1913
  3. Jessie R. McIlroy b. 3-27-1912
  1st Married H.R. Harver
  2nd Married J.L. Smith
    1. Robert Lee Harver b. 7-5-1931
    2. James Lewis Smith b. 10-27-1940
  4. Gerald W. McIlroy b. 7-17-1915
  Married Helen Wilder on 4-18-1940?
    1. Kenneth Dale McIlroy b. 1-26-1941
    2. Retta Grace McIlroy b. 10-7-1942

12. Thomas A. McIlroy b. 8-23-1881 d. 12-6-1957
Married Mattie Kerr (b. 7-20-1885 d. 8-10-1968) on 11-4-1903
  1. Valera Mae McIlroy b. 5-28-1905 d. 9-5-1976
  Married Jarvis
  2. Opal M. McIlroy b. 12-7-1907 d. 2-18-1959
  Married J.R. Finley
  3. Coy McIlroy b. 10-4-1914
    1. James Coy McIlroy b. 1948
      1. James Coy McIlroy III

4. Charles Ray McIlroy
5. T. Douglas McIlroy
13. William White McIlroy b. 2-16-1884 d. 1959
Married Winnie Hooper (no children)
14. Bilbrey Dean McIlroy b. 7-10-1886 d. 3-12-1868
Married Obie May Makamson
  1. V. Maxine McIlroy b. 11-7-1912 d. 12-2-1956
  2. Mary Jane McIlroy b. 6-15-1913
    1. Charles W. Crowder b. 1947
    2. Joyce b. 1955
  Married Joel Crowder
  3. Claudean McIlroy b. 3-15-1915
  Married Claude Starr
    1. Kim Starr
  4. Iva McIlroy b. 3-26-1917
  Married W.H. Mansfield
2. Thomas Jefferson McIlroy[7] b. 7-3-1840 d. 9-23-1895
Married Mary "Polly" White (b. 1-25-1843 d. 12-30-1920) on 1-18-1861
  1. William Thomas McIlroy b. 9-4-1864 d. 3-14-1927
  Married Mary P. Dalton (b. 4-4-1886 d. 4-2-1953) on 4-4-1886
    1. Bessie McIlroy b. 8-2-1886 d. 9-21-1896
    2. Willie McIlroy b. 10-26-1898 d. 4-3-1904
  2. Nora Elizabeth McIlroy b. 1-7-1866 d. 11-23-1956
  1st Married Colonel James Dalton (b. 3-5-1865 d. 6-25-1896)
    1. Nora Ella Dalton b. 5-22-1888 d. 11-27-1965
    Married U.A. Pond
      1. Ruth Elizabeth Pond b. 2-24-1918
      Married Harley Wiggins in 1942
      (no children)
  2nd Married Joseph Dalton (b. 1865 d. 1941) in 1899
    2. Daisy Dalton b. 8-26-1901
    (Never married)
    3. Jesse Earl Dalton b. 1903
    Married Ila Inez McCauley on 4-28-1928
      1. Joe Edward Dalton b. 6-27-1933

---

7   Thomas Jefferson McIlroy was a veteran of the Civil War and a very successful farmer. He also learned a hatter's trade from his father and grandfather and worked in the family shop until he was grown. He made some hats after he was married and let his sons manage the farm.

1st Married Ruth Buford on 6-23-1957
2nd Married Ruth Kennon on 5-26-1972
   1. Jennifer R. Dalton b. 2-23-1973
3. Robert Lee McIlroy b. 3-14-1868 d. 1-5-1953
Married Susie Bailey (b. 10-28-1872 d. 8-12-1957) on 2-7-1892
   1. Cecil Theodore McIlroy b. 11-19-1892 d. 6-11-1893
   2. Alma McIlroy b. 9-9-1894
   Married Houston Brown on 12-18-1912
      1. Lloyd Brown
      Married Maude Roach
      2. Lola Brown b. 2-14-1918
      Married Kincade
      3. Raymond Brown
   3. Verner McIlroy b. 12-9-1896 d. 11-9-1899
   4. Lela McIlroy b. 6-17-1898
(Never married)
   5. Hite H. McIlroy DVM. b. 2-11-1901 d. 6-1986
Married Marie Moore on 3-31-1923
      1. Mozel McIlroy b. 10-1923
      1st Married _____ Lanbick
      2. James McIlroy b. 12-24-1927
      3. Vernell McIlroy b. 1931
      Married Wesley N. Bert Jr.
         1. Kolett Bert
         2. Kim Bert
         3. Kyle Bert
   6. Clara McIlroy b. 8-4-1904
Married Alvin Tyler on 11-6-1923
      1. Alvin Tyler Jr. b. 6-21-1924
   7. Ava Mae McIlroy b. 10-24-1907
Married Virgil Crawford on 1-20-1928
      1. Cloyce Crawford b. 5-18-1930
      Married Bardree
      2. Weldon Crawford b. 6-24-1935
      Married Francis _____
      3. Shirley Crawford b. 6-22-1943
      Married Eddie Mehl
   8. Irene McIlroy b. 6-18-1909 d. 4-5-1944
Married Wells L. Waddell on 3-7-1926

1. Gerald M. Waddell
9. Paulene McIlroy b. 1-8-1912
Married Groves Milam on 11-8-1933
   1. Carrie Milam
   2. Wanda Milam
   Married Eddie Long
   3. Thomas Milam b. 3-20-1935
   4. Mary Milam b. 6-23-1944
10. Ira Lee McIlroy b. 3-24-1915
Married Peggy F. Kerley
   1. Peggy Lou McIlroy b. 2-14-1943
   Married Richard Lonor
4. Henry Murray McIlroy b. 9-18-1869 d. 8-22-1937
Married Della Crim (b. 10-26-1879 d. 5-11-1967) in 1903
   1. Lillian McIlroy b. 6-27-1904
   Married Leonard Stubblefield in 1921
      1. Clara Jean Stubblefield b. 12-10-1925
      Married Arthur Muller on 1-28-1945
         1. Beverly Muller b. 8-5-1947
         2. Virginia Muller b. 12-17-1948
   2. Lytell Clyde McIlroy b. 3-16-1909 d. 1-23-1986
   1st Married Nola Brown
   2nd Married Adele Dalton in 1977
      1. Thomas L. McIlroy b. 11-28-1936
      Married Mary Lee Smith on 8-16-1958
         1. Kimberly McIlroy b. 10-9-1960
         2. Jeffrey McIlroy b. 2-4-1962
         3. Kerry Jean McIlroy b. 2-16-1965
5. James Irvy McIlroy (twin) b. 9-18-1869 d. 10-9-1891
6. Sarah Adaline "Addie" McIlroy b. 3-25-1872 d. 3-22-1946
Married Samuel Copeland (b. 10-2-1866 d. 3-22-1924) in 1891
   1. Mac Copeland D.Y.
   2. Hugh Copeland
   Married Ethel Henson
   3. Leon Copeland
   Married Henrietta Scott
      1. Robert Copeland
   4. Alma Copeland
   Married Paul Meek
      1. Jean Meek

5. Pearl Copeland
Married James D. Walley
   1. James Walley
6. Thelma Copeland
Married Leonard F. Patterson
   1. Billy F. Patterson
   Married ____
      1. Billy F. Patterson Jr.
7. Mary Francis "Molly" McIlroy b. 8-12-1875 d. 2-22-1946
Married James Copeland (b. 10-21-1868 d. 4-15-1948) on 8-8-1896
   1. Mamie H. Copeland b. 11-12-1897
   Married Rex Day
      1. Ester "Louise" Day b. 6-27-1928
      Married James F. McLaughlin
         1. James Michael McLaughlin
         Married Pat Gazda
            1. Karen McLaughlin b. 1-27-1976
         2. Patricia McLaughlin
         Married Robert Tucker
            1. Alicia Rene Tucker b. 4-1977
         3. David Rex McLaughlin
   2. Emmett Carson Copeland b. 10-1899 d. 5-29-1974
   Married Ethel Henson
      1. Donald Copeland
      2. Nancy Copeland
   3. Edith Gay Copeland b. 7-25-1903 d. 7-12-1977
   Married Anthony Minceau
      1. Beverly Minceau
      2. Richard Minceau
   4. Ina Grace Copeland b. 8-26-1906
   Married J.W. Rhoads
      1. Joyce Rhoads
   5. Willie Mae Copeland b. 9-15-1910
   Married W.C. Croutch
      1. Max
      2. Carson
      3. Mary
      4. Aubrey

3. Martha A. McIlroy b. 1842 d. 8-3-1884
Married James Newton Robinett[8] (b. 3-22-1840 d. 10-5-1908) on 5-3-1865
>1. Henrietta "Rettie" Robinett b. 3-12-1867 d. 9-4-1908
Married Samuel Houston Thomason on 10-27-1889
>>1. Martha Letetia Thomason b. 11-21-1890 d. 8-15-1979
Married Raleigh Bonebreak on 6-14-1913
>>>1. Anadean Bonebreak
Married Jon Headrick
>>>>1. George Hubert Headrick
>>>>2. Bonnie Marie Headrick
>>>>3. Kenneth Headrick
>>>>4. Jerry Headrick
>>>>5. Kermit Headrick
>>>>6. Barbara Headrick
>>>>7. Gary Headrick
>>>2. Marie Bonebreak
Married Earl Carmack
>>>>1. David Carmack
>>>>2. Radean Carmack
>>>3. Murrel Bonebreak
Married Francis Dickman
>>>>1. Gregory Bonebreak
>>>>2. Pat Bonebreak
>>>>3. Allen Bonebreak
>>>>4. Errick Bonebreak

---

8    After the Civil War ended, James N. Robinett, a Confederate soldier, tired, hungry, and broke, started back to his home in Missouri. His horse was barely alive from lack of food. After several days of traveling, they came to the old Military Road and after a few hours, they approached a peaceful-looking plantation home. James had nothing to lose, so he approached the house and was greeted by an older man who asked what he wanted. After telling him of his plight, this man greeted him warmly. He fed and took care of his horse and gave James a place to stay for the night. The man taking care of him was Hammet McIlroy, who had two sons that fought for the South. That night they talked, and Hammet found that James was a little worried about how he would be perceived at home, where there was a mixture of people for the North and for the South. Hammet mentioned to him that he was now hiring workers for his farmer's operation, and that there was a place for him if he wanted fifty cents per day plus room and board. This offer was accepted, partly because James had nothing else to look forward to but also because Hammet had several pretty daughters. A few months later, James Newton married Martha McIlroy, one of Hammet's daughters.

  5. Aneta Bonebreak

2. Harriet Amberzine "Amy" Thomason b. 6-21-1892 d. 3-24-1961

Married Bruce Prewit in 1961

  1. Allen Devere Prewit

  Married Alma Malone

    1. Allen Devere Prewit Jr.

    2. Willard "Red" Prewit

    3. Shirley Prewit

    4. Ray Prewit

  2. Athol Walton Prewit

  Married Hazel Iola "Peggy" Fairbarin

    1. Edlon Dean Prewit

    2. Harry Alvin Prewit

  3. Glen Estel Prewit

  Married Verda Mae Russell

    1. Glenda Prewit

    2. Tommy Prewit

    3. Beverley Prewit

    4. Gary Prewit

    5. Linda Prewit

  4. Loyd Early Prewit

  Married Isobel "Belle" Lowe

    1. Unnamed Girl D.Y.

    2. Thelma Pearl "Cookie" Prewit

    3. Shirley Fay Prewit

  5. Arzetta Prewit

  Married Bud Slatter in 1960

    (no children)

3. Dora Berzilla Thomason b. 6-10-1896 d. 9-23-1970

Married Carl Cleveland Payne on 5-24-1924

  1. Jannetta Payne

  Married Ed Smith

    1. Carl Smith

    2. Linda Smith

4. James Wilford Thomason b. 9-3-1898 d. 2-27-1956

Married Cora Thompson on 2-27-1918

  1. Loyd Thomason

  Married Audry Weaver

(no children)
2. Leo Thomason
Married Grace Stump
   1. Betty Thomason
   2. Carrol Thomason
   3. Jimmy Thomason
3. Lois Thomason
Married Jesse Weaterman
   1. Carlean Weaterman
   2. Wanda Weaterman
   3. Anita Weaterman
5. Minnie Pearl Thomason
Married Steward P. Dalton
   1. Vera Dean Dalton
   Married Clark Hagler
      1. Keith Hagler
6. Clara Gertrude Thomason b. 8-27-1903 d. 5-19-1918 of spinal meningitis
7. Joseph Thomason b. 5-14-1906 d. 9-1906
2. Joseph Hammet Robinett b. 10-9-1869 d. 12-29-1947
Married Samantha Upshaw (b. 1-5-1877 d. 4-10-1952) in 1908
   1. Ailyce Agness Robinett b. 1-3-1903
   Married Daniel Boyce on 6-28-1936
      1. Major Ronald J. Boyce
      2. David R. Boyce
   2. Edna Mae Robinett b. 12-7-1903 d. 6-10-1963
   3. Martha Jewell Robinett b. 12-14-1910
   4. Joseph Pharaoh (J.P.) Robinett b. 1-30-1914
   Married Wanda Gamble
      1. Glen Edward Robinett
      2. Melvin J. Robinett
      Married Grace Cusing on 11-30-1979
3. Letetia Robinett
Married Johnny Martin
   1. Bessie Martin
   Married Warren Triplett
      1. Letha Triplett
      Married Alton Kissock
         (no children)
      2. Beuna Triplett

Married Roscoe "Ross" Mahan
   1. Donna Fay Mahan
   2. Roy Mahan
   3. Donald Triplett
2. Hazel Samantha Martin
Married Otis Wallis
   1. Beverly Kay Wallis
3. Lois Martin
Married Pharris Mahan
   1. Jannette Mahan
   2. Barbara Mahan
4. Margaret Martin
Married Reverend Bill Grey
5. Elba Martin
6. Oscar Martin
4. Martha Louiza Robinett
Married John Twillman
   1. Raymond Twillman
   Married Helen _____
      1. David Twillman
      2. Carrol Twillman
      3. Anita Twillman
5. Moses "Mozie" Robinett
Married Bertha Martin
   1. Glen Robinett
   2. Opal Robinett
6. Jasper William Robinett
Married Agness Payne
   1. Vera Robinett
   Married Wilford Lord
      1. Emely Lord
      2. David Lord
   2. I. Robinett
   Married Lorenzo "Swinnie" Hartman
      1. Donald Hartman
   3. Harold Robinett
   Married Verna Varvis
      1. Jannette Robinett
      Married _____

(2 daughters)
4. Monera Robinett
Married Albert Martin
   (2 daughters)
5. Archie Robinett
Married Norma Williams
   (no children)
4. Mariah L. McIlroy b. 1846 d. 1871
Married Columbus G. Fry
   1. Harriet Fry b. 1868
   2. Hammet Fry b. 1870
5. Archibald Yale McIlroy b. 10-1847 d. 6-1-1922
Married Mary Elizabeth Vandergriff (b. 3-25-1850 d. 3-12-1934) on 8-26-1866
   1. Ursula McIlroy b. 1869
   Married Bowers
      1. Pomp Bowers
      2. Troy Bowers
   2. Maggie McIlroy b. 1871 D.Y.
   3. Joseph Lee McIlroy b. 10-1-1874 d. 3-25-1952
   Married Lennie May Huffstedler (b. 5-24-1875 d. 8-20-1960) on 7-16-1893
      1. Della Lee McIlroy b. 8-2-1894
      Married Willie Lawing on 4-15-1914
         1. Harry Claude Lawing
         2. Mary Lawing
         3. Frieda Jane Lawing b. 11-11-1923
         Married C.E. Harrington
            1. Carol Ann Harrington b. 5-7-1943
            2. Charles K. Harrington b. 9-3-1948
         4. Jack Lawing b. 6-8-1925
         Married Evelyn Krause
            1. John Keith Krause b. 4-10-1954
         5. Billy Max Lawing
      2. Homer Claude McIlroy b. 7-7-1887 d. 11-1-1969
      Married Gertrude Hughes on 9-2-1922
         1. Homer Claude McIlroy Jr. b. 9-17-1923
         Married Carol Aurand
            1. David Scott McIlroy b. 8-8-1951
            Married Karen Mercer

     1. Christopher McIlroy b. 8-5-1973

     2. Scott McIlroy b. 11-24-1975

   2. Jennifer McIlroy b. 5-23-1954

   3. Cathy Sue McIlroy b. 10-25-1956

  2. Valery Mae McIlroy b. 10-31-1925

Married Walter Farmer (b. 9-1-1925) on 11-25-1944

   1. Walter L. Farmer b. 6-2-1947

   2. Claudia Ann Farmer b. 8-10-1952

   Married Gregg A. Nixter

3. Walter Earl McIlroy b. 9-15-1888

Married Ora Burton

  1. Ora Earlene McIlroy b. 11-26-1921

Married Bill Warren on 7-21-1943

   1. Sandra Warren

   2. Harry Warren

   3. Sharon Warren

   4. William Warren

   5. Annetta Warren

   6. David Warren

  2. Robert Joe McIlroy b. 9-11-1924 d. 2-19-1944

Married Wanda Shefner on 12-25-1942

   1. Robert Joe McIlroy Jr. b. 11-28-1943

  3. Burton Ted b McIlroy. 12-14-1925

Married Wanda Shefner McIlroy

   1. Burton Carl McIlroy b. 2-18-1947

   2. Becky Dean McIlroy b. 6-14-1957

4. William Clyde "Jake" McIlroy b. 5-2-1906

(Never married)

5. Chrystell McIlroy b. 2-3-1908

Married R.D. Peters on 4-7-1928

  1. Betty

Married _____

   1. Cheryl b. 5-21-1949

   2. Herbert b. 8-16-1951

   3. Terry b. 9-5-1954

6. Archibald Yale McIlroy b. 10-25-1915

Married Iris Fern Elliott

  1. Barbara Fern McIlroy b. 12-13-1940

   1. Weldon Brown b. 10-16-1960

    2. Patricia b. 6-12-1965
    3. Pamela b. 3-28-1968
  2. Janet Kay McIlroy b. 9-24-1944
  Married W.D. Henson on 5-25-1963
    1. Susan Lynette Henson b. 1-25-1966
    Kathryn Lynn Henson b. 8-13-1969
    Lisa Henson b. 1975
    James Henson b. 1976
  3. Archibald Yale McIlroy III b. 4-1-1946 d. 2-8-2005
  Married Betty Jean Duncan on 8-26-1966
    1. Lori Michelle McIlroy b. 3-20-1971
    Married Mark Holdorf
      1. Madison Holdorf
      2. Grant Holdorf
    2. Kerri McIlroy
    Married _____ Gleaves
      1. KyLeigh Gleaves
      2. Keaten Gleaves
    3. Tamara McIlroy
    Married Greg Gunta
      1. Matt Gunta
      2. Kaitlyn Gunta
      3. Morgan Gunta
  4. Karen Lynn McIlroy b. 12-8-1950
  Married Gary Sullivan
4. Mattie McIlroy b. 1875
Married John Akers
5. Marion McIlroy b. 1877
1st Married ____McIntosh
2nd Married Matie McGuire
  1. Grace McIlroy
  Married Forrest Morris
  2. Atha McIlroy
  3. Marion McIlroy
  Married Bruce Fagan
6. Lott McIlroy b. 1879
Married Ella Coleman
  1. Laurence McIlroy
  Married ____ Lipp
    1. Martha

2. Cecil McIlroy
Married T.W. McCullum (No children)
3. Harley McIlroy
Married Leona Perkins
    1. Harley Leon McIlroy
    Married Dorothy _____
        1. Ronnie McIlroy
        2. Kerry McIlroy
        3. Kevin McIlroy
4. Mable McIlroy
Married F. White
    1. Wayne
        1. Pam
        2. Carol
5. Lela McIlroy
7. Elmo McIlroy b. 1881 D.Y.
8. Maude McIlroy b. 1883
Married Virgie McIntosh
    1. Olin McIntosh
    2. Floy McIntosh
9. Thomas Archibald McIlroy
    1. Aubrey McIlroy
        1. Dale
    2. Howard McIlroy
    Married Johnnie
        1. Diana
        Married _____ Starnes
        2. Howard Wayne
    3. Alvone McIlroy
    Married _____ McManus
    4. Haskell McIlroy
    5. Mary McIlroy
    Married Bob Boyce
    6. Sue McIlroy
    Married Lewis Craw
    7. Jack McIlroy
    8. Morris McIlroy
    Married _____
        1. Monte McIlroy

6. Elizabeth Jane McIlroy b. 1-3-1849 d. 4-19-1927
1st Married John W. Vandergriff on 1-28-1866
   1. James (Jim) R. Vandergriff b. 3-31-1866 d. 4-22-1949
   Married Lanora "Nora" Stubblefield
      1. Myrtle Vandergriff
      Married _____ McKinzey
         1. Mildred Vandergriff
         Married Ray Young
         2. Wayne Vandergriff
         3. Loretta
         Married Leslie Sutton
         4. Loice Vandergriff
         Married D.E. Conner
         5. J.R. Vandergriff
         6. Beatrice Vandergriff
         Married Dewey Dixon
         7. John Mack Vandergriff
      2. Willie Vandergriff b. 4-17-1892
      Married _____
         1. Wayne Vandergriff
      3. Lola? Vandergriff b. 1907 d. 3-26-1959
   2. Joseph Ruffin Vandergriff b. 8-27-1871 d. 9-11-1929
   Married Jane Elizabeth Hopkins
      1. Amy Vandergriff b. 11-6-1896
      (Never married)
   3. Jane Ada Vandergriff b. 9-2-1874 d. 12-13-1928
   Married S.G. Nettle
      1. Lorah Nettle (no children)
      2. P.V. Nettle Jr.
      Married Margerie Wrepe
         1. Child D.Y.
         2. P.V. Nettle Jr.
         Married _____
            1. Shawn Nettle
   4. Minnie Florence Vandergriff b. 1876 D.Y.
   5. John Thomas Vandergriff[9] b. 1878 d. 1-1-1965

---

9    John Thomas Vandergriff moved to Carrolton, Texas about the same time his cousin Sam moved to Hill County, Texas. He was a blacksmith, the same occupation as his father in Randolph County, Arkansas, for several years until he became a Chevrolet dealer. He managed the business until his sons were old enough to take over. After I (J.R. McIlroy) became

Married Mollie Hugins
1. William Thomas Vandergriff (Hooker)
Married C. Mays
   1. Thomas Joe Vandergriff
   Married Anna _____
      1. Vanessa Vandergriff
      2. Victor Vandergriff
      3. Valoria Vandergriff
      4. Vanaca Vandergriff
   2. Virginia Sue Vandergriff
   1st Married Jake Hopeman
   2nd Married Jerry Deartnig
2. Gordon "Smokey" Tilman Vandergriff
3. Dorothy Vandergriff
Married _____ O'Dell
4. Jack Vandergriff
Married J. Echols
   1. Jack Vandergriff
   Married Marylou _____
      1. Sue Ann Vandergriff
      2. David Vandergriff
      3. Dean Vandergriff
      4. Dale Vandergriff
   2. Peggy Vandergriff
   Married _____ DeSola
      1. Darek DeSola
      2. Dana DeSola
      3. Dug DeSola
5. Bobbie Lavern Vandergriff
Married C.E. Collins
   1. Charlene Collins
   2. Melinda Collins
   3. Amy Kate Collins
6. Jesse Vandergriff b. 11-26-1880 d. 7-12-1964
(Never married)
2nd Married Calvin Hagger in 1883

---

a Chevrolet dealer, he came to visit me several times. This family served as close friends to my grandparents, Samuel and Amanda McIlroy, and we visited them several times when I was a young boy.

7. Alan Hagger b. 1883 D.Y.
8. Alpha Zelotus Hagger
Married Reta Harris
   1. Joe Alan Hagger
3$^{rd}$ Married William Baker in 1888
9. Oregon Baker b. 1-14-1889 d. 7-8-1969
Married _____ Grady
   1. Paulene Baker b. 12-21-1918
   Married Henry Brewer
      1. Wanda Brewer
      2. Henry Brewer Jr.
10. Maggie Baker D. Y.
7. Chloe T. McIlroy b. 1853 d. 1-5-1927
Married W.C. (Conley) Byrd on 2-25-1872
   1. Hampton Byrd b. 1873 d. 1879
   2. Mariah Byrd b. 1875 d. 1880
   3. Mont Byrd b. 1877 d. 1951
   Married Mattie _____
      1. Grace Byrd b. 6-1899
   4. Effie Byrd b. 1880 d. 1900
   Married Thomas W. Turner
   5. Mattie Byrd b. 1882
   Married _____ Byrd
   6. Archie Byrd b. 1884
   7. William M. Byrd b. 10-24-1887 d. 1-21-1969
   Married Lurah A. Williams on 11-2-1913
      1. Paul C. Byrd b. 1914
      2. C.W. Byrd b. 1918
      3. Omar Byrd b. 1922
      4. Robert Byrd b. 1924
8. Bell McIlroy b. 1857 (no children)
3. Alexander McIlroy[10] b. 6-4-1813 d. 1-4-1862
Married Francis Kennedy (b. 1816 d. 6-5-1886)

---

10   Alexander McIlroy was the only son of Samuel that did not live within a few miles of 11-Point River. He had moved to Green County, an adjoining county. He had a country store and did quite well, mostly because he had a still in the back of the store that enabled him to sell liquor. Francis Kennedy, his wife, was a devout Baptist. A story has it that she prayed every morning and night that he would get rid of that still. A few days after he died, she did. At least two of their children became Baptist pastors, and her granddaughter became the dean of women at Baylor University.

1. Vandalia Prewitt McIlroy b. 1-23-1840 d. 1-14-1862
Married Sarah _____
2. Fernando "Bud" Colombus McIlroy b. 4-8-1844 d. 9-19-1865
3. Ezra Vespusus McIlroy b. 11-17-1842 d. 2-5-1874
Married Sarah "Callie" McIlroy Lankford on 9-19-1869
    1. Sarah Ann McIlroy d. 8-12-1872
    2. Gus McIlroy b. 1873
4. Oregon Dallas (O.D.) "Polk" McIlroy[11] b. 2-17-1845 d. 5-17-1925
Married Lucearchy C. Burke (b. 5-23-1853 d. 2-6-1939) on 12-24-1974
    1. Rufus McIlroy b. 11-26-1875 d. 5-2-1876
    2. Sallie Lula McIlroy b. 10-25-1878 d. 8-13-1957
Married James Lafayette Roberson on 3-31-1901
        1. James Lafayette Roberson b. 2-23-1902 d. 5-28-1976
Married Lola Howell
            1. James H. Roberson b. 6-28-1922
1st Married Annie Myrle Hendon on 2-2-1944
            1. Nancy Myrle Roberson b. 4-15-45
Married John W. Jones on 8-12-1966
                1. Hollis Ray Jones b. 9-30-1969
                2. Ryan C. Jones b. 6-22-1975
            2. Stefin Lynn Roberson b. 1-26-1952
Married Harly Greer III on 10-10-1970
                1. Harry Greer IV b. 5-16-1971
                2. Scott R. Greer b.1974
                3. Shari Lynn Greer b. 1-29-1976
2nd Married Suzy Wild
            2. Newton C. Roberson b. 2-8-1927
Married Joyce Koontz (b. 4-5-1930)
            1. Lee Ann Roberson b. 11-10-1958
            2. William David Roberson b. 1-27-1956
            3. Carol Jean Roberson b. 10-13-1957
        3. Maddie D. Roberson b. 2-16-1929
Married Olin Ralph Vernon
            1. Lorrine Vernon b. 9-5-1952

11 Oregon Dallas was one of the most popular of all the McIlroys. The family had moved to Rains County after the death of his father, and he farmed for awhile, but later on he became editor of the newspaper at Burnet, Texas and was a part-time Baptist pastor. Every time I talked to my older kin about their family, they all remembered him. My grandmother named her second son Dallas after Oregon Dallas.

2. Dennis Ralph Vernon b. 11-15-1957
3. Betty Douglas Vernon b. 6-8-1974
4. James Andrew Vernon b. 6-1974
2. Herman Dallas Roberson b. 8-7-1903 d. 6-22-1967
1st Married Laura Etta Oney
  1. Ella Louise Roberson b. 12-10-1926
  Married Ralph O. Wortham
    1. Ralph O. Wortham Jr. b. 11-26-1942
    Married Ruby Moreen
    2. Betty Jean Wortham
    Married Leo Thornley
      1. J. Lee Thornley
      2. Melissa Thornley b. 9-17-1972
2nd Married Dolly Woodall
  2. Herman Dallas Roberson Jr. b. 8-24-1933
  1st Married Wanda Hall
    1. Aubrey Roberson
  2nd Married Gerold Dean Price
    2. Elaine Roberson b. 2-24-1959
  3. Wallace Carol Roberson b. 6-15-1936
  Married Fay Chambless
    1. Lisa Roberson b. 7-28-1963
    2. Nicole Roberson b. 10-11-1974
  4. Jimmie LeRoy Roberson b. 7-8-1938
  Married Roberta Nabors
    1. Jimmie Roberson Jr. b. 3-24-1972
    2. Adora Roberson b. 11-20-1973
  5. Nancy Ann Roberson b. 6-14-1945
  Married Willis Newman
    1. Cynthia Newman b. 4-16-1961
    2. Julie Newman b. 1-28-1963
    3. Ben Newman b. 11-19-1964
    4. Bobbie Newman b. 7-24-1967
    5. Shanna Newman b. 7-17-1974
3. B.L. "Jack" Roberson b. 10-9-1905
Married Hettie Jewel McCosland
  1. Doris Dean Roberson b. 6-18-1930
  1st Married Charlie E. Bradford
  2nd Married Billy McCauley
    1. Donald Edward McCauley

        1. Donald McCauley b. 9-19-1968

        2. Andy McCauley b. 8-1-1970

3rd Married Paul Tanner

2. Walter Gene Roberson b. 7-22-1932

Married Wanda Stevens

    1. Roberta Roberson b. 3-7-1951

    Married Paul Hightower

        1. Laurie Ann Hightower b. 3-1-1973

        2. Julie Lynne Hightower b. 3-13-1975

    2. Joyce Roberson b. 10-12-1953

    3. Jerry L. Roberson b. 11-28-1956

    4. Lois J. Roberson b. 2-23-1951

    5. Sandra Roberson b. 7-21-1963

    6. Stephen G. Roberson b. 7-19-1968

3. Myrtle Marie Roberson b. 1-6-1936

Married Willie Lee Thatcher

    1. Patsy Marie Thatcher b. 5-11-1951

    2. Gary Lee Thatcher b. 5-23-1952

    Married Judy Kay Citty

        1. Andrea Marie Thatcher b. 1-30-1975

        2. Amy Elizabeth Thatcher b. 3-8-1977

    3. Linda Kay Thatcher b. 5-21-1953

    Married Nolan E. Janes

        1. Tina Marie Janes b. 10-5-1978

    4. Debrah Joan Thatcher b. 6-8-1956

    5. Vickie Oran Thatcher b. 6-26-1963

4. Hershall Charles Roberson b. 8-18-1907 d. 9-23-1943

5. Maurice E. Roberson b. 7-5-1910

Married Verdia Ellen McCasland

    1. Jack Roberson b. 12-10-1931

    Married Ella Mactalley

        1. Sharon Kay Roberson b. 2-3-1959

        2. James R. Roberson b. 5-1-1965

    2. Ralph Roberson b. 12-30-1934

    Married Vera Allen

        1. Michael Edward Roberson b. 1-7-1959

        2. Deborah Lynn Roberson b. 8-26-1962

        3. Mary Ellen Roberson b. 9-20-1971

    3. Harold Wade Roberson b. 5-5-1939

Married Norma Burton
   1. David Lee Roberson b. 2-16-1959
   2. Deana Sue Roberson b. 2-16-1959
4. Maurice Ray Roberson b. 5-5-1939
Married Patricia Sara Otero
   1. Kurt Maurice Roberson b. 4-3-1962
   2. Marlene Renee Roberson b. 5-15-1963
5. Loretta Fay Roberson b. 4-6-1941
Married Neil Thomas Keyes
   1. Lorane Lee Keyes b. 3-10-1961
   Married Terry Jones
      1. Jacquline Lee Jones b. 12-9-1979
   2. Elizabeth Ellen Keyes b. 4-17-1965
3. Chester Ashley McIlroy b. 6-16-1881 d. 1-22-1960
Married Bettie McMillon (d. 1-11-1967) on 8-1-1906
   1. Chester Britton McIlroy b. 11-3-1907 d. 5-5-1978
   Married Odessa Brown
      1. Byron Ashley McIlroy b. 12-29-1955
   2. Lavirgie Irene McIlroy b. 1-16-1909
1st Married Clarence Martin Brummett
   1. Shirley Jean Brummett b. 11-4-1930
2nd Married William Stahlheber
   1. William L. Stahlheber b. 8-9-1933
   Married Frieda Loraine Hoague
      1. William Patrick Stahlheber b. 6-27-1958
      Married Gina Leeper
         1. Christopher Allen Stahlheber
         2. Cynthia Ann Stahlheber
      2. Christopher Allen Stahlheber b. 3-22-1960
      3. Gina Melissa Stahlheber b. 12-7-1969
3. Lanora Addie McIlroy b. 3-3-1911
Married Leslie Dee Morgan
   1. Bonnie Sue Morgan b. 7-10-1931
   Married Marvin Albert Schwarz
      1. Sherri Sue Schwarz b. 6-1-1950
      Married Benny Lynn Cherry
      2. Gary Morgan Schwarz b. 10-5-1952
      Married Marilee Ann Whitley
         1. Blair Morgan Schwarz b. 3-23-1980
      3. Mark Albert Schwarz b. 2-26-1956

Married Jami Lynn Welch (b. 8-28-1957)
  4. Brad Dee Schwarz b. 9-3-1957
  Married Susan Michelle Sparron
 2. Patricia Joyce Morgan b. 6-19-1940
 Married Robert Glenn Jarvis
  1. Jeffrey Glenn Jarvis b. 3-31-1963
  2. Robert Todd Jarvis b. 6-22-1965
  3. Tate Morgan Jarvis b. 11-6-1970
4. Jessie Lou McIlroy b. 10-13-1913
Married James John Newbauer
 1. Yvonne Antoinette Newbauer b. 4-19-1937
 Married James Edward Nordmeyer, Sr. (b. 5-17-1936)
  1. James Edward Nordmeyer, Jr. b. 8-16-1958
  2. Rebecca Susan Nordmeyer b. 11-15-1962
 2. Janette Newbauer b. 9-17-1942
 Larry Don Perkins
  1. Shari Diane Perkins b. 2-15-1963
  2. Pamela Kay Perkins b. 12-21-1964
 3. Michael James Newbauer b. 7-13-1948
 1st Married Lynn Ann Martin Newbauer
  1. Jody Newbauer b. 4-1-1970
  2. Jenny Lynn Newbauer b. 8-5-1971
 2nd Married Alice Lorraine Stevens (b. 2-15-1940)
5. Glenn McIlroy b. 1-17-1916
6. Lin McIlroy b. 1-17-1916 d. 12-31-1978
Married Mary Lou Adam (b. 3-22-1931)
 1. Jimmy Ray McIlroy b. 8-15-1948
 Married LaDonna Freeman
  1. Adam Cary McIlroy b. 10-5-1972
  2. Brooke McKenzie McIlroy
 2. Linda Lou McIlroy(twin) b. 3-9-1950
 Married William David Cucinello
  1. Shelly Ann Cucinello b. 1-4-1979
 3. Glin Davis McIlroy(twin) b. 3-9-1950 d. 3-9-1950
 4. Mary Ann McIlroy b. 9-26-1951
 Married Richard Lynn Stout
7. James Burke McIlroy b. 2-26-1918 d. 7-2-1939
8. Alma Bernice McIlroy b. 4-27-1921 d. 8-6-1977
Married William Cecil Peck

9. Jack Radford McIlroy b. 9-19-1923 d. 8-6-1977
Married Betty Ann Geraughty (b. 2-29-1928)
   1. Debora Lee McIlroy b. 9-8-1947
   2. Jack Redford McIlroy Jr. b. 1-12-1950
   1st Married Terry Lynn Holbrook
      1. Jennifer Lynn McIlroy b. 3-28-1972
      2. Jackie Lee McIlroy b. 1-7-1974
   2nd Married Kathryn Ann Bomer (b. 10-28-1948)
   3. Penny Gail McIlroy b. 8-26-1955
   Married Gary Wayne Canipe
      1. Ashley Ann Canipe b. 11-8-1978
10. Robert Lanor b. 9-20-1926
1st Married Theresa Brilliant
   1. Robert Chester Lanor b. 7-5-1950
   2. Debra Ann Lanor b. 9-4-1952
   3. Sheila Lanor b. 3-31-1959
   4. Christopher Lin Lanor b. 8-26-1960
   5. June Marie Lanor b. 6-17-1964
2nd Married Doris May Graham
4. Francis Jeanette McIlroy b. 2-27-1882 d. 1-1-1951
Married Orlander Haskell Crews on 4-20-1908
   1. Dallas Alline Crews b. 2-21-1909
   Married James Walton (b. 5-21-1910 d. 8-27-1967) Jordan Sr.
      1. Lana Jeanette Jordan b. 11-13-1943
      2. James Walton Jordan Jr. b. 7-5-1946
      1st Married Barbara L. Branch (b. 1-25-1947)
         1. Jill Jordan b. 11-10-1968
      2nd Married Sallie Ruth Hubbard Wilson
         1. James Walton Jordan III b. 4-19-1972
         2. Lawrence Cary Jordan b. 9-18-1979
   2. Ruby Lou Crews b. 6-26-1910
   Married B.C. Johnson
      1. LaJunta Jeaneane Johnson b. 10-4-1933
      Married Guy Harold Farmer
         1. Guy Michael Farmer b. 10-4-1951
         Married Glenda Kay Elredge (Gillispie)
         (b. 3-16-1947)
            1. LaJunta Kay Farmer b. 5-31-1978
         2. Marshall B. Farmer b. 1-12-1953
         Married Emily Marie Fornie (b. 8-5-1954)

      1. Tracy Lynette Farmer b. 5-31-1976

      2. B.C. Farmer b. 1-14-1979

      3. LaJunta Michelle Farmer b. 2-27-1955

      Married James Edward Rios (b. 9-26-1954)

         1. Jamie Edwards Rios b. 12-25-1978

   3. Francis Marion Crews b. 6-7-1913 b. 7-19-1929

   4. Ella Louise Crews b. 8-21-1915 d. 3-3-1974

   Married Joe Edward Batis

      1. Ramona Jo Batis b. 4-25-1943

      Married Harold Knight (b. 11-17-1939)

         1. Marie Monique Knight b. 12-26-1968

         2. Kevin Heath Knight b. 11-28-1970

      2. Kathryn Francis Batis b. 9-14-1945

      Married Keith John Ekberg, Sr. (b. 11-2-1943)

         1. Keith John Ekberg, Jr. b. 12-30-1968

   5. Marshall Woodrow Crews b. 7-11-1917

5. Martha Jane McIlroy b. 2-27-1882

Married William Frederick. Shotwell

   1. Fannie Lucille Shotwell b. 10-2-1905 d. 9-14-1906

   2. Frederick Delwyn Shotwell b. 8-21-1906

   Married Mary Opal Powers

      1. Patti Lynn Shotwell b. 10-22-1958

   3. Leona Shotwell b. 4-27-1909

   Married Edward Warren Kelley

      1. Don Warren Kelly b. 6-9-1952

   4. Lula Irene Shotwell b. 10-24-1911

   Married Woodrow Marshall Shaddix, Sr.

      1. Glenda Muriel Shaddix b. 11-28-1942

      Married Joe Marvin Ellis, Jr.

         1. Sharon Kae Ellis b. 9-11-1960

         2. Teresa Gay Ellis b. 11-22-1962

      2. Woodrow Marshall Shaddix, Jr. b. 10-18-1946

      Married Patsy G. Williams

         1. Cassie Lynn Shaddix b. 10-5-1965

         2. Douglas Wayne Shaddix b. 3-21-1968

   5. J.D. Shotwell b. 10-28-1913 d. 12-1-1957

   6. Marvin Lou Shotwell b. 11-6-1915 d. 7-29-1960

   7. Effa Ella Shotwell b. 4-24-1918

   Married Otis Paul Robinson

1. Jerry Weldon Robinson b. 2-18-1940
Married E.V. Dodson
   1. Brandi Lea b. 6-28-1963
   2. Scott Allen b. 2-8-1967
2. William Paul Robinson b. 10-2-1945
Married Mary Frances Hall
   1. Jeffrey Jay Robinson b. 2-12-1964
   2. William Keith Robinson b. 3-31-1967
   3. Jamie Sue Robinson b. 8-6-1968
3. Martha Susan Robinson b. 5-24-1949
4. Leslie Gene Robinson b. 2-10-1952
Married Deborah Irene Byrd
   1. Russell Steven Robinson b. 10-31-1972
   2. Julie Colleen Robinson b. 4-19-1976
8. Mattie Shotwell b. 3-28-1922
Married Edward C. Foster, Sr.
   1. Edward C. Foster, Jr. b. 12-18-1946
   1st Married Norma Jean Nally
      1. Melissa Jane Foster b. 4-9-1965
   2nd Married Linda Dell Cozby
      1. Michael James Foster b. 11-11-1972
      2. David Gregory Foster (twin) b. 12-4-1977
      3. Tamara Lynn Foster (twin) b. 12-4-1977
   2. Lois Jane Foster b. 11-11-1948
Married Nelson James Huffman
      1. Nelson Skeeter Huffman b. 9-7-1974
      2. Casey Ryan Huffman b. 10-14-1975
      3. Janie Jaye Huffman b. 11-7-1976
   3. Vicki Linn Foster b. 6-5-1952
6. Carol Ross McIlroy b. 6-21-1887 d. 6-16-1963
Married Willie Mabel Shaw (b. 1-3-1891 d. 1-3-1958) on 9-27-1908
   1. Carol Rupert McIlroy b. 10-20-1909
   1st Married Omega Earl Hagins
   1. Betty Carolyn Hagins b. 4-29-1936
Married James Roger Vind
      1. Debra Kaye Vind b. 5-19-1955
Married Samuel David Blake
         1. Justin B. Blake b. 7-9-1975
         2. Bradley David Blake b. 12-28-1977

2. Roger Dale Vind b. 3-6-1957
Married Denise Marie Kraft
    1. Laura Nicole Vind b. 8-21-1978
2nd Married Gladyth Mae Rhodes Walter
2. Oscar Leo McIlroy b. 9-20-1911
Married Rowena Cook Baker
    1. Carol Ashley McIlroy b. 11-15-1946
    Married Vivian Marie Oden
        1. Shannon Denise McIlroy b. 1-14-1970
3. Ross McIlroy Jr. b. 8-29-1919
Married Mary Nell Morgan
    1. Kenneth Ross McIlroy b. 7-19-1950
    Married Donna Jo Rowe
    2. James David McIlroy b. 9-10-1952
    Married Bonita Jean Binch
        1. Mark David McIlroy b. 11-4-1978
4. O. Dee McIlroy b. 10-2-1928
Married Sybil A. Eason
    1. Peggy Ruth b. 1-17-1949
    Married Larry Dean Hedgpeth
        1. Kimberly Dawn b. 1-31-1968
        2. Kinley Earl b. 10-5-1970
        3. Kevin Dee b. 10-5-1970
    2. Stephen D. b. 4-24-1955
    Married Jackie Arlene Dethridge
7. Ella Alice Victoria McIlroy b. 12-1-1890 d. 8-18-1963
Married Joseph Bartlett on 11-21-1908
    1. Joseph Wayne Bartlett b. 9-17-1909 d. 8-9-1976
    Married Huldah Myrtle Byars
        1. Joseph Estes Bartlett b. 11-16-1931
        2. Wanda Jeanette Bartlett b. 7-4-1934
        3. Minnie Ella Bartlett b. 6-25-1933
        4. Norma Jewell Bartlett b. 12-5-1937
        1st Married Bobby Alfred Roden
            1. Thomas Anthony Roden b. 10-15-1954
            2. Martha Wayne Roden b. 3-1-1956
            3. Bonnie Susan Roden b. 7-29-1957
        2nd Married George A. Russell
        5. Larry Wayne Bartlett b. 10-9-1949

2. Harry Leonard Bartlett b. 3-1-1911 d. 4-5-1972
3. Kenneth Warren Bartlett b. 2-7-1921 d. 5-19-1967
Married Betty Fay Owens
    1. Linda Kay Bartlett b. 1-28-1942
2nd Married Christine Land
    1. Kenneth Wayne Bartlett b. 10-18-1944
3rd Married Pauline Elizabeth Thorn
    1. Jerry Dwayne Bartlett b. 12-24-1949
    Married Brenda Irene Allen
        1. Jerry Dwayne Bartlett, Jr. b. 1-9-1979
    2. Terry Joe Bartlett b. 3-30-1952
    Married Lenora June Sanders
        1. Tonja Lynn Bartlett b. 6-14-1976
        2. Tamra Naomi Bartlett b. 6-24-1978
    3. Kenneth Warren Bartlett Jr. b. 5-8-1961
5. Louisa Elizabeth McIlroy b. 6-4-1847 d. 12-4-1856
6. Chester Ashley McIlroy b. 1-9-1849 d. 1926
Married Mary Francis LaCoe
    1. Chester McIlroy d. 6-18-1965
    Married _____
        1. Edith
        2. Dorothy
    Married Walter Isham
    2. Delwin McIlroy
    (no children)
    3. Lillie McIlroy b. 1-24-1887 d. 8-21-1958
    Married James B. Russell
        1. Mary Claudia Russell
        Married _____ Standish
    4. Minnie McIlroy b. 9-14-1890 d. 1-19-1979
    (Never married)
    5. Alva McIlroy b. 9-16-1892
    Married _____ Spears
    6. Mary Lula McIlroy b. 6-13-1897 d. 9-19-1975
    Married _____ Doyle
        1. Betty Doyle
        Married _____ Norwood
            1. Elizabeth Norwood
7. Amanda Florida McIlroy b. 5-23-1850 d. 9-21-1911
Married Jacob Jeremiah Gregg on 3-13-1886

1. Jerry Emmett Vandalia Gregg b. 1-13-1888 d. 3-8-1960
Married Flora Nations (d. 10-1959)
    1. Erma Gregg d. 1960
    2. Nina Gregg d. 5-10-1955
    Married George W. Hogen in 1935
        1. Paddy Hogen b. 5-6-1935
        1st Married D.G. Gardner in 1956
        2nd Married W.W. Littlefield in 6-1976
            1. David R. Gardner b. 11-14-1962
            2. Susan L. Gardner b. 8-26-1965
    3. Conrad E. Gregg b. 1913 d. 1918
    4. Geraldine Gregg b. 1915 d. 1955
    Married _____ Wilson
    5. John Gregg b. 1920 d. 12-1960
    6. Mary N. Gregg b. 1-1-1923 d. 12-17-1978
    Married John L. Wilson
2. Mary Elizabeth Gregg b. 1-27-1890 d. 4-30-1960
Married Thomas William Jones (b. 9-15-1886 d. 3-2-1972) on 10-23-1907
    1. Garnie Irene Jones b. 4-17-1909
    Married Osie Danley
        1. Thomas A. Danley b. 1-18-1938
        Married Dana Pender
            1. Joel T. Danley b. 12-30-1960
            2. Jason L. Danley b. 5-24-1962
    2. Pansey Pearl Jones b. 4-13-1911
    Married Vincent M. Lee (b. 12-12-1911 d. 3-26-1965)
        1. Vincent Lee b. 4-30-1940
        Married Linda Tinkrey
            1. Vanessa Lee b. 4-18-1967
            2. Stewart Lee b. 4-18-1868
        2. Judith Lee b. 5-31-1942
        Married Jim Blair
            1. Jamie Blair b. 6-6-1964
            2. Eugene Blair
            3. Kimberly Blair
        3. Jackie Lee b. 4-9-1943
        Married Larry Smith
            1. Vincent Smith b. 1971

2. Larry J. Smith b. 1977
3. Lilie Francis Jones b. 6-18-1912
Married Ike "Chalk" Norton
   1. Mary Joe Norton b. 1-27-1935
   Married Tom Joy
      1. Thomas Joy b. 1955
      2. Michael Joy b. 1958
      3. Kayla Joy b. 1963
4. William Thomas Jones b. 1-18-1915
Married Panzey Courtney (b. 11-18-1919)
(no children)
5. Olive Mary Jones b. 10-23-1916
Married John Stephens (b. 1-15-1909)
   1. Mary E. Stephens b. 10-12-1936
   Married Robert Bishop
      1. Sheron L. Bishop b. 9-30-1957
      2. Robert Bishop Jr. b. 6-1-1955
6. Thomas G. Jones b. 11-18-1918
Married Marcelle Nelson (b. 3-10-1921) on 3-9-1940
   1. Susan Jones b. 3-31-54
   Married Robert Lingnety
      1. Crystal Lingnety b. 1-17-1978
   2. Lynn Jones b. 9-24-1955
   3. Karen Jones b. 12-12-1956
   Married Bill J. Landerson on 3-1-1975
7. Emmett Jones b. 7-21-1926
Married Patricia Jenkinson b. 6-4-1927
   1. Janet Mae Jones b. 3-7-1955
   Married Stephens Adams
      1. Laura Adams b. 5-10-1977
   2. Gail Jones b. 6-24-1956
   3. Leah Jones b. 1-20-1960
   4. Marcie Jones
   5. Thomas W. Jones
8. Sarah Jane McIlroy b. 3-2-1853 d. 9-14-1854
4. Archibald McIlroy b. 1815 d. 1815
5. John McIlroy b. 11-15-1816 d. 11-1863
1st Married Sally Job
(no children)
2nd Married Caroline Edwards

3rd Married Mary Ann Jones[12] (daughter of Polly Russell and Benjamin Jones) on 8-29-1843

1. Francisco McIlroy b. 1843 d. 6-24-1856
2. Kerlue McIlroy b. 11-9-1845 d. 2-7-1847
3. Sarah Caroline "Callie" McIlroy[13] b. 12-20-1846 d. 4-15-1888

1st Married Jordan Lankford (b. 6-7-1822 d. 4-15-1865) on 6-13-1864

2nd Married Ezra "Ves" McIlroy (b. 6-11-1843 d. 2-5-1874) on 4-19-1969

1. Gus McIlroy b. 9-23-1873

Married Mary _____

1. Vera McIlroy

3rd Married Albert W.W. Brooks (b. 9-22-1832 d. 4-22-1894) on 9-29-1874

1. Fannie Brooks b. 8-6-1880

Married James Surridge

---

12 Many of the older McIlroys that I talked to knew Mary Ann Jones (McIlroy) and have quoted stories told by her. Mary Ann was raised on the farm east of the 11-Point River that joined the John McIlroy place. When Mary Ann was sixteen, John McIlroy asked her to marry him. She told him that her mother was not well and she had to help take care of the children. Mary Ann's mother, Polly, and her father did die a few years later. In the meantime, John had married Sally Jo, who died the year after, probably at childbirth, and Caroline Edwards, a marriage that was also shortly over. Soon after Caroline died, Mary Ann wrote John McIlroy a note saying that if he still wanted to marry her, she thought her brothers and sisters were old enough to take care of themselves. They were married and had ten children and thirty-five grandchildren. Another story told by Mary Ann was about her mother's family, the Russells. They were living in Yorktown when Cornwallis surrendered the British army, which virtually ended the Revolutionary War. She said it was the most glorious day, that both armies had their full dress uniforms on and the British marched into town and stacked their arms. Mary Ann said that Sam (my grandfather) was very young when his father died and was very hardheaded. She said his older brothers had to tell him to do opposite of what they wanted him to do in order to get him to do anything. She also said that they had gone to Ravendale Springs and bought Christmas presents one year and came back to the 11-Point River ford and water had come across it. They told Sam, who was driving, not to cross, but he said that they would or die. They almost did he turned over the wagon and lost all the Christmas presents. Mary Ann also left a letter that described her children, and she said that her daughter Callie was a very pretty girl with auburn hair and some freckles, "like a Scotch girl is supposed to have."

13 Callie McIlroy was married in 1864 to her neighbor, Jordan B. Lankford, who soon died on a trip back to Robinson County, Tennessee. She then married her cousin, but he died shortly afterwards. Later, she married W.W. Brooks, who supposedly was the wealthiest man in Randolph County¬ he owned 8,000 acres of land that bordered the Current River.

1. Naomi Surridge
1st Married G.B. Unstedd on 1-10-1917
    1. G.B. Unstedd
    2. James S. Unstedd
2nd Married Forrest Grimes
3rd Married _____ Mitchell
4. Cicero Dekalb "Bud" McIlroy b. 4-24-1850
Married Lavina Ellis (b. 1-18-1851 d. 3-1-1899) on 3-16-1876
    1. Eunice McIlroy b. 8-12-1877 d. 5-25-1907
    Married Laura Davis
        1. Ethel McIlroy
        Married _____ Pruett
        2. Edna McIlroy
    2. Boy D.Y.
5. Mary Elizabeth McIlroy b. 12-30-1852 d. 1-16-1891
Married John E. Amos (b. 1850) on 2-24-1869
    1. Ransom Amos (no children)
    2. Dell Amos d. 1905
    (Never married)
    3. William Amos
    Married Parthena Haynes
        1. H.D. Amos
        Married _____Thornton (no children)
        2. Guy Amos[14]
        1st Married Eileen Goeing
        2nd Married Jane Halton
        3. Chris Amos(no children)
        4. Clyde Amos (no children)
        5. Eva Amos
        Married Willie Johnson
            1. Billy Amos Johnson
    4. Bernie Amos
    Married Bob Lynch
        1. Robert Lynch
        2. Ray Lynch

---

14    Guy Amos was one of the most popular men in Randolph County. For years, he was a barber in Pocahontas, then was elected as sheriff, and later served several terms as county judge. He promised that if the people elected him for his last term, he would never run again. He told me that he regretted that statement because he really wanted to run again. He stayed with his word and went back to being a barber. (J.R.M.)

    3. Parrish Lynch

    5. Robert Amos

    6. Gertrude Amos

Married Hugh Bishop

    1. Printice Bishop

    2. Novell Bishop

    3. Paulene Bishop

    4. Van Bishop

6. Alexander Hamilton McIlroy b. 3-26-1854 d. 3-6-1904

Married Willis Thompson (b. 3-26-1865 d. 10-22-1952) on 2-28-1888

    1. Elmo McIlroy[15] b. 3-6-1893 d. 2-4-1930

Married Idella "Della" Graham[16]

    1. Marie McIlroy b. 12-13-1919

Married Ray Burrow

        1. Allie Ruth Burrow b. 10-25-1941

    Married Gale Clark on 6-28-1969

        2. Laura Burrow b. 10-20-1944

    Married Morris McMillion on 7-13-1964

        1. Carl McMillion b. 10-17-1966

        2. Lora McMillion b. 12-19-1971

        3. Patricia Burrow b. 8-4-1946

    Married Robert Holt

        1. Robert Holt

        4. Nancy Burrow b. 1-16-1948

    Married Russell Hall on 2-1-1969

        1. Don Hall b. 3-16-1974

        2. Jill Rae Hall b. 2-4-1977

    2. E.M. McIlroy b. 6-16-1921

Married Dorothy Gebhardt

    1. Catherine McIlroy b. 11-13-1951

    2. Samuel McIlroy b. 9-3-1953

Married Peggy Boling on 12-29-1973

---

15    Elmo McIlroy was known all over Randolph County as a progressive, successful farmer. He had a good standing in his community as a citizen and his credit at the county banks was unquestioned. He was educated in the county schools and spent two years at the Jonesboro A&M College.

16    Idella "Della" Graham (McIlroy) taught in Randolph county schools for thirty years and participated in all church and community activities.

      3. David Lewis McIlroy(twin) b. 10-13-1954
      Married Wanda Teague on 12-11-1977
      4. Robert Lewis McIlroy (twin) b. 10-13-1954
      Married Patricia Ann Coburn in 2-1978
      5. Ann McIlroy b. 6-22-1957 d. 7-7-1959
    3. James McIlroy b. 11-27-1922
    Married Susan Tyler
      1. Mary E. McIlroy
      Married C.J. Bradford
      2. Laurie Kay McIlroy
      Married Gregory S. Escue
      3. Stephen J. McIlroy
      Married Alma Norton
  2. Maude Wells McIlroy b. 3-23-1897 d. 4-11-1978
  Married H. McAnelly
    1. Katherine McAnelly b. 12-13-1935
    Married Darwin Damon
      1. Michael D. Damon b. 7-18-1957
      2. Kelly Joe Damon b. 4-25-1959 d. 10-27-1975
      3. Todd Raymond Damon b. 10-5-1963
      4. James Patrick Damon b. 10-9-1966
    2. Shirley McAnelly
    Married Allen Ricketts on 10-17-1954
      1. Janice Ricketts b. 6-18-1957
      2. Karen L. Ricketts b. 12-3-1959
  3. Tola McIlroy b. 8-24-1899
  Married Bryson Waddell
    1. Patsey Waddell
    Married Victor Clark
      1. Patricia Clark
      2. Vickie Clark
      3. Mary Clark
      4. Victor Clark
  4. John McIlroy b. 2-2-1902 d. 2-12-1989
  Married Lula Graham (b. 1-4-1897 d. 1-27-2000)
    1. Betty Joan McIlroy b. 1-17-1935
    Married E. Erickson
      1. John Erickson b. 3-31-1959
      2. Erik Erickson b. 6-19-1963
7. Penelope Golden "Nep" McIlroy b. 10-12-1855 d. 2-17-1928

Married Jasper Vandergriff (b. 3-17-1852 d. 1910) on 1-31-1878
1. Mary "Jennie" Vandergriff
Married Frank Smith
  1. Jessie Smith
  Married Claud Snow
  2. Tressie Smith
  Married Joe Snow
  3. Exie Smith
  Married Larry Lowell
    1. Sammy Lowell
    2. Tommie Lowell
  4. Lou Dean Smith
2. Sular Vandergriff
Married Kate Tiner
  1. Edna Vandergriff
  Married Millard Crawford
    1. Golde Fay Crawford
    2. Dallas Crawford
    3. Thomas Crawford
  2. Alma Lee Vandergriff
  Married Henry Kildow
    1. Wilma Kildow
    2. Thurlow Kildow
    3. Francis Kildow
    4. Perry Kildow
  3. Kenneth Vandergriff
  Married Irene Sparling
    1. Helen Vandergriff
    2. Elvis Vandergriff
    3. Wanda Vandergriff
    4. William Vandergriff
  4. Alouis Vandergriff
  Married Cecil Thatch
    1. Ben Thatch
    2. Lavanta Thatch
    3. Peggy Thatch
  5. Avis Vandergriff
  Married Joyce Peterson
    1. Patsy Vandergriff

    2. William Vandergriff
    6. Joe Vandergriff
    Married Glenda White (no children)
    7. Dennis Vandergriff
    Married Bernie Rau
    8. Bonnie Vandergriff
    Married Herman Bukenback
    9. Clyde Vandergriff
    Married Charlene Thatch
        1. Bobby Joe Vandergriff
        2. Darrell Vandergriff
        3. Darlene Vandergriff
        4. Laverne Vandergriff
    10. Clay Vandergriff
3. Claudia Vandergriff
1st Married Will Brooks
    1. Charles Brooks
2nd Married _____ Johnson
    2. Lorene Johnson
    Married Lehman Kellett
        1. Helen Kellett
        2. Dwayne Kellett
        3. Shirley Kellett
        4. Doyle Kellett
        5. Jim Kellett
        6. Anna Kellett
    3. Anna L. Johnson
    Married Troy Russell
    4. Ada Johnson
    Married Sherman Hager
4. Augustus Vandergriff
Married Donna Boling
    1. Lorell Vandergriff
    Married Chester Billings
        1. Harold Billings
        2. Thomas Billings
        3. Neal Billings
        4. Burley Billings
        5. Sharon Billings
    2. Duvall Vandergriff

Married Lucille Riddle
   1. Bill Vandergriff
   2. Alta Vandergriff
3. Cecil Vandergriff
Married Ethel Mars
4. Juanita Vandergriff
Married Adam White
5. Glenn Vandergriff
Married Helen Jones
6. Rayford Vandergriff
Married Zelda Booth
7. Daisy Vandergriff
5. Ollie Vandergriff
Married Henry Tweedy
   1. Julane Tweedy
   Married Orlie Melton
      1. Maxine Melton
      2. Raney Melton
      3. Rhoda Melton
      4. Bridget Melton
   2. Hazel Tweedy
   Married Jewel Early
   3. Paul Tweedy
   Married Vida Thomas
   4. Carl Tweedy
   Married Mary Adams
   5. Harold Tweedy
   (Never married)
   6. Helen Tweedy
   Married James Pratt
6. Willie Vandergriff
Married _____ Jones
   1. Cletus Vandergriff
   Married Mae Crawford
   2. Curtis Vandergriff
   Married Faye White
   3. Essie Vandergriff
   Married Arthur Blackwell
   4. Dessie Vandergriff

Married Jack Eaton
7. Minnie F. Vandergriff b. 10-6-1976 d. 3-5-1977
Married _____
   1. Lorell
   Married Chester Billings
      1. Harold Billings
      2. Thomas Billings
      3. Neal Billings
      4. Burley Billings
      5. Sharon Billings
   2. Duvell
   Married Lucella Riddle
   3. Cecil
   Married Ethel Mars
   4. Juanita
   Married Adam White
      1. William White
      2. Alta White
   6. Rayford
   Married Zelda Booth
   7. Daisy
8. Robert J. McIlroy b. 8-24-1857 d. 3-13-1929
Married Sarah Vandergriff (b. 1-18-1852)
   1. Walter R. McIlroy b. 8-6-1855
   Married Myrtle Jackson
   2. Vess McIlroy b. 1-18-1890 d. 2-11-1898
   3. Clyde McIlroy b. 12-1893 (no children)
   4. Emmett McIlroy b. 4-15-1900 d. 3-9-1963
   5. Grace McIlroy b. 3-16-1889 d. 7-10-1976
   Married Paul Roehr in 1922
      1. Paul Roehr Jr. b. 1924
      2. Bertha Roehr b. 1926
      3. Dorothy Roehr b. 1928
      4. Sarah Roehr b. 1930
      Married William B. Head
   6. Earl McIlroy b. 1896 d. 1971
   Married Agnes Schoenfelt
      1. Robert Earl McIlroy Jr. b. 2-27-1931
      Married Carolyn Hoyt on 6-9-1956
         1. Nancy Jane McIlroy b. 8-24-1957

Married Ricky Maurey
   1. Rebecca Maurey b. 4-20-1980
   2. Craig E. Maurey b. 8-16-1982
   3. Robert J. Maurey b. 12-20-1985
  2. Robert E. McIlroy b. 2-23-1959
Married Pamela K. Johnson on 5-16-1981
   1. Misty McIlroy b. 8-28-1982
   2. Robb Early McIlroy b. 6-24-1982
   3. Scott Hoyt McIlroy b. 6-28-1983
  3. Penny Gail McIlroy b. 4-5-1962
Married Ronnie Hampton on 12-27-1980
   1. Ronnie J. Hampton b. 3-22-1983
   2. Benjamin E. Hampton b. 5-21-1985
 2. William D. McIlroy
Married Barbara Matthews
   1. Yvonne Gennetta McIlroy
   2. Diana Lynn McIlroy
7. Ted McIlroy b. 12-8-1904 d. 1970
   1. Patricia McIlroy
9. Evaline McIlroy b. 3-6-1859 d. 10-23-1940
Married Gideon Thompson (b. 10-25-1857 d. 7-9-1914) on 8-30-1883
   1. Mazie Thompson b. 8-27-1884 d. 3-25-1937
Married Charles A. Dixon on 5-2-1903
   1. Dorothy Dizon b. 11-1-1908
Married M.V. Hatchet
   (no children)
   2. Helen Dixon b. 1-7-1914 d. 2-1-1993
Married Harold Bly on 12-31-1942
   1. Linda Bly b. 12-10-1950
   3. Mariam Dixon b. 10-8-1916
Married Lewis Sanders on 12-14-1942
   (no children)
 2. Daly Thompson
Married Ouida Blankenship
   1. Daly Thompson Jr.
Married Jeanne H. Scott in 8-1958
   2. Sarah E. Thompson b. 10-3-1933
Married Dan Finch in 6-1956

1. Michael Finch
2. _____ Finch
3. Roy Thompson
Married Sarah Hopkins
1. Ross H. Thompson
Married Harriet _____
2. Margaret F. Thompson
Married John Murdock
1. Glen Murdock
2. Ellen Murdock
10. Samuel Benjamin McIlroy[17] b. 10-27-1860 d. 2-9-1910
Married Amanda Lewis (b. 10-6-1866 d. 5-15-1944) on 10-11-1883
1. I.V. McIlroy b. 10-1-1886 d. 1963
Married Ida Bell Brown
1. Emma Dee McIlroy b. 10-16-1906 d. 7-14-2004
Married Homer H. Beene
1. Lorenda Beene b. 5-25-1933
Married Joe Howard
1. Marsha Howard
Married Gary Hubbard
1. Matthew Hubbard
Married Gerron _____
2. Meliah Howard
3. Scott Howard
2. Thelma Mae McIlroy b. 1911
1st Married _____ Pritchett
2nd Married _____ White
(no children)
2. Essie McIlroy b. 4-2-1890 d. 1956
Married Tom G. Foster b. 1-31-1885 d. 1941
1. Thomas Elmer Foster b. 8-17-1914
(Never married)
2. Thurman Norris Foster b. 1915
Married Lillie Anna Hegar

---

17    I never knew my grandfather, Samuel Benjamin McIlroy, and my father was only six years old when Sam died. I did talk to several people that remembered Sam¬ one was Herma Hawley, who was his niece by marriage. She had come to Texas with the McIlroys and she lived with them for awhile. She said that Sam was a good man, a hard worker, and a good manager. She also said that if he had not died at fifty, he would have owned the whole community.

(no children)
3. Leona Estaline Foster b. 1918
1<sup>st</sup> Married H.D. Woodruff on 6-26-1945 (no children)
2<sup>nd</sup> Married Cloyd Cartwright on 9-30-1950
    1. Barbara Cloylene b. 11-23-1954
    Married Jerry Kelm
        1. Jerry Dale Kelm
        2. Melissa Kelm
    Married Andrew Tucker
3. Dallas McIlroy b. 6-3-1892 d. 1965
1<sup>st</sup> Married Annie Acton (b. 1890 d. 1929)
2<sup>nd</sup> Married Anna Sears (d. 1970)
    1. Lottie Lee McIlroy b. 9-29-1914
    Married Orla Dugger on 4-16-1933
        1. Della Dugger b. 12-23-1935
        Married Kenneth Anderson on 3-23-1958
        (3 children)
        2. Howard Dugger b. 3-1-1938
        Married Susanne Nelson on 12-20-1964
        3. Anita Dugger b. 4-8-1945
        4. Troy Lee Dugger b. 1-18-1950
    2. Birdie Bee McIlroy b. 12-10-1915
    Married T.F. Ramsey on 12-29-1935
        1. Francis Ann Ramsey b. 10-18-1936
        Married Charles M. Tyson on 3-15-1957
        2. Gloria Kay Ramsey b. 11-1942
        Married Keith Lamb in 6-1958
    3. Martha McIlroy b. 1-12-1917
    Married M. Douglas White
        1. Douglas Ray White b. 3-15-1937
        2. Jerry Don White b. 1-4-1939
    4. Dorothy Dee McIlroy b. 8-23-1921
    Married Thomas Sherrod
        1. Sandra Ann Sherrod b. 3-23-1943
        Married Clyde Smith on 5-30-1959
4. Lewis McIlroy b. 9-7-1897 d. 7-13-1973
1<sup>st</sup> Married Della Francis Rainbolt (b. 1897 d. 9-11-1930) in 1916
    1. Dorcas McIlroy b. 6-13-1917
    1<sup>st</sup> Married Carl Brustrom

      1. Norman Dale Brustrom b. 10-1-1939

2nd Married William Shales

      1. Dari Lynn Shales

2. Samuel McIlroy b. 10-3-1921 d. 8-6-1971

Married Clora Long

      1. Della Eileen McIlroy

      2. Lewis Dwayne McIlroy b. 2-1951

      3. Samuel Wayne McIlroy b. 2-1951

3. James Aubrey McIlroy b. 2-19-1924 d. 9-11-1967

Married Kathleen Fivelash on 12-10-1947

      1. Patricia Claudine Dossett b. 2-27-1945 d. 1985

      (step-daughter)

      2. James A. McIlroy Jr. b. 3-19-1951

      1st Married Debra Kay Nelson

            1. Brandi Michelle McIlroy b. 4-13-1973

            Married Bradley Anderson

      2nd Married Barbara G. Wells

            1. Misty Dawn McIlroy b. 3-2-1977

            2. James A. McIlroy b. 1-31-1980

            Married Nicole Taylor

      3. Frank Lewis McIlroy b. 9-3-1954 D.Y.

      4. Richard Edward McIlroy b. 5-4-1959

      1st Married Sherry Lynn Wright

            1. Jodie Lynn McIlroy b. 10-10-1981

            2. Shelly Kathleen McIlroy b. 5-15-1983

      2nd Married Kara Lousie Francis

      (no children)

      3rd Married Patricia Lynn Mosley

            1. Brook Lenanell McIlroy b. 7-18-1995

4. Frank McIlroy b. 10-5-1928 d. 9-10-1984

Married Freida Hazlett

      1. Brenda Darlene McIlroy

      2. Edwin McIlroy

      3. Linda Gaylene McIlroy

5. S.B. McIlroy[18] b. 4-9-1904 d. 7-23-1968

---

18   S.B. McIlroy was a very intelligent and successful farmer. As my mother told me, he finished school ahead of her and went back to teach math for one year. He would do algebra and trigonometry at home just for the fun of it. He was not only intelligent, but he also had great skills. He built the first radio in Vaughn Community and had a shop where he had various tools including a lathe, welder, forge, and surveying equipment. Whenever

Married Linna L. Hooker (b. 2-26-1904 d. 2-14-1995) on 8-12-1923
1. James Roland McIlroy b. 6-6-1924
Married Margaret Virginia Thomas (b. 9-15-1924) on 6-30-1947
  1. Mary Elizabeth McIlroy b. 1-31-1950
  1st Married Randy Birge
    1. Eric Birge b. 11-1-1971
    Married Jessica Houston
      1. Natalie Birge(twin) b. 4-9-2004
      2. Nathan Birge(twin) b. 4-9-2004
    2. Sarah Birge b. 12-28-1978
    3. Adam Birge b. 11-4-1981
  2nd Married Ernest Chesney (7-28-1948)
    1. Rachel Chesney b. 11-27-1987
  2. James Thomas McIlroy b. 6-29-1951
  Married Rebecca Pence (b. 11-13-1951)
    1. Jennifer McIlroy b. 12-7-1973
    Married Ed Reynolds
      1. Cole Edward Reynolds b. 10-13-2004
      2. Sidney Reynolds b. 4-24-2006
    2. Kimberly McIlroy b. 1-12-1981
    Married Luke Mohon
      1. Bryden Mohon b. 5-11-2005
  3. John David McIlroy b. 9-17-1960
  1st Married Martha Brown
    1. Jessica Leigh McIlroy b. 8-26-1986
    2. Amy Elizabeth McIlroy b. 5-9-1991
  2nd Married Laurie Luetkemeyer
  4. Charles Robert McIlroy b. 2-20-1962
  Married Stacey Smith (b. 11-16-1966) on 1-3-1987
    1. Margaret Abigail "Abby" McIlroy b. 8-10-1996
    2. Daniel Wilson "Will" McIlroy b. 4-28-1998

---

the neighbors needed any terracing or land measurements, he could help them with that. When rural electricity came to the community, he wired the houses in the community. If someone was building a barn or house around him, they always came to him to cut the angles on the rafters. His farming was so clean and neat that if he ever had a crooked row, he went back and re-did it. After my father's funeral, I had a neighbor say to me that he did not know what he would do without my Daddy. He said that S.B. knew when to plant, plow, spray, and harvest, so he watched when he did this and did the same.

2. Barbara McIlroy b. 3-1-1926
Married Malcolm Harper
  1. Malcolm Harper Jr. b. 1-30-1948
  Married Deborah Brooks
    1. Carl Malcolm Harper
    2. Jill E. Harper
    Married Ehren Wetzell
  2. Brenda Kay Harper b. 1-25-1952
  1st Married _____ Shockley
    1. Michael Shockley b. 5-29-1978
  2nd Married _____ Mitchell
    2. Amanda Mitchell b. 11-12-1984
  3rd Married John Hunnicutt
  3. Monica Jan Harper
  1st Married Jim Ford
    1. Mollie Jan Ford b. 12-20-1985
    Married Clifton Paine
    2. Mary Christine Ford b. 4-6-1987
    3. Megan Alice Ford b. 9-20-1993
  2nd Married Mark Sanders
  4. Samuel A. Harper b. 9-7-1957
  Married Cathy Shannon
    1. Andrew "Andy" Harper
    2. Miranda Harper
    Married Jonathan Boddie
3. Ralph Earl McIlroy b. 7-31-1933
Married Shirley Leonard on 3-14-1958
  1. DeAnna McIlroy
  Married David T. Basden
    1. Brittney Ann Basden b. 11-26-1988
    2. David Sterling Basden b. 7-28-1990
    3. Alyssa T. Basden b. 3-13-1997
11. John McIlroy Jr. b. 3-28-1863 d. 9-5-1869
6. William McIlroy b. 1818 D.Y.
7. Andrew McIlroy[19] b. 9-10-1821 d. 12-24-1896
Married Sarah Ann Davis (b. 3-15-1823 d. 12-19-1897)

---

19  Andrew McIlroy attended common country schools in his youth and acquired a fair knowledge. At the age of twenty, he was driving stock. The following year he took charge of the
state line from Frederickstown, Missouri south to Reeves Station. Two years later, he bought
forty acres of land on the east side of the 11-Point River and gradually accumulated land

1. Margaret Elizabeth McIlroy b. 12-25-1845 d. 12-23-1903
Married John C. Williams on 2-7-1875
   1. Dora Williams D.Y.
   2. Tula William b. 10-15-1878 d. 12-24-1955
   Married Erestus Ezra Tyler (b. 1-17-1879 d. 7-1-1941) in 1899
      1. Alma Lorine Tyler b. 1-31-1902
      1st Married Luther Harndnen
         1. Charles Harnden b. 3-10-1934
         2. Helen E. Harnden b. 3-23-1938
         3. Daniel T. Harnden b. 3-23-1938
      2nd Married Ralph Jackson
      2. Harold B. Tyler b. 5-15-1904
      Married Etalka Hite
      3. Charles Tyler b. 3-1900 D.Y.
      4. Sarah Virginia Tyler b. 5-7-1908
      Married Carl Byrd
      5. Everett Glendon Tyler b. 12-1910
      Married Meredith Thomas
      6. Jewell Tyler b. 8-15-1913
      Married William Frazier
         1. Phyllis Frazier
         2. Neal Frazier
      7. Phillip Tyler b. 4-2-1919
      Married Marilyn _____
      8. Joe Dan Tyler b. 2-14-1922
      Married Carol Connell
2. Mary Susan McIlroy b. 9-12-1847 d. 4-26-1916
Married James Norris Lewis (b. 8-26-1849 d. 6-6-1931) on 4-2-1874
   1. John N. Lewis
   Married _____
      1. Maxine
   2. Dr. Everett Lewis
   3. William Lewis D.Y.
   4. Frank Lewis D.Y.
   5. Lelia Lewis D.Y.
3. Amanda C. McIlroy b. 7-3-1849 d. 6-26-1938
Married J. Robert Ross on 4-16-1889

until he owned 950 acres. He was a mason, a staunch member of the Baptist church, and a Democrat. Previous to the Civil War, he was postmaster at Lima for seven years.

(no children)

4. James Franklin "Frank" McIlroy[20] b. 4-1-1851 d. 2-6-1913

(Never married)

5. Daniel Webster McIlroy[21] b. 12-24-1853 d. 7-30-1892

1st Married Martha Gross

2nd Married _____ Hatley

  1. Frank McIlroy b. 12-1881 d. 1963

  Married Lee Luttnel

    1. Euell Franklin McIlroy b. 3-26-1906

    Married Dorothy French

      1. Barbara McIlroy

      2. Daniel McIlroy

      3. Margaret McIlroy

    2. Maxine McIlroy

    1st Married Aubrey Thompson (d. 1971) in 11-1938

      1. Bruce Kelsey Thompson

      Married Linda Mezzell on 11-14-1964

        1. Jeffrey Thompson

        2. Janelle Thompson

        3. Michael Thompson

      2. Sandra Marie Thompson

      Married Virgil Curry on 3-31-1961

        1. William Robert Curry

        2. David Wayne Curry

        3. Stephen Curry

        4. Diana Marie Curry

      3. Katherine Leora Thompson

      1st Married Denman Wherlie

        1. Troy Wherlie

      2nd Married Edd Bare

---

20  James Franklin McIlroy never married and became very prosperous. He owned several hundred acres of land and bottom of the Current River. A year or two before he died, he decided he wanted to visit all of his relatives. As I was researching the McIlroys and visited my kin, they all told me about Frank coming to visit them. My grandmother Amanda told me that Frank still spoke with a Scottish brogue.

21  Daniel Webster McIlroy was a prosperous farmer, owned a ferry on Current River, and owned a gin and several hundred acres of land. He died young when he was killed by his neighbor. The story goes that they had gone to town to court and were drinking and got in an argument in the wagon on the way home. When Daniel let the man off, the neighbor went in the house, got a gun, and killed him.

4. Deborah Lynn Thompson
Married James Ray Sellers
2. Iva McIlroy b. 1-1-1892 d. 4-1949
1st Married Caudle Glass 1-28-1908
  1. Raymond H. Glass b. 5-25-1909 d. 1-1970
  2. Buell Glass b. 1916 d. 3-13-1936
2nd Married _____ Witchar
3. Cora McIlroy D.Y.
4. Gertrude McIlroy
Married Austin M. Johnson
  1. Malisa Johnson
  Married Bill Zosso
  2. Daniel Johnson
  Married Maggie Davidson
    1. Shirley Johnson
    2. Jane Johnson
    3. Danny Johnson
  3. Ernest Johnson
  Married Pauline _____
    1. David Johnson
6. Martha Josephine McIlroy b. 4-4-1854 d. 2-1-1935
Married Dr. John T. Johnson
(no children)
7. Sarah Ann McIlroy b. 6-1-1860
(Never married)
8. John A. McIlroy b. 6-1-1860 d. 9-6-1872
8. Thomas McIlroy
(Never married)
9. Samuel B. McIlroy b. 1825 d. 1865
Married Francis Elizabeth Jones
  1. Mary C. McIlroy b. 1850 d. 1886
1st Married Aaron Jenkins on 2-2-1871
2nd Married Peter Laplace on 11-7-1884
  1. Mary Jane Jenkins
  Married "Doc" Miller
    1. Birdie Mae Miller
    Married M.C. Matthews
      1. May Matthews
      2. Eva Lewis Matthews

3. Clarence Matthews
4. Macy Matthews
   Married Nate McAbee
5. Rachel Mae Matthews
6. Robert Mathews
7. Jeff Otto Matthews
2. Lucinda Jenkins
Married Bush Wilson
  1. Bertha Wilson
  Married _____ King
3. Lavender Jenkins b. 5-1-1876
Married Myrtle Beck
  1. Homer b. 1906
  2. Canzada b. 1908
  3. William b. 1910
  4. J.J. b. 7-1912
  5. Vera J. b. 10-3-1914
  Married A.E. Hert
  6. Helen b. 1918
  7. Aaron b. 1920
  8. Wilson b. 1922
  9. Lester b. 1927
2. Anna McIlroy b. 1-6-1851 d. 1945
Married John W. Huffstedler on 1-5-1871
  1. Lula Huffstedler
  2. Leona Huffstedler
  Married _____ Rogers
  3. Lute Huffstedler
3. Mellisa D. McIlroy b. 1853 d. 1870
(Never married)
4. Columbus "Bud" McIlroy b. 2-9-1856 d. 8-26-1936
1st Married Martha Humphries on 10-21-1875
  1. Minnie McIlroy b. 1-8-1878 d. 1961
  Married John Layle
    1. Guy Layle b. 1896
    Married _____
      1. Guy Layle Jr.
    2. Gabe Layle b. 1-15-1898
    Married _____
      1. Terry Layle

        1. John
      3. Myrtle Layle b. 9-19-1899 d. 11-12-1974
      Married _____ Green
         1. James L. Green
      4. Hulet Layle b. 2-16-1902 d. 6-17-1978
         1. Hulet Layle Jr.
      5. Essie Layle b. 12-17-1904
      1st Married _____ Lehman
      2nd Married _____ Schopel
         1. Richard Lehman
      6. Johnnie Layle b. 12-9-1907
         (no children)
      7. McIlroy "Mack" Layle b. 1-31-1910
         1. Barry Layle
            1. Brett Adam Layle b. 5-12-1966
      8. Martha Layle (triplet) D.Y.
      9. Mike Layle (triplet) D.Y.
      10. Marcie Layle (triplet) D.Y.
2. Ruff Frank McIlroy b. 12-15-1879
Married Myrtle Pruit
      1. Ruth McIlroy b. 12-31-1907
      Married T.B. Williams on 6-22-1930
         1. Catherine Williams b. 6-10-1931
         Married _____ Yarber
            1. Ruth Yarber b. 1952
            2. Tommie Yarber b. 1954
            3. Child
         2. Carl Williams b. 11-8-1916
         Married Marie Childers on 1-23-1943
         (no children)
         3. William H. Williams b. 12-26-1920
         Married F. McCord
            1. Frank Williams b. 1956
3. Francis "Fannie" Elizabeth McIlroy b. 2-16-1881
Married Josephus Fry on 7-2-1899
      1. Edeth Fry b. 3-28-1903
      Married G.E. Songer on 12-9-1923
         1. Marian Songer b. 1925
         Married J. Warren

2. Mae Ann Songer b. 1931
2. William H. Fry b. 9-29-1905
Married Eleanor Williams on 12-7-1924
   1. Francis Williams b. 1927
   2. Ola Williams b. 1934
   3. Karen Williams b. 1940
   4. Linda Williams b. 1942
3. J. Lynn Fry b. 11-22-1908
Married Essie Dagus on 10-5-1929
   1. Mary Fry
   2. Laura Fry
   Married _____ Busby
   3. Pattie Fry
   Married _____ Soong
4. Benjamin McIlroy b. 1884 d. 1921
Married Pearl Holder
   1. Carrington McIlroy
   2. Printiss McIlroy
   3. Vera McIlroy
5. Ann McIlroy's stats to born 12-24-1887 and died 9-26-1961
Married Leonard Boyd on 4-2-1905
   1. Ruby Boyd b. 1907
   Married Leo Rickman
      1. Lillian Rickman
      2. Len Rickman
   2. Sherman Boyd
   Married Betty Hartfiel
   3. Lillian Boyd
   Married Will Raines
      1. Elizabeth Raines
      Married Reding Bugh
         1. Scott Bugh b. 1959
         2. Bryan Bugh b. 1961
6. Marion McIlroy b. 2-1891
Married Lela Riley
   1. Earl McIlroy
   2. Blanch McIlroy
   3. Fern McIlroy
   4. Joyce McIlroy
   5. Jimmie McIlroy

    6. Jean Avon McIlroy

    7. Willie May McIlroy b. 8-1894

Married Fred "Red" Riley

      1. Max Riley

      2. Robert Lee Riley

2nd Married _____

    8. Marvin McIlroy b. 1904 d. 1904

2nd Married Betty Ann Dame (Martin) (b. 11-20-1867 d. 1-4-1942)

    9. Vinnie Estelle McIlroy b. 9-20-1905

Married Ted Cox on 11-4-1923

      1. Wanda Joe Cox b. 1-14-1925

      Married Paul Murphy

      2. Jesse D. Cox b. 3-28-1926

      1st Married J. Abston

      2nd Married Velma Vlyles

      3. Darwin Cox b. 12-10-1927

      Married Gala _____

        1. Randy Cox

        Married Bobby Rederick on 3-28-1968

          1. Misty Cox b. 7-1970

          2. Darwin Cox b. 12-10-1973

        2. Byron Cox b. 12-18-1956

        3. Anthony Cox b. 9-9-1959

    10. Lloyd McIlroy b. 10-10-1908

Married Lorene Townsley on 12-13-1935

    (no children)

    11. Luster Leroy McIlroy b. 1-6-1913 d. 1-17-1978

Married Lora South on 11-11-1934

      1. Jimmie McIlroy b. 11-6-1935 d. 6-27-1958

    (Never married)

      2. Harold McIlroy b. 2-6-1938

      Married Linda _____

        1. Stacy McIlroy b. 3-29-1968

        2. Lee Carlton McIlroy b. 6-3-1971

5. Ruff Vandergriff McIlroy b. 3-8-1857 d. 2-25-1950

Married Mary Jane Blackwell (b. 12-22-1864 d. 10-9-1950) on 8-25-1881

    1. Cora McIlroy b. 8-15-1882 d. 2-26-1916

Married Alex Jack

1. Sular Jack b. 12-1899 d. 6-1900
2. William Jack b. 1901 d. 5-25-1915
3. Evaline Jack
4. Glen Jack
5. Gladys Jack
2. Martha McIlroy b. 12-1883
Married L.H. Schiller
3. Bell McIlroy b. 8-6-1887
Married S.F. King (b. 1-10-1883 d. 5-25-1950) on 10-23-1907
(no children)
4. Lee McIlroy b. 6-6-1886 d. 4-23-1944
(no children)
5. Della McIlroy b. 8-23-1895
Married Elvin Hatley on 6-29-1918
   1. Hellen Hatley
6. Ada McIlroy b. 1898
Married Sular Graham on 12-16-1916
   1. Iris Graham b. 5-31-1919
   2. Barbara Graham
   3. Dale Graham
7. Tolbert E. McElroy *(note spelling change)* b. 1890 d. 1971
Married Nancy Seagroves (b. 1896)
   1. Thursaye McIlroy
   Married Roberts
   2. Imogene McIlroy
   Married John Rush
   3. Mae McIlroy
   Married O. Little
   4. Carence McIlroy
8. Charles McIlroy b. 2-25-1903
Married Leslie Merriet (b. 1906 d. 1927)
   1. Melba JaneMcIlroy
   Married Willis White
      1. Tim White
      2. Kim White
   2. Francis McIlroy
   Married Jack Bower
      1. Jack Bower Jr.
   3. Dwayne McIlroy
   Married Pattie Williams

(2 adopted children)
9. Pearle McIlroy b. 8-12-1900 d. 10-1976
Married Charles Merriet on 11-5-1922
  1. Raymond Merriet b. 8-2-1925
  Married Emma Hampton on 9-6-1952
    1. Stephen Ray Merriet b. 4-15-1955
  2. Roland Lee Merriet b. 8-13-1927
  Married Mabel Carroll on 4-8-1956
    1. Keith Merriet b. 1-9-1961
  3. Doris Merriet b. 8-24-1930
  Married Olen Hunt on 1-13-1955
    1. Alan Hunt b. 6-14-1956
    2. Lelia Hunt b. 6-6-1959
    3. Bonnie Hunt b. 6-29-1962
6. Emily Francis McIlroy b. 1860 d. 1898
Married Erastus Hill on 12-26-1887
  1. John Hill b. 10-1879
7. Samuel B. McIlroy b. 1864 d. 1-1935
1st Married Ella Jones on 12-7-1882
2nd Married Mattie W. Wallace (b. 1877)
  1. William A. McIlroy b. 1884
  2. Edward McIlroy b. 6-8-1890
  Married _____
    1. James Kirby McIlroy
    2. Carnie McIlroy
    3. Mary McIlroy
  Married _____ Blue
    4. C.W. McIlroy
    5. Calvin McIlroy
    6. Carlos McIlroy
    7. John Lehman McIlroy
    8. William Gerald McIlroy
    9. Jewel Hurst McIlroy
    10. Autsie McIlroy b. 1935
    11. Lawrence K. McIlroy D.Y.
    12. Coleman A. McIlroy
8. Daniel McIlroy b. 1865 D.Y.

9. Martha Ellen McIlroy *(This is not proven and I have some doubts, but some of the McIlroys and Davises think that she was the daughter of Samuel and Elizabeth, so I am including it.)*
Married Solomon Davis on 1-12-1829
    1. James Denton Davis
    2. Jasper Davis
    3. Mary Caroline Davis
    4. Rebecca Davis
    5. Molly Emedia Davis
    6. Elijah Davis
    7. Solomon Franklin Davis
    8. Martha Elizabeth Davis
    9. Sarah Emily Davis
    10. John Lott Davis
    11. Malinda J. Davis
    12. Henry Denton Davis
    13. William A. Davis
    14. Robert M. Davis

# Samuel McIlroy
# Descendants of Note

## Lily Russell, granddaughter of Alexander McIlroy

Lily Amanda McIlroy Russell, born Kerrville, Texas, January 24, 1887, daughter of Chester Ashley and Mary Frances McIlroy. B.A. Baylor 1911, M.A. 1931; studied University of Chicago, summer 1914; married Junius Brown Russell, May 4, 1917 (divorced 1929); one daughter, Mary Claudia. Teacher elementary grades, Brandon, Texas 1909-1910; Latin and German teacher, Vernon High School, 1910-1912; teacher English, Baylor Academy 1912-1917; Instructor English, Baylor University 1918-1919 and 1922-1924; assistant dean of women 1925-1931; dean of women, 1931-1940; director of public relations, 1940-1948; dean of Baylor University Union Building, 1948-1954?. Appointed in 1940 director of Baylor University Centennial Celebration 1945; executive secretary Baylor University Citizenship Inst., 1940; president of William Tyron Chapter, Daughters of Republic of Texas, 1934-1936; chairman edn. 14th District. Women's Missionary Union of Texas 1934-1936; chairman speakers' bureau, Texas Division, AAUW, 1937-1939; chairman resolutions committee 1939-1941; member Waco Convention Bureau 1941; Democrat, Baptist. Club: Baylor Round Table, contributor to the Baptist Standard and The Baylor Century.

# Sherman Douglas McIlroy, grandson of Hammet McIlroy

A Newspaper Article After his Death

S.D. (Tex) McIlroy died at 12:15 o'clock this morning in a San Antonio hospital where he has been since July 16, when he was stricken with a severe heart ailment. Funeral services will be conducted at 4 o'clock Tuesday afternoon at Tolar, the old McIlroy family home in Hood county and burial will be in the family plot in Stroud Creek Cemetery.

Mr. McIlroy was 74 years of age and spent the greater part of his life in the excitement of a gold field or an oil field. His big success came late in life in the Panhandle oil field, where he was one of the very first operators. His Dixon Creek No. 1 well on the Smith ranch in Hutchinson County was the first big commercial producer in the Borger field and the spark that set off the oil boom of 1926 here.

Tex, as he was known to his friend and acquaintances, was without doubt one of the best known and best liked men in the Panhandle oil industry. His word was as good as his bond, and he helped many a hard hit oil man to an easier position in life. His charities were legion, but he kept that part of his life strictly to himself. Every civic enterprise that needed financial support received his aid. The smaller churches, the Maverick Club, the Community Chest, every war relief agency found the going made easier by reason of his thoughtful help. He liked people and people liked him.

Mr. McIlroy was one of the most successful independent oil operators in the Southwest. He, with his brother White McIlroy, organized three local oil companies, and every stockholder in every one of the companies was well repaid for investment in these enterprises.

The Dixon Creek Oil Company, with its dividends and sale price, paid out over 700 per cent. The McIlroy Oil Company, on the same basis paid out over 600 per cent and the Cockrell—McIlroy Company, 700 per cent. It took a lot of hard work and a lot of plain honesty to make that record, but the record stands.

He was the third of 11 children born to William McIlroy and Mary C. McIlroy. His birth place was Randolph County, Ark. The family moved to Hood County, Tex. in 1886 and settled on a farm 10 miles west of Granbury. He was married to Kathryn Byrd of San Antonio at Hot Springs, Ark., in 1900.

In 1889 Mr. McIlroy left the family home in Hood County and went to Fresno, Cal. He remained there until 1897 when he joined the gold rush to

Alaska. He landed in Dawson City in the Yukon Territory and while they were living there, Hazel McIlroy was born, the first white child born in the Yukon Territory. Later after the moved to Fairbanks, a second daughter, Kathryn, was born. Hazel is now Mrs. T.G. Nichols of Amarillo and Kathryn is Mrs. F.G. Antonio of Helotes, Texas.

He left Alaska in 1914 and came to Amarillo, where he entered partnership with his brother, W.W. McIlroy, who was then engaged in the meat and grocery business here.

The McIlroys brothers were among the first to become interested in the gas and oil discovery that broke here in 1919, and the Dixon Creek Oil Company was organized. The Dixon Creek No. 1 Smith Ranch came in during the latter part of 1925 for 14,000 barrels a day and the oil boom was on.

Drilling more producers and gradually adding to their holdings, the McIlroy interests became the dominant producers in the field and held that position during the early days of the development.

Later transferring activities to the West Pampa field, these pioneer operators drilled the second well in that area and acquired some 1, 800 acres of leases. When the Dixon Creek interests were sold in 1932 to the King Royalty Company of Wichita Falls, the company had built up a daily production of 2,500 barrels.

Discovery and development was a prominent trait of S.D. McIlroy, and up until the last he kept in close touch with the Panhandle field and with the oil business in general.

Soon after he sold the Dixon Creek holdings he bought a large cattle ranch in the vicinity of his old Hood County home, to which much of his latter attention and interest were devoted.

Mrs. McIlroy could not live in the high altitude of Amarillo and made her home much of the time in Columbus, Tex., and with her daughter, Mrs. Antonio, in Helotes, near San Antonio. It was while on a visit there that Mr. McIlroy was stricken with the heart ailment that resulted in his death.

He is survived by the widow, two daughters and two granddaughters, Nancy and Dawn Nichols, in the immediate family. Also by six brothers, E.M. and H.S. of Hood County, G.W. of Dublin, T.A. of Hood County, W.W. of Amarillo and B.D. McIlroy of Fort Worth. Two sisters, Mrs. Betty Campbell and Mrs. Willie Hufstedler and two brothers. A.H. and R.B. McIlroy, are dead.

# Tom J. Vandergriff, great-grandson of Hammet McIlroy

"Vandergriff Closes a Legendary Career: Mayor, Congressman, Judge, Helm of Region's Growth" (The Dallas Morning News, 2006)
Additional Information from the City of Arlington Website

Tom Vandergriff entered politics in 1951 as the ambitious "Boy Mayor" of Arlington. Friday, he leaves the county judge's office in Fort Worth as a legend who says he's nearing the end of his public life.

The 80-year old former car dealer spent 44 years as mayor, U.S. representative and Tarrant County judge. He ushered in Arlington's great boom, briefly served in Washington, and suffered his only political defeat thanks to the "Reagan Revolution" which involved the changing of districts and putting him in a rapidly growing county that always voted Republican.

For the second half of the 20$^{th}$ century, Mr. Vandergriff's life was intertwined with the history of North Texas. He helped bring General Motors, Six Flags Over Texas and the Texas Rangers to Arlington.

He pushed for construction of Lake Arlington, Dallas-Fort Worth International Airport, the Tarrant County College district and Interstate 30, and he was the first president of the North Central Texas Council of Governments.

Former U.S. House Speaker Jim Wright, once dubbed Weatherford's "Boy Mayor," said that Mr. Vandergriff is a giant.

"If we were required to name five humans who in the last century contributed to the healthy growth and development of the region, Tom Vandergriff would have to be on the list," Mr. Wright said.

The story of one of Tarrant County's most famous politicians actually started in Carrolton, where Mr. Vandergriff was born. His father was a prominent car dealer who moved to Arlington in the 1930s.

By his mid-20s, Mr. Vandergriff was already the Chamber of Commerce president in Arlington, a town of about 7,500 residents and 4 square miles at the time. In 1951, Arlington voters turned out in record number-999 went to the polls—to choose a new mayor, and it was a landslide.

Arlington's modern era had begun.

General Motors

Mr. Vandergriff said he first thought about running for mayor after hearing rumors from Detroit. His father's car dealer contacts said that GM planned to build a new assembly plant in the South or Southwest.

He reasoned that having someone with "GM blood" at City Hall could only help.

"This might not be the best intentions for why someone should run for office," Mr. Vandergriff admitted, chuckling.

But he won and started wooing GM from his new office.

Two months later, the city began annexing six square miles near the Grand Prairie border. Two months after that, GM bought 255 acres of the newly annexed property and announced it would build a plant that would employ 6,000 to 10,000 people—a workforce the size of Arlington's entire population.

"I'm not really sure that proved to be a deciding factor," Mr. Vandergriff said about whether his new position affected Gm's move. Still, he couldn't argue with the results.

The legend of Mr. Vandergriff—whom friends call both gentlemanly and shrewd—was growing just months after his first election.

Landing the plant meant more than just good-paying jobs, Mr. Vandergriff said. There also was a cachet to having the auto giant in town.

"If GM thought it was a good location, then it has to be for me, too," he said, explaining the conventional wisdom.

Within two decades, Arlington had grown to more than 90,000 residents, and today it has a population of 363,050 spread over nearly 100 square miles.

Six Flags Over Texas

GM made Arlington an industrial town. Southern California made Arlington a tourist destination.

Mr. Vandergriff graduated from the University of Southern California in the 1940s with plans to be a broadcaster but instead became fascinated with the astonishing post-war growth around Los Angeles.

In the 1950s, he visited the newly opened Disneyland.

"I became a fan myself," Mr. Vandergriff said of the amusement park, "so much so that I convinced the Great Southwest Corporation this was worth exploring."

The company was planning a large industrial park in Arlington and Grand Prairie, but Mr. Vandergriff told developer Angus Wynne Jr. that he should also go look at Disneyland.

"You only had to see it once back in those days to know you would like to have it in your hometown," Mr. Vandergriff said.

He met with Walt Disney and tried to convince him that his next theme park should be in Arlington, and Mr. Wynne offered land for the project.

That effort went nowhere, but Mr. Wynne decided to build his own park called Texas Under Six Flags.

Several years, $10 million and one name change later, Six Flags Over Texas opened in August 1961.

Mr. Vandergriff's not-so-small town was suddenly in the tourism business.

On its first day, nearly 8,400 visitors paid about $3 each to play at the petting zoo, listen to Dixieland band performances and experience the handful of rides, according to Parktimes.com and the Six Flags Over Texas Web site.

Since then, Arlington has become a tourist destination, and Six Flags—which draws 3 million visitors to the Arlington park each year—became a national brand.

Texas Rangers

Before Six Flags opened, Mr. Vandergriff—known as the area's "get-it-done man"—already had his eye on his next big project. It would take him 13 years to complete.

As a child, Mr. Vandergriff was a fan of the Texas League's Dallas Steers and Fort Worth Cats baseball teams. While in college, he worked on broadcasts of the minor league Los Angeles Angels.

In 1958, Mr. Vandergriff created a committee to bring professional baseball to the Dallas-Fort Worth area. Every time the major leagues expanded or a team was rumored to move, Arlington was in the mix.

"We came close a time or two, but we just couldn't get the votes we needed," Mr. Vandergriff said.

Tarrant County spent $1.5 million to build Turnpike Stadium on what is now I-30, and Arlington landed the minor league Dallas-Fort Worth Spurs. At the same time, Mr. Vandergriff courted Kansas City Athletics owner Charles O. Finely before he moved the team to Oakland, and Arlington was mentioned when Cleveland, Cincinnati, and Pittsburgh owners considered moving.

The persistence paid off in 1971 when Mr. Vandergriff successfully courted the Washington Senators to move to town, where they became the Texas Rangers. His years of lobbying and behind-the-scenes wrangling overcame opposition from the baseball commissioner and President Richard Nixon.

"That was one of the most exciting experiences in my life," he said. "We all worked together as a single region to get a major league club to come our way."

Baseball continued to play a big part in Mr. Vandergriff's life. He lent his authoritative and measured voice to the Rangers broadcasts during the 1970s, and his latest office in Fort Worth provided him a daily reminder of his childhood. The office faces north, with a clear view of LaGrave Field, where the Fort Worth Cats play.

Life after Mayor

He remained a private citizen for only a few years before winning a seat in the U.S. House of Representatives in 1982 in one of the closest and most expensive races in the nation. Two years later, the Republican tide swept the Democrat out of office, replacing him with future congressional leader Dick Armey.

Again, Mr. Vandergriff was out of office, having suffered his only loss at the polls.

But a few years later, at age 63, the conservative Democrat re-emerged as a Republican and ran for Tarrant County judge. He won easily in 1990 and has remained in office ever since.

## TOMMY JOE VANDERGRIFF

Born: Jan. 29, 1926, in Carrolton
Graduated: University of Southern California, 1947
Career: Arlington mayor, 1951-778; U.S. House, 1983-85; Tarrant County judge, 1991-2006

## CAREER OF A POLITICAL LEGEND

1951—Tom Vandergriff is elected Arlington mayor at age 25; General Motors announces plans to build n assembly plant in Arlington

1954—GM's new plant opens

1957—The Dallas—Fort Worth Turnpike opens, running through Arlington

1958—Mr. Vandergriff forms a committee to pursue a major league baseball franchise

1961—Six Flags Over Texas opens

1965—The Dallas—Fort Worth Spurs minor league baseball team plays its first game in Arlington's Turnpike Stadium

1971—Washington Senators owner Bob Short announces he's moving his team to Arlington and renaming it the Texas Rangers

1972—Seven Seas, a city-owned aquatic theme park, opens. It's a financial failure and closes after three years.

1977—Mr. Vandergriff resigns as mayor.

1982—Mr. Vandergriff runs for the U.S. House as a Democrat and wins. He loses two years later to political novice Dick Armey.

1990—Mr. Mr. Vandergriff resigns as mayor runs for Tarrant County judge as a Republican and wins.

2005—Mr. Vandergriff announces he'll retire after his current term is over.

Tom J. Vandergriff was the great grandson of Hammet McIlroy and probably the best known man in North Texas.

Born in Texas, January 29, 1926, Tommy Joe Vandergriff, also known as Tom J. Vandergriff, was born in Carrolton, Dallas County, Texas.

Arlington was a town with a population of less than 8,000 when Vandergriff began his 26 year term as Mayor. During that period of time, he was involved with such major endeavors as the elevation of the University of Texas at Arlington to senior college status, construction of the Dallas-Fort Worth International Airport and development of the region's giant tourist industry.

Judge Vandergriff has served on White House Commission on Urban Problems. He was the founding President of the North Central Texas Council of Governments and the first Chairman of the Board.

# Daniel McIlroy, Jr.

Daniel McIlroy Sr. and his family moved to Ross County, Ohio about 1803. Years later, after his father's death, Daniel McIlroy Jr. moved to Green County, Ohio.

3. Daniel McIlroy Jr. b. 1781 in Laudon County, Virginia d. 9-26-1850 in Green County, Ohio
Married Grizzle Roat Johnson (b. 3-10-1794 d. 10-25-1850)
   1. Gavin J. McIlroy b. 3-2-1816 in Green County, Ohio d. 4-19-1878 in Green County, Ohio
   Married Jane Miller
      1. Sarah McIlroy b. 1-2-1849 in Green County, Ohio
      2. Daniel McIlroy b. 8-24-1851
      3. Emily Jane McIlroy b. 12-20-1853
      4. Samuel McIlroy b. 4-24-1856
      Married Rebecca Chalmer
         1. Gavin B. McIlroy
         Married Emma Miller
            1. Helen McIlroy
            Married Stuepel Baughley
               1. Donna Baughley
               Married Benjamin Wagner
                  1. Clinton Wagner
      5. Joseph McIlroy b. 7-13-1859
      6. William C. McIlroy b 12-10-1863
   2. Elizabeth J. McIlroy b. 9-18-1818 d. 9-18-1903
   Married Milton Scott (b. 1811 d. 1900)
   3. Archibald J. McIlroy[22] b. 7-16-1819 d. 3-7-1908

---

22    Archibald J. McIlroy was a millwright by trade and followed that business until middle age when he turned his attention to farming. His last days were spent upon 123 acres of land that for many years was known as the McIloy farm. He served in the War of 1812 and at all times was as loyal to his country as when he wore the nation's uniform. Archibald pursued his education in a log schoolhouse near Cedarville Township. He belonged to the Reformed Presbyterian Church and its principles were the guiding spirit of his life. He witnessed the

Married Mary Ellen Little (b. 1826 d. 11-2-1881) in 1855
1. Mary C. McIlroy
2. John R. McIlroy
1st Married _____ Morris
  1. Daniel McIlroy
2nd Married Minnie Cline
  1. Kenneth McIlroy
3. Daniel W. McIlroy
4. David McIlroy
5. Elnora McIlroy
4. Robert J. McIlroy b. 1-16-1823
Married Elizabeth _____
5. Jane Scott McIlroy b. 4-20-1825 d. before 1903
Married Thomas Bromagen in 1845
  1. William Samuel Bromagen b. 3-15-1846 d. 12-12-1912
1st Married Nancy Criswell (d. 5-1873)
2nd Married Hannah Townsley on 10-10-1875
    1. Martha Jane Bromagen b. 3-13-1871
    2. Walter Bromagen D.Y.
    3. Mabel Bromagen b. 1876 d. 9-22-1883 in Gibson County, Indiana
    4. Bessie Bromagen b. 1881
Married George Hampton Harvey (d. 2-2-1951) on 9-8-1904
    1. Ester Harvey b. 1906 d. 2-2-1951
    (Never married)
    2. Hazel Harvey b. 8-1908
Married Durwood Simms on 8-1908
    1. Donald Lee Simms b. 10-1943
Married Linda Joe Urban
      1. Katherine Louise Simms b. 1-28-1971
      2. Douglas P. Simms b. 11-1-1973
      3. Matthew Simms b. 7-15-1976
    2. Richard Franklin Simms b. 7-18-1946
Married Joyce L. Rose in 8-1973
    3. Charles S. Harvey b. 2-14-1916

---

marvelous growth of Greene county throughout many years, and his aid and cooperation were never withheld from any movement or measure which he believed would contribute to the general good. His honorable career, embracing the strongest traits of an upright manhood, gained for him respect and veneration.

4. George E. Harvey b. 9-26-1919 d. 2-16-1952
Married Verlie Dale Ahlemann on 4-14-1941
    1. Nan L. Harvey b. 4-25-1953
    Married Alex S. Dailey on 2-16-1980
        1. Benjamin S. Daily b. 12-17-1981
        2. Michael E. Daily b. 1-5-1963
5. Samuel Arthur Bromagen b. 2-3-1885 d. 7-24-1886
    1. Robert Lee Bromagen b. 8-11-1923
    Married Helen Gentry
        1. Ronald Lynn Bromagen b. 1944
        Married Linda K. Oswald
            1. Robert Bromagen Jr. b. 1966
            2. Carol Bromagen b. 1968
            3. Stephanie Bromagen b. 1970
            4. Kathleen Bromagen b. 1976
        2. Tressa Ann Bromagen b. 9-15-1951
        Married R.L. Hooker
            1. Dawn Hooker b. 10-28-1970
            2. Ryan L. Hooker
2. Margaret A. Bromagen b. 1848
Married William Goodrich (d. 9-22-1902) in 1875
    1. Myrtle Goodrich b. 1876
    Married _____Clark
    (no children)
    2. Carrie Goodrich b. 1886 d. 11-12-1967
    Married Howard Rigby
    (no children)
    3. Gertrude "Madge" Goodrich b. 8-1858
    Married Fred Smith
    (no children)
3. Roat "Kate" Grizzell Bromagen b. 1851 d. after 1924
1st Married Matthew Crewis (b. 11-28-1889 in Gibson County, Indiana)
2nd Married _____ Wismore
4. John A. Bromagen b. 5-8-1853 d. 5-3-1918
5. Sally Jane Bromagen b. 5-8-1856 d. 5-3-1918
Married Hugh M. Grace on 10-30-1878
    1. Claud Grace b. 12-11-1884
    Married Laura Mitchell on 6-17-1909)
        1. Margaret Mitchell

Married Edwin Rinehart
1. Mary Joe Rinehart b. 10-5-1931
Married Oscar Swador
  1. Stephen A. Swador b. 11-12-1951
  Married Rita _____
    1. Yvonne Swador b. 1-20-1974
    2. Jacqueline Swador b. 4-20-1977
  2. Louella G. Swader b. 4-15-1973
  3. Jennifer Swader b. 11-5-1954
  Married _____ Seay
  4. Arthur J. Swader b. 3-1-1956
  5. Thomas R. Swader b. 2-17-1964
  6. David Swader b. 10-12-1966
2. Roselyn S. Rinehart b. 6-28-1934
Married Jesse Hughes Jr.
  1. Elizabeth A. Hughes b. 9-28-1954
  2. Deborah J. Hughes b. 2-13-1958
3. Edwin Rinehart b. 3-11-1940
Married Joe Ann Vandever
  1. Richard J. Rinehart b. 10-20-1967
  2. Kelly Ann Rinehart b. 7-21-1971
6. Mary A. Bromagen b. 1862 d. before 1912
Married William C. Polk on 3-9-1882
1. Female b. 9-20-1884
2. Female b. 5-20-1887
7. Jennie Bromagen b. 1865 d. 2-13-1898
Married William P. Lucas
(no children)
6. Dr. John J. McIlroy b. 10-14-1827 in Green County, Ohio
Married _____
1. Nelta M. McIlroy b. 11-1-1861
Married Reverend A.G. Bergen in Mattoon, Illinois
2. John Howard McIlroy b. 1863
Married Cora M. Allen
7. James Roat McIlroy b. 4-2-1830 in Green County, Ohio d. 5-9-1898
8. Mealancthon "Lank" McIlroy b. 9-13-1833 d. 10-18-1921 in Green County, Ohio
Married Matilda Moudy
1. William McIlroy b. 10-2-1859 d. 10-8-1936 in Blairstown, Iowa

Married Elizabeth McClerin
 1. Lincoln McIlroy b. 7-8-1918 d. 6-5-1962
 Married Leva Akeson
  1. William McElroy
  Married Ida _____ in Mason City, Iowa
   1. Douglas McIlroy
   2. Twin
 9. Alexander McIlroy b. 10-27-1836
 Married Mary Ellen Hawley
  1. Margaret McIlroy
  Married _____ Westbrook in Paxton, Iowa
  2. John H. McElroy b. 1-29-1867 in Chicago, Illinois
 10. William McIlroy b. 2-4-1839 d. 2-19-1878
4. Isabella McIlroy b. 2-28-1783 in Loudon County, Virginia
5. Deborah McIlroy b. 6-16-1786 in Loudon County, Virginia
 1st Married Robert Brownfield in 6-1807
 2nd Married Philomen Davis in 10-1817 in Adams County, Ohio
  1. Rebecca Brownfield
  Married James McNutt
  2. Angeline
  Married Dan J. Sears
  3. Joseph
6. Jane McIlroy b. 9-10-1789 in Laudon County, Virginia
Married James Watts on 2-27-1812 in Ross County, Ohio
  1. Alexander Watts
  2. Daniel L. Watts b. 3-6-1817 d. 11-12-1848
  Married Julia M. Bingham on 11-23-1848

# The Lewis Family

The story of my McIlroys could not be complete without including the Lewis family.

The Lewis name is associated with that part of Great Britain that is called Wales. Many of the Welsh moved to the English plantations in Ireland about 1650. At this time, the people from Scotland were doing the same. The children of the Scots that were born in Ireland were called Scotch-Irish. This group began to migrate to the Americas soon after 1700. By that time, the Welch Lewises had married into the Irvines, Campbells, Mitchells, McIlroys, McDaniels, McDowells and other families and had in fact become Scotch-Irish of Presbyterian faith.

Some have thought our Lewis family was Scotch-Irish but I don't believe that it is true. They came to America directly from England about 1650. Most think there were two brothers, David and John. There are some records that show that they were in Pennsylvania early—before William Penn, in fact, and that they were associated with him.

John's great-grandson John moved to Randolph County, North Carolina where he died in 1802. David Lewis, his son, fought in the Revolutionary War. David married Ann Beeson, a Quaker, and she was dropped from the Church because of this marriage.

Our line continues from Isaiah, a son of the above mentioned David and Ann. Isaiah was born in Gilford County, North Carolina where he married Nancy Julian. Isaiah moved with his father to Pendleton, South Carolina about 1799 where he remained for seven years before moving to Warren County, Kentucky. His brothers Neriah and Joab came with him. Eight years later, in the spring of 1814, he sold his land and moved to what is now Lawrence County, Illinois. He bought one hundred and sixty acres of land three miles west of Lawrenceville on the Old State Road.

Isaiah had a large family, as did most at that time. Five children were born in South Carolina, four in North Carolina, and two in Kentucky. Isaiah was active in community affairs. He served on the first jury, taught school, and also helped survey the village of Lawrenceville and was county commissioner for one term. After completing his term as commissioner, he moved to Vigo County, Indiana where he died in 1837. His wife returned to Lawrenceville after his death and remained until she and her son David died of the Black Tongue Plague (cholera).

Isaiah was the ancestor of most all the Lawrenceville County Lewises. He left several children and grandchildren (we will show some of the kin at the end of this section). He and Nancy had eleven children, Paul born a twin in 1800, and Isaiah Lewis (Paul's nephew) born in 1812 became my grandmother's grandparents.

Paul married Ann Stewart on Mary 16, 1820. He operated the first linseed oil mill in Lawrence County. It was operated by ox power, the tread being sixty feet in diameter. Paul was of a literary type and accumulated a large library. He was a Universalist in belief and preached on several occasions. In 1846, he moved to Arkansas. Late in 1845, Paul sold his land and other holdings to his son Perry in preparation of their move to Hot Springs, where he was taking his wife Ann for treatment. A few of his younger children moved with them, including Martha, my great—grandmother, who was six at that time. Ann lived for several more years. After her death, he married his cousin's widow Mary Smith Lewis. Her husband Isaiah Lewis, son of Joab, had died early in 1850 after living in what became Randolph County, Arkansas. His son William Martin Lewis married the last child of Paul, Martha Lewis, who became William's fourth wife. Martha had been married previously-probably two or three times. The last before marrying William Martin was named Hassell. She was known as Martha Lewis Hassell. As far as I can tell, she had no children (maybe one) before her last marriage to William Martin Lewis.

David Lewis b. 12-4-1694 in Maryland
Married Mary Crawford
    1. David Lewis
    2. Crawford Lewis
    3. John Lewis b. 3-21-1720 d. 1802 in Randolph County, North Carolina
    Married Pricilla Brooks
        1. David Lewis b. 3-21-1747 d. 1822 in Anderson County, South Carolina
        1st Married _____
        2nd Married Ann Beeson
        3rd Married Penelope _____
        1. Isaiah Lewis b. 9-4-1769
        Married Nancy Julian
            1. Rebekah Lewis b. 1-2-1789 d. 1855
            Married Eli Noel
            2. David Lewis b. 1791 d. 1845 (cholera)

Married Elizabeth Hedricks in 1815
   1. Neriah Lewis
   1st Married _____ Paine
   2nd Married Nancy Fonner McDonald
   2. Thomas Lewis
   3. Mary Ann "Betsy" Lewis
   Married David Ousborn
   4. Isaiah Lewis b. 1821
   Married Sally Umfleet on 2-28-1840
      1. Francis Marion Lewis b. 1842
      Married Sarah Raycop
         1. Amanda Lewis
         2. Manuel Lewis
         3. Amelia Lewis
         4. John W. Lewis
      2. Byaka Lewis
      3. David Lewis
      4. Mary Jane Lewis
   5. Peter Lewis
   Married Mahala Swango
   6. Nancy Lewis
   Married Benjamin Anthony
   7. John L. Lewis
   Married Harriet Milburn
   8. William M. Lewis b. 1826 d. 1876
   Married Amanda White
      1. William Lewis b. 1861 d. 1936
         1. Roy Lewis
   9. Sarah Lewis
   Married James Hayes
   10. Phillip Lewis
   Married Elizabeth Lagmage
2. Peter Lewis
Married Mahala Spencer
   1. James Allen Lewis
   Married Jennetta Tritt
      1. William R. Lewis b. 5-5-1840 d. 5-12-1892
      2. Nancy M. Lewis b. 5-21-1841 d. 11-4-1892
      3. Sarah R. Lewis b. 1-29-1847 d. 6-1897

4. Alice W. Lewis b. 9-21-1852
5. Infant born dead 2-15-1862
4. Paul Lewis b. 1-1800 d. 1872
Married Ann Stewart on 3-16-1820
  1. Perry Lewis b. 3-30-1821
  Married Mary Jane Musgrove
    1. Lydia Lewis b. 12-15-1846 d. 5-15-1921
    Married E.B. Price
      1. Perry Price
      2. Glenn Price
      3. Guy Price
    2. John Paul Lewis b. 12-24-1842 d. 6-19-1915
    Married Sarah Dunlop
    3. Joseph Battenfield Lewis b. 2-4-1850 d. 3-24-1929
    Married Mary Ellen Lake on 2-1-1880
      1. Bryan Ray Lewis b. 11-18-1880
      Married Suella Eaton on 7-4-1910
      2. Cornelia O. Lewis b. 1882 d. 10-16-1898
      3. Whitney L. Lewis b. 4-20-1885 d. 11-28-1898
      4. Lydia B. Lewis b. 10-9-1887 d. 11-7-07
      5. Franklin Lewis b. 3-10-1888 D.Y. (1889)
      6. Roger Q. Lewis
      Married Clara B. Stiner
        1. Mary Ann Lewis
        Married G. Simms
        2. Margaret Lewis
        Married Fred Nayberry
        3. Martha Lewis
        Married Walter Watke
        4. Bryan R. Lewis
        Married Barbara Cox
      7. Ruth Ellen Lewis b. 4-23-1893
      Married V.E. French
    4. James Potts Lewis b. 3-24-1852 d. 10-29-1872
    5. Mary M. Lewis b. 1-6-1856 d. 10-6-1936
    Married Charles Spencer
      1. Ralph Spencer
    6. George Marshall Lewis b. 9-6-1858 d. 3-8-1941
    1st Married Floury Abernathy on 12-6-1880
    2nd Married Marietta Barnate in 1908

1. Carl Vernon Lewis
Married Lena _____
    1. Gladys M. Lewis
    2. George A. Lewis
2. Bert Elmer Lewis
3. George Marshall Lewis Jr.
4. Mary Jane Lewis
5. Lydia Ann Lewis
Married Ray Buchanan
    1. James Buchanan
    2. George Buchanan
7. Edwin Morrison Lewis b. 12-20-1860 d. 6-30-1942
Married Anna Black in 1884
    1. Maggie Jane Lewis b. 11-16-1885
    2. Perry S. Lewis b. 4-9-1887
    3. Phillip H.E. Lewis b. 11-19-1889
    4. Nellie Lewis b. 1-9-1902
8. Cornelia Lewis (twin) b. 8-11-1864 d. 1-24-1953
Married Thornton Combs
    1. Lewis Combs b. 1891
9. Cornelius Lewis (twin) b. 8-11-1864 d. 10-29-1889
10. Sarah E. Lewis b. 12-30-1867 d. 12-2-1896
11. Alice Lewis b. 6-14-1871 d. 8-31-1951
1st Married Theodore Hazelton
2nd Married _____ Haltom
2. James Stewart Lewis b. 1823
Married Angelina Watson on 6-10-1841
    1. William Lewis b. 1842
    2. James Lewis b. 1843
        1. John Lewis b. 1870
        2. Nancy Lewis b. 1873
    3. Oliver Lewis b. 1862
    4. Mary Lewis b. 1864
3. Matilda Lewis b. 1827
Married Asa Mays in 1845
    1. Eliza Mays
    2. Ann Mays b. 1845
    3. Mary Mays b. 1847
    4. Paul Mays b. 1853

4. Phillip Howard Lewis b. 2-8-1826
(Never married)
5. Nancy Lewis b. 1839 d. 1839
6. John Lewis b. 1828 d. 4-23-1848
7. Margaret Lewis b. about 1830 d. about 1830
8. Voltaire Lewis b. 1831 d. 1840
10. Martha Lewis b. 8-1-1840 d. 2-20-1919
1st Married John Hassell
    1. Lizzie Hassell
    Married Jess Ford
2nd Married William Martin Lewis
11. Paul Alexander Lewis b. 1831 d. 1840
5. Phillip Lewis (twin) b. 1-1800 d. 2-4-1873
1st Married Mary Craven (13 children)
2nd Married Hester Clean (2 children)
3rd Married Martha Black Brinier
    1. Elizabeth Lewis b. 12-23-1824 d. 7-10-1880
    Married William Neal on 6-31-1847
    2. Lousia Lewis b. 8-20-1826 d. 12-26-1883
    Married William Buffy on 7-20-1842
    3. William Melton Lewis b. 6-19-1828 d. 2-3-1882
    Married Catherine Eaton (b. 12-25-1836 d. 11-4-1899)
        1. Henry Howard Lewis b. 1-14-1855
        2. Mary Lucinda Lewis d. 4-3-1851 d. 12-20-1861
        3. Harlie V. Lewis b. 1-9-1859
        1st Married Hattie H. Ray on 10-5-1881
        2nd Married Annie Halton
            1. William Thomas Lewis b. 9-3-1882 d. 2-9-1886
            2. Ray Vernon Lewis b. 1-25-1885 d. 12-7-1910
            3. Noel Adair Lewis b. 9-19-1886 d. 11-7-1891
            4. Paul Fredrick Lewis b. 8-21-1888 d. 6-29-1948
            Married Julia Smith on 2-22-1919
            5. Russell Marvin Lewis b. 4-14-1891 d. 4-15-1943
            Married Elizabeth Gray on 4-3-1912
            6. Floy M. Lewis b. 9-13-1893 d. 9-13-1893
            7. Victor A. Lewis b. 10-29-1895
    4. Sigel D. Lewis b. 3-4-1862
    Married Elizabeth Steed in 1889
        1. Willis Lewis b. 7-4-1890 d. 12-14-1890
        2. Hugo Sigel Lewis b. 10-5-1891

3. Francis Lewis b. 11-2-1893
4. Albert Lewis b. 3-5-1896 d. 2-2-1899
5. Dr. Udolph S. Lewis b. 5-10-1864 d. 2-1904
Married Kate Wolf in 1888
   1. L.E. Lewis b. 10-22-1890
   2. Irma Lewis b. 5-3-1894
   Married Floyd Moore
   3. Kate Lewis b. 9-18-1905
   Married Haywood Jones
   4. K. Lewis
   Married A.A. Wood
6. Dr. Caius Marius Lewis[23]
1st Married Bertha C. Benefield (b. 1872 d. 1901) on 10-16-1895
   1. Chester Delvey Lewis b. 3-12-1899 d. 4-7-1976
   Married Ruth I. Tracy (b. 1904 d. 1970) in 1930
      1. Tracy D. Lewis b. 1935
      Married Judith Abels in 1956
         1. Sandra A. Lewis b. 1957
         Married Steven W. Taylor
            1. Gary M. Taylor b. 1975
            2. David L. Taylor b. 1981
         2. James M. Lewis b. 1958
         Married Ana Cancan
            1. Samantha A. Lewis b. 1996
2nd Married Anna C. McNeill (b. 1877 d. 1962)
   2. William Marvis Lewis b. 3-21-1904 d. 5-30-1923
4. Pricella Lewis b. 5-7-1830 d. 4-25-1852
Married George Whittaker (b. 1851)
5. Mary Ann Lewis b. 6-7-1832 d. 1893
6. Erwin Lewis b. 5-20-1834 d. 12-22-1855
7. Franklin Lewis b. 11-7-1836 d. 9-22-1908
Married Ann Keller on 3-13-1868
8. Cynthia Lewis b. 12-23-1838 d. 6-14-1904
Married James Eaton on 5-13-1855

---

23   Dr. Caius Marius Lewis was born at Bridgeport Township in Lawrence County, Illinois and obtained his primary education at schools of his district and in Bridgeport. He graduated in the class of 1898 at the University of Indianapolis in Indiana. His wife, Bertha, taught school for a few years before they married.

9. Martha Lewis b. 2-11-1841 d. 2-26-1902
Married Sam Besley in 1865
10. Elenor Lewis b. 5-6-1843 d. 2-22-1877
Married John n. Griggs
11. Comedore P. Lewis b. 7-20-1845 d. 2-5-1898
1st Married Lydia Hamilton
2nd Married Jane Moore
12. Julian Lewis b. 5-18-48 d. 10-19-1848
13. Caroline Lewis b. 2-9-1850
14. Samuel D. Lewis b. 4-6-1852 d. 1923
Married Maggie Lane on 1-17-1876
   1. Pearl Lewis
   Married Leslie Endicolt
15. Levi Lewis b. 1857 D.Y. (1859)
16. John B. Lewis b. 1856 d. 11-3-1927
Married Alvina Cummings on 11-24-1878
17. James Lewis b. 10-1-1858 d. 5-31-1952
Married Mary Jane Bickell
   1. William Henry Lewis
   2. Perney Mae Lewis
   3. John Phillip Lewis
   4. Twin D.Y.
   5. Hattie V. Lewis
   6. Martha R. Lewis
   7. James B. Lewis
   8. Lillie Fern Lewis
18. Robert Lewis b. 9-16-1860 d. 1-26-1934
Married Minnie Lake on 12-23-1880
6. Jacob Lewis b. 1-27-1802 d. 3-5-1889
Married Rebekah James on 5-6-1824
   1. Alfred Lewis b. 3-8-1825
   Married Nancy Douglas on 8-30-1843
      1. Ellen Lewis b. 1845
      2. Andrew L. Lewis b. 1848
      3. Martin Lewis b. 1850
      4. Jacob Lewis b. 1852
      5. Henry Lewis b. 1857
   2. Alvin J. Lewis b. 8-29-1826
   Married Orillia Baird Passman b. 11-23-1847
      1. Daughter

Married _____ Thompson
3. Calvin Perry Lewis b. 1-20-1828
4. Jacob Lewis Jr. b. 1830 d. 1830
5. Emsley Lewis b. 6-9-1832
Married Elizabeth Laws
   1. Casper L. "Cap" Lewis b. 2-8-1872
   Married Linda Miller in 1884
      1. Merle E. Lewis b. 1895 d. 1963
      2. Edna Lewis
      Married _____ McCroskey
      3. Paul Lewis
      4. Paulene Lewis
      5. Kathryn Lewis
      Married J. Lewis
      6. Guy Lewis b. 1921 d. 10-10-1987
      7. Gail Lewis b. 4-30-1913
6. Adaline Lewis b. 4-8-1835
7. William J. Lewis b. 4-7-1837
Married _____ Smith
   1. Samuel Lewis b. 12-26-1873
   Married _____ Spencer
   2. Effie Lewis b. 8-11-1875
   Married Leslie Gray
   3. George M. Lewis b. 2-15-1877
   Married _____ Adams
8. Jacob Lewis
9. Samuel Perry Lewis b. 2-23-1839
10. Emeline Lewis b. 6-30-1841
Married Absolon Loos
   1. George Loos
   2. William Loos
   3. Amanda Loos
   4. Hattie Loos
   5. Charles Loos
11. Milton Lewis b. 12-12-1843
12. Martha Lewis b. 3-13-1848 d. 1933
Married Robert Bershire
   1. Elmer Berkshire b. 1868
   2. E.M. Berkshire b. 1872

3. Carrie Berkshire b. 1874
4. Homer Berkshire b. 1882
7. John L. Lewis b. 1804
Married Matilda Stewart
  1. Mary L. Lewis b. 1-9-1826
  Married James Hall
    1. James Hall
    2. Clinton Hall
    3. William Hall
    4. Joseph Hall
  2. Martha L. Lewis b. 8-8-1827
  Married William Hardwick
    1. Ada Hardwick b. 10-22-1868
    2. Mary L. Hardwick b. 3-24-1871
  3. Abner H. Lewis b. 2-5-1829
  1st Married Mary McCorkle
    1. William A. Lewis b. 1855
    2. Sarah Lewis b. 3-7-1857
    3. Abner Lewis Jr.
  2nd Married Louisa Ackers
    1. Louisa Lewis
    2. John Lewis b. 4-21-1864
    3. Martha J. Lewis
    4. Emma Lewis
  4. Joseph M. Lewis b. 10-1832
  Married Elizabeth Burkhart
    1. Mary M. Lewis
    1st Married Charles Webber
      1. Charles Webber Jr. b. 7-17-1878
      1st Married Gertie Hitchcock
        1. Cecil Gale Webber b. 4-9-1878
      2nd Married Abram Caudle
        1. Effie Caudle b. 2-24-1882
        Married Alvie Sebright
          1. Harry Sebright
        3. Daisy Caudle b. 8-27-1883
        Married Otto Vangilder
        4. Anne E. Caudle b. 9-7-1885
        5. Ethel V. Caudle 3-7-1887
        6. Emerson J. Caudle b. 4-15-1889

2. James T. Lewis b. 9-14-1861
Married Eva Lackley on 5-22-1884
  1. Nina E. Lewis b. 6-27-1885
  Married B.W. Babcock in 1903
  2. John S. Lewis b. 10-10-1886
  3. Earl Lewis b. 9-10-1889
  4. Etta Lewis b. 1-1884
5. Allen J. Lewis b. 1830
6. Nancy Ann Lewis b. 1834
Married George Lehr
  1. James C. Lehr b. 1-6-1856
7. Margaret E. Lewis b. 1836 D.Y. (1838)
8. John W. Lewis b. 1840
Married Jane Couchman
9. James Paul Lewis b. 6-2-1842
Married Amelia Couger on 12-20-1862
  1. John Lewis
  2. Alfred Lewis
8. William M. Lewis b. 8-23-1806
Married Martha Craven
  1. Addison Lewis b. 10-25-1829 d. 9-18-1885
  Married Hannah Pierson
  2. Crawford Lewis b. 5-10-1831
  Married Lucinda Paine
  3. Emmeline Lewis b. 5-28-1834 d. 12-11-1898
  Married Isaac Potts
  4. Permilia Lewis b. 9-9-1836
  Married Joseph Lawson
  5. Elizabeth E. Lewis b. 5-13-1838
  1st Married James Musgrave
  2nd Married C.E. Stamper
  6. C. Perry Lewis b. 1841 d. 9-10-1845
  7. William Hardin Lewis b. 7-2-1847 d. 1-19-1917
  Married Annie Paddock
    1. W.M. Melton Lewis
    Married Emma Moon
      1. Eddie Lewis b. 3-11-1891
  8. Jasper Lewis b. 1-2-1850 d. 3-9-1915
    1. Della Lewis b. 4-9-1872

      2. Floyd Lewis b. 2-7-1874
      3. William H. Lewis b. 2-1-1878
      4. Carrie M. Lewis b. 2-7-1880
      5. Ira Allen Lewis b. 10-27-1883
      6. Tenna Lewis b. 10-1-1885 d. 9-1886
9. Ann Lewis
Married Andrew McMahan
10. Mary Lewis
11. Isaiah Lewis Jr. b. 1813
Married Mary Smith
      1. Joab Lewis b. 1829
      Married Lousie McCarthy
         1. John Lewis
         2. Sue Anna Lewis
         Married T.M. Brown in 1875
         3. Cynthia Lewis
         Married John Glass
            (4 daughters)
         4. Elizabeth Lewis
         5. David Lewis b. 1809
2. Persilla Lewis b. 4-7-1770
Married Thomas Fields
3. Jacob Lewis b. 3-14-1772 d. 8-4-1857
Married Ailsie Leonard on 2-22-1782
      1. David Lewis b. 1-10-1793
      Married Nancy Williams
      2. Joseph Lewis b. 1794
      3. Abner Lewis b. 2-8-1797
      Married Marcy B. Gibson
      4. Mary Lewis b. 3-20-1799
      Married Richard Baker
      5. Joab Lewis b. 1-12-1801
      1st Married Elizabeth House
      2nd Married Vilante Cobb
      6. Ann Beeson Lewis b. 12-18-1803
      Married William Alexander
         1. Francis Alexander b. 1828
         2. Ailsey Alexander b. 1830
         3. Mary Alexander b. 1832
         4. Elizabeth Alexander b. 1834

5. James T. Alexander b. 1836
6. Catherine Alexander b. 1838
7. Maulia Alexander b. 1840
8. William Alexander b. 1842
7. Elizabeth Lewis b. 9-7-1805
8. James Lewis b. 9-7-1807 d. 3-26-1863
Married Mary Stewart
   1. Leonard Lewis b. 1829
   2. Sarah Ann Lewis b. 1833
   3. John Tarleton Lewis b. 2-8-1837
   4. Elizabeth Lewis b. 1835
   5. Jane Lewis b. 1839
   6. Ailsie Lewis b. 1841
   7. Malinda Lewis b. 1843
   8. Katherine Lewis b. 1845
   9. Phalaba Lewis b. 1847
   10. Henry Lewis b. 1849
   11. Malissa Lewis b. 1852
   12. Margaret Lewis b. 1854
   13. Robert Stewart Lewis
9. Katherine Lewis b. 10-7-1810
Married James Alexander
10. Jacob Lewis b. 4-1813
Married _____ Stewart
4. Joab Lewis b. 12-23-1773
Married Katherine Leonard
   1. Leonard Lewis
   Married Sarah Williams
   2. Isaiah Lewis b. 1808 d. 1850
   Married Mary "Polly" Wright in 1828
      1. William Martin Lewis
      1st Married Elizabeth Biggers in 1848
         1. James Norris Lewis b. 1850
         Married Mary Susan McIlroy (b. 9-12-1848 d. 9-8-1889)
            1. James F. Lewis b. 5-1-1877 d. 8-31-1878
            2. John N. Lewis
            Married Ethel Durham
               1. Maxine
            3. Dr. Everett Lewis(lived in Tulsa, Oklahoma)

4. William Lewis b. 7-4-1875 d. 7-22-1879
5. James Lewis b. 5-7-1877
6. Frank Lewis b. 1877 d. 1879
7. Lela Lewis b. 1-2-1879 d. 8-5-1879
2. William Franklin Lewis b. 1854 d. in Arkansas
Married Emily Richardson in 1876
    1. J.J. Lewis b. 1881
    Married Ida Lang in 1904
        1. Aidene Lewis
        2. Alford J. Lewis
        3. George Lewis
        4. C.P. Lewis
        5. Tommie Ruth Lewis
3. Ben Wiley Lewis
Married Vicey Wilson in 1884
2nd Married Mary Jane Hassell
4. Thomas Marion Lewis
1st Married Emily Tisdale (d. 1876) in 1876
2nd Married Francis C. Pratt (b. 5-26-1856 d. 8-25-1894)
3rd Married Nancy Flannery (b. 11-30-1870 d. 1959)
(Mother of Last 5 children)
    1. Matthew Lewis b. 11-26-1874 d. 1889
    2. James M. Lewis b. 1876 d.1878
    3. Laura Lewis b. 1878 d. 1967
    Married M.L. Buce
        1. Mavoreen Buce
        Married _____ Dexter
    4. Robert Newton Lewis b. 1881
    Married Arkie Matilda Mondy (b. 5-3-1884 d. 1960) in 1901
        1. Ed Lewis(twin) D.Y.
        2. Fred Lewis(twin) D.Y.
        3. Rex C. Lewis
        Married Jessie _____
        4. Robert M. Lewis
        Married Mabel _____
        5. Ruby Lewis b. 1904
        Married Homer Ruyle
            1. Mary Ruyle
            Married K. Hudson

2. John Ruyle
Married Debbie _____
6. Ruth Lewis b. 1914
1st Married J. Lytle Martin
  1. Nancy Martin
  Married _____ Stewart
  2. Lewis Martin
2nd Married _____ Parsons
5. Thomas S. Lewis b. 12-5-1882 d. 9-26-1918
Married Ella McDaniel
6. Ella Lewis b. 1-24-1884 d. 3-2-1919
Married J.E. Skinner
7. Joseph Frank Lewis b. 12-11-1886 d. 6-23-1968
  1. Fred Lewis
8. A.G. "Pete" Lewis b. 8-14-1889 d. 1-29-1925
9. Edgar Lewis b. 8-7-1894 d. 8-25-1899
10. Chris Lewis
11. Harvey Lewis
12. Earl R. Lewis
13. Burtie Lewis
Married _____ Partridge
14. Myrtie Lewis
Married _____ Davenport
5. Mary Lewis
Married James Ford
3rd Married Miss Fowler
6. Joe A. Lewis
Married Sally Pratt in 1890
  1. Herma Jane Lewis
  Married John Hawley
    1. Bob Hawley b. 3-11-1915
    2. Mary Hawley b. 6-5-1916
7. Daughter D.Y.
4th Married Martha Lewis Hassell (second cousin, b. 1840)
8. Paul Martin "P.M." Lewis b. 1863
Married Clara Frazier (b. 1865) on 10-17-1886
  1. Martin Lewis b. 1890
  2. Isabella Lewis b. 1893
  3. Grover Lewis b. 1894

Married Blanch \_\_\_\_\_
  1. Avis Lewis b. 1919
4. Pearl Lewis b. 1898
9. Phillip Lewis b. 1865
Married Ella Williams
  1. Ernest Lewis b. 1890 in Arkansas
    1. Calvin Lewis
    2. Fritz Lewis
  2. Lula May Lewis b. 1887 d. 1891
  3. Earl "Ark" Lewis b. 1892
    1. Earlenne Lewis
  4. Dan Lewis b. 1899 in Texas
  5. Carl Lewis b. 1901 in Texas
  Married Artie
    1. Daughter
  6. Maggie Lewis b. 1903 in Texas
  Married Reverend Sheehan
    1. Gerald Sheehan
    2. Child
    3. Child
    4. Bill Sheehan (lived in Durmas, Texas)
10. Amanda Lewis [24] b. 1867
Married Samuel Benjamin McIlroy
  1. I.V. McIlroy

---

24  The marriage of Amanda Lewis and Samuel B. McIlroy resulted in seven children, one of whom was my grandmother Amanda, who was born on October 3, 1867. The family lived about three miles west of Pocahontas at 5 Mile Spring. After William Martin's death and after Martha's brother Howard had left her a considerable inheritance, Martha bought land (about one hundred acres for each of her living children P.M., Phillip, Perry, and Amanda). Amanda and Sam moved to Hill County, Texas in 1900, the boys a few months earlier.

Amanda had married Samuel Benjamin McIlroy on October 11, 1883. They had four children born in Randolph County, Arkansas I.V., Essie, Dallas, and Lewis. The 5th, S.B., was born on April 9, 1904 in Hill County, TX. Samuel McIlroy had sold his land in Randolph County, Arkansas, so he had money to buy and add to the farm given to them by his mother-in-law Martha. He accumulated about 600 acres by the time of his early death in 1910 at the age of 50. Martha Lewis lived with her youngest son Perry until he went to Arkansas and married Lottie Ford and moved her to Texas. Afterwards, Martha lived and rotated between the children. Soon, P.M. and Philip Lewis sold their land in Hill County and moved to Childress, Texas where the land was cheaper and the climate was dryer. Philip was having health problems, which corrected after the move. One or two of Martha Lewis's stepsons also moved to Hill County, Texas. They had large families and many of their descendants still live in Texas.

  2. Essie McIlroy

  3. Lewis McIlroy

  4. Dallas McIlroy

  5. S.B. (initials only) b. 4-9-1904

 11. Jeff Lewis b. 1869 D.Y.

 12. Lucy Lewis b. 1876 D.Y.

 13. Myrtle Lewis b. 10-13-1873 d. 11-15-1889

 14. Perry Lewis b. 1877

Married Lottie Ford

  1. Ralph Lewis b. 1909

  2. Martha Hazel Lewis b. 1-30-1905 d. 10-5-1999

  Married Harry Morgan on 9-12-1924

   1. Helen Graves Morgan

   2. Elizabeth Ann McGee Morgan

   3. Harry Glenn Morgan

  3. George Lewis b. 1910

  4. Herbert Lewis b. 1913

  5. Harold Lewis b. 1915

  6. Ruth b. Lewis 1917

 15. Alice E. Lewis b. 8-7-1878 d. 9-17-1890 in Randolph County, Arkansas

2. Charles Lewis b. 1836

1st Married _____ Stockell

 1. Sarah Lewis

 2. Mahala Lewis

 3. Charles Lewis

 4. Louisa Lewis b. 1868

 5. Perry V. Lewis b. 1871

 6. Isaiah Lewis b. 1874

2nd Married _____ Haloker

3. Joab Lewis b. 1832

1st Married Martha Kelly

2nd Married Behema Covanter on 5-24-1866

3rd Married Nancy Jane Dennis

 1. Paul A. Lewis b. 1861

 Married Lula Witt

 2. Jane Lewis b. 1854

1st Married Green Johnson

2nd Married Bill Ingram

3. William Lewis
4. Charles W. Lewis b. 1860
Married Jane Kelly
5. James Lewis b. 1863
6. Rebecca Lewis b. 1866
Married John F. Ruff
    1. Jesse Ruff
7. George F. Lewis b. 1868
8. Mollie Lewis
Married Dan Sketes
4. Neriah Lewis
(Never married)
5. Abner Lewis b. 9-22-1775
6. Neriah Lewis b. 6-25-1778 d. 11-27-1843
Married Mary Moss (b. 1775 d. 1844)
    1. Ann Lewis b. 12-21-1800 d. 1876
Married Ellis Wilcox in 1823
    2. Martha Lewis b. 3-6-1802 d. 5-3-1842
Married Travis More
    3. Benjamin Lewis b. 4-22-1803 d. 10-30-1838
Married Joannah Ryons
        1. Mary Frances Lewis b. 1827
        2. John M. Lewis b. 1829
        3. William Crawford Lewis b. 1830
        4. Martha Lewis b. 1833
Married S. Bingham
        5. Sarah Lewis b. 1835
Married G. Davis
        6. Rebecca Lewis D.Y.
        7. Samuel Lewis b. 1810
        8. Elizabeth Lewis b. 1812
        9. David Lewis b. 1814
        10. Neriah Lewis b. 1816
        11. Byron Lewis b. 1818
        12. Mary Lewis b. 1820
Married M.J. Blackburn
7. Benjamin Lewis b. 5-26-1781
8. Elizabeth Lewis b. 9-21-1783
9. Cozby Lewis b. 6-17-1785
Married John Woodall

10. Tarleton Lewis b. 8-11-1787
1st Married Rachel Williams
    1. James Lewis b. 10-13-1807
    2. Ann Beeson Lewis b. 1-10-1810
    3. Ruth W. Lewis b. 10-7-1811
2nd Married Penelope _____
    1. Margaret Lewis b. 1-24-1815
    2. David Lewis b. 10-7-1818
11. Hannah Lewis b. 10-2-1789
Married Ezekiel Harlon Perry
    1. Nathan W. Perry
    2. Amos N. Perry
12. David Lewis b. 1-12-1814
13. Rosannah Lewis b. 10-26-1815
2. Jocob Lewis b. 5-24-1750 d. 12-3-1812
Married Sarah Nolan
    1. David Lewis b. 2-25-1770
    2. John Lewis b. 9-3-1771
    Married Jane Hurley
    3. Mary M. Lewis b. 2-25-1773
    Married Manseh Womack
    4. Pearce A. Lewis b. 10-4-1774
    Married Phebe Langon
    5. Roseanna Lewis b. 10-17-1776
    Married John Dugent
    6. Jacob Lewis b. 5-25-1778
    7. George Lewis b. 1-2-1780
    Married Katherine Brooks
    8. Aberham Lewis b. 11-8-1783
    9. Sarah A. Lewis b. 4-10-1786
    Married John Womack
    10. Nolan R. Lewis b. 9-21-1791
3. Rosannah Lewis b. 7-5-1752
Married _____ West
4. Jean Lewis b. 7-15-1755
Married John Campbell
    1. Balam Campell
    2. William Campell
    3. Sarah Campell

4. Joab Campell
6. John Campell
7. David Campell
8. David Campell
5. Stephen Lewis b. 6-4-1757 d. 1791
Married Susannah _____
    1. Stephen Lewis b. 1781
    2. David Lewis b. 1783
    3. Susanne Lewis b. 1784
    4. Brooks Lewis b. 1785
    5. Eleanor Lewis b. 1787
    6. Deliah Lewis b. 1789
    7. Priscilla Lewis b. 1791
6. Richard Lewis b. 6-4-1759
Married Lydia Fields
    1. Lydia Lewis b. 1783 d. 1825
    Married Judge Erwin
    2. Jonathan Lewis b. 1785
    3. John Lewis b. 1787
    4. William Lewis b. 1789
    5. Robert Lewis b. 1792
    6. Priscilla Lewis b. 1794
    Married John Scott on 2-12-1813
    7. Jane Lewis b. 1796
    Married J.W. Clark
    8. Richard Lewis b. 1799
    9. Crawford Lewis b. 1802
    Married Elizabeth Neal
    10. David Lewis b. 1806
    11. Levina Lewis b. 1808
7. John Lewis b. 1-15-1763
Married Sarah Ruckman
    1. Hanna Lewis b. 1782 d. 1848-1849
    Married Thomas Lamb
    2. Richard Lewis b. 8-6-1784
    Married Laverne Hall
    3. Sarah Lewis b. 7-19-1787
    4. Isaiah Lewis b. 12-26-1789
    5. John Lewis b. 1-6-1792
    6. Joseph Lewis b. 2-6-1794

7. Naomi Lewis b. 7-30-1796
Married James Harris
8. Martha Lewis b. 1-12-1799
Married Samuel K. Boyd on 4-10-1817
9. Priscillia Lewis b. 7-13-1801
Married David Martindale
10. Lawson Lewis b. 10-30-1805 d. 1806
11. Allen W. Lewis b. 6-14-1809
Married Lucy Hallinsworth on 5-30-1839
8. Sarah Lewis b. 1-15-1763
Married Isaiah Ruckman

**John Lewis** was living in the county of Randolph, North Carolina when his will was appraised in 1802. The home place was on Pole Cat Creek in the northern part of the county—he was probably born in Frederick County, Virginia and moved before 1755 to North Carolina

His wife Priscilla Brooks was the daughter of Jacob Brook and Rosanna Warren. This was wild country then—there were not many neighbors—the boys of John and Priscilla were described as big-strong and somewhat unruly. They loved to fight and most everyone in the neighborhood was afraid of them. It was written that they ran their cattle where they wanted to, raided others' fish traps, and dared anyone to cross them. They were all liked by the girls and most married well. It was probably good that John's son David married Ann Beeson (a Quaker), for they produced preachers and good citizens.

John, the father of David, lived in 1738 in Frederick County, Virginia. He had secured two Farifax grants in Opequion Creek. This land adjoined that of Jacob Brook, the father of Priscilla, who married David's son John. About 1756, David and Mary Crawford sold their land and moved to South Carolina.

David was probably born in Maryland or Pennsylvania and most likely was the second generation of this Lewis family born in America. There is belief that they had come to America about 1650. This was only forty years after the Jamestown settlement, so you can see that they did not have an easy time settling in this country. They probably lived in Maryland or Pennsylvania before removing to the wilds of Virginia and North Carolina.

Isaiah Lewis, son of David and Ann Beeson, was born in Randolph County, North Carolina. His wife was Nancy Julian and they located near Pickens, South Carolina for several years. In 1807 they moved to Warren County, Kentucky and then to Edwards County, Illinois, which later became Randolph. He located between Lawrenceville and Bridgeport (3 miles west of Lawrenceville).

Isaiah took an active part in this location which was just developing—he served on the first petite jury, was an early school teacher, helped survey the village of Lawrenceville and was county commissioner in 1829. At the completion of his term, he moved to Vigo County, Indiana where he died in 1837.

There is no doubt that Isaiah Lewis's large family in most part remained in Randolph County and populated that county with Lewises.

Family tradition has it that Isaiah was away from home with his team when the twins Phillip and Paul were born. He had a dream to return home quickly, which he did, and he gave them the same names that they had in his dream. He probably was hauling for his father David, who was a merchant. Isaiah was a large stocky man and quite fleshy. While lighting his pipe, he let a coal of fire fall on one of his feet. He had on low shoes, but no stockings. This turned into erysipelas, resulting in his death.

**Paul Lewis** lived for a long time in a log house on the land entered by Peter Lewis and but a short distance from the house of his father Isaiah Lewis. This house was nearer the State Road than that occupied by Isaiah. Paul then moved to a farm in what is now the eastern edge of Richland County, locating on a stream named Paul Creek for himself. The move was probably made around 1824 or 1825, for Phillip Lewis bought out his father in the later years.

The location on Paul Creek was probably near the road that was viewed from Shaker Mills (Charlottesville) to the State Road. This road is mentioned in the County Commissioner's records for 1822 and later we find Paul Lewis named as a surveyor. This road ran by the Pargin and Elliot settlements. Peter Pargin settled on Elm Creek, later turned Pargins Creek. He was the first settler in what is now Petty Tup. His son Isaiah was of the same age as Perry Lewis. The latter remembered as a mere boy that his father took him to the Pargin home four miles distant through the timber.

Paul Lewis sold his land on Paul Creek to a man named John Laws (patented July 27, 1824) and entered land from the U.S. government. The land was located four miles west and north of Lawrenceville. He lived on the land until 1846, then he sold out to his son Perry and went to Hot Springs, Arkansas for the benefit of his wife's health. He went away in a covered wagon and consumed several months on the way—so precarious was the health of his wife, who lay upon her bed in the wagon. He began the journey on October 8, 1845 and it took three days to make it to Olney, which was then a place of five hours. He reached Springfield, Missouri on December 24, 1845, and spent some time with his son James. He reached Hot Springs in the spring of that year.

Paul was a Universalist in belief and preached on several occasions. Paul farmed but he also built and operated the first linseed oil mill in Lawrenceville

County. It was operated by ox power. It was operated for many years after Paul left for Arkansas, probably by his brother-in-law Daniel Payne.

Matilda, Mary, and Martha were the only ones of the children who accompanied him to Arkansas. When he left Lawrence County, Paul Lewis took with him a bookcase which was laid down in the wagon to make the support for the bed. These books, along with others that were secured later, were scattered and torn up after the Civil War. Paul became an ardent reader and student in middle life. He was well versed in the Bible and preached the doctrine of the Universalists.

Paul Lewis and family, which included that of his daughter, Matilda Ann Lewis-Mayes, lived in Jefferson Township, Independence County, Arkansas.

Paul's land was sold to his older son Perry. This was the land that he planted an orchard on when he moved there. Today, some of the trees are still standing. Paul's creek is still named after him and runs across the end of the tract of land.

**Ann Stewart** died in a few years after the moved to Arkansas. Paul continued to live in Randolph County, Arkansas until his death many years later. He was not alone there. His first cousin Isaiah (son of Joab) had moved there about the same time. Isaiah's widow married Paul after Isaiah's death. Also, Isaiah's son William Martin married Martha and became Paul's son-in-law.

**Perry Lewis**, first son of Paul and Ann, lived to be over 90 years old. He bought his father's place when Paul took Ann to Hot Springs in 1845. By trade, he was a millwright. He built the water mill at Charlottesville, the first mill at Lawrenceville, and many more. He also built bridges and was superintendent of the Plank Tollroad from Lawrenceville to the Wabash River.

Perry was described as a very energetic man, straight-forward, honest. With only a few months schooling, he began carpenter work at age 14 and became an excellent millwright. He built houses, barns, and many bridges—framing then with timber. He also was an excellent farmer, accumulated 800 acres of land, and was the first west of the Ambrose River to own a self binder. His children followed in his footsteps and became well-known and useful citizens. Most remained in Lawrence County.

**Phillip Howard**, the younger brother of Perry and the son of Paul and Ann Lewis, never married but left an impact on this family. He was outfitted with help from Phillip to go to California for the gold rush around 1850. He had very little success there and moved up the coast, staying about a year in Oregon and in 1852 returned to Seattle (a small town of only a few thousand) where he took up a homestead claim which became the Newcastle coal mines. Years later, he sold this mine and bought and sold real estate in Seattle. Howard never forgot his early home and returned at times. His niece, Linda Price (and husband) went to Seattle and worked with Howard as did Elmer Lewis (a nephew), who died there at the age of 25. When Phillip Howard died, he left his estate to Lydia Price, to Perry who helped him financially, to his brother James P. Lewis (of Green County, Missouri), and to his sister Martha Lewis. His estate at that time was about $200,000, or about $4 million today (2007). Martha received $35,000 and bought land in Hill County, Texas for her four living children. As stated before, Martha and her three boys moved soon to Hill County. Martha's daughter Amanda and her son-in-law Sam McIlroy arrived in the fall of 1900. A few of Amanda's step-children later came near to where they lived in Hill County, Texas.

**William**, son of Phillip, was active and an industrious citizen of Bridgeport. He was a gifted carpenter like his father and brother. He was foreman and builder of several railroad stations. He built the first depot in Bridgeport and was a station agent. He had the first hardware store in Bridgeport and was an early grain dealer. Two of his sons became physicians. Dr. H.V. was county coroner as was his brother. Dr. H.V. Lewis began his practice in Bridgeport and later moved to Lawrenceville.

**Joseph Battenfield**, another son of Perry, was a carpenter and built several railroad bridges and depots.

**Martha Lewis**, the youngest daughter of Paul, moved to Arkansas in the fall of 1845-spring 1846 to take her mother Ann to Hot Springs, Arkansas for treatments. She was six years old—her mother lived a few more years, but Martha was mostly raised without a mother. She married at age 16 to John Hassel and had one daughter, Lizzie. A few years later, she married her second cousin William Martin Lewis, son of Isaiah, son of Joab, her grandfather Isaiah's brother. He had been married three times and had family by all. Martha had eight children by William, but only four reached maturity—Paul Martin, Philip, Amanda b. 1867, and Perry b. 1877. By the spring of 1899, the three boys and Martha were in Hill County, Texas. Amanda McIlroy and Sam, her husband, moved there later in 1900. Before 1910, the two older boys moved to nearby Childress—my father said she lived with each of the children after they left Arkansas. She died in 1919, probably from the flu that killed so many in 1918-1919. I found records In Hillsboro papers that said five from the Lewis family died within a year from this epidemic.

**Phillip Lewis**, son of Isaiah, was twin to Paul. About 1859, he sold his land to his son-in-law John Grigs and moved to Arkansas where his twin brother lived, but he stayed only one year and in 1861 returned to Illinois. He bought the new place on the Old State Road about four miles west of Lawrenceville.

His first home place was purchased from his father Isaiah and he built a fine residence. Other than farming, he was a blacksmith and wagon maker.

**William Lewis**, son of William-son of David-son of Isaiah, was well-known and highly regarded in Lawrenceville for many years. He was city clerk for thirty years and also the town clerk and newspaper compositor for a time and operated his own job printing plant. He also was a director of the building and loan association.

**Paul Lewis**, son of Dr. H.V. Lewis, was associated with his father in the drugstore business for several years. The Lewis Drugstore was located on the northeast corner of the square. Paul was a traveling agent for a drug company for several years.

**Lydia Ann**, daughter of Perry-son of Paul, was born December 15, 1846 (the oldest of Perry's eleven children). She married E.B. Price on November 13, 1879 and they had three children—the youngest died very young and the oldest disappeared in Seattle in later years. A few years after they married, the moved to Seattle (Washington territory). They joined her uncle Howard Lewis, who was a pioneer and one of the founders of the city. Mr. Price died in July 1904 and she returned to Lawrence County in January of 1913.

# My (James Roland McIlroy's) Kin Hyde-Baggett-Hooker-McLean

## The Hydes

This is a seven-generation pedigree of our Hyde line. These facts were taken from various sources: family Bibles, censuses, family records, and more. I feel they are fairly correct but I cannot document them. There may be some errors.

The first record I have is Richard Hyde who came to America in 1636 from England and died in Surrey County, Virginia in 1659. This was early, only thirty years after the founding or Jamestown. Richard and his brother John came together with their passage paid for by Edward Minter. They had to work out this obligation before they could operate on their own. Richard I moved to Surrey County, Virginia and married Judith _____ about 1651. They had a son Richard II, born in 1652. This Richard married Mary _____ and had Richard III about 1678. Richard III became a pirate (under Edward Teach who was called Black Beard). After Black Beard was killed in 1718, he came home and gave up his ways. He had a son named Richard IV who was a guide to the Indian Country. The story is told that his father worked for him and got in trouble with the Indians and had his ears cut off. We will start our story with this Richard IV.

1. Richard Hyde IV b. about 1718 d. 1762
Married Mildred Hartwell (b. 1720 d. 1795) in 1744
    1. Ann Hyde b. 1745
    2. Sophia Hyde b. 1747
    3. Letichia Hyde b. 1749
    4. John Hyde b. 1750

5. Henry Hyde[25] b. 1753 in Northampton County, North Carolina d. 1812 in Tennessee
Married Elizabeth Warren
    1. John Hyde b. 1780 in North Carolina d. 1838 in Tennessee
    Married Elizabeth Emmerson on 10-11-1799
        1. John Hyde b. 6-20-1804 d. 10-5-1845
        Married Permelia Kelly
          (5 children)
        2. Child
        3. Franklin Hyde D.Y.
        4. William H. "Willis" Hyde b. 6-17-1806
        Married Marina Shaw
        5. Henry Emerson Hyde b. 5-11-1808 d. 5-13-1877
        Married Margaret Watson
          1. I.B. Hyde b. 5-1848
          2. Penola Hyde
          3. Rufus Hyde
          4. Dick Hyde
          5. Alice Hyde
          6. Ann Hyde
          7. May Hyde
          8. Margaret Hyde
          9. Sallie Hyde
          10. Henrietta Hyde
    2. Henry Hyde Jr. d. 1818
    Married Mary Drake on 11-12-1799
        1. Elizabeth Hyde
        Married James Green on 12-12-1835
        2. Wesley W. Hyde
        3. Mary D. Hyde
        Married A.W. Butler on 6-3-1829
        4. Maria W. Hyde b. 1805
        Married A.D. Carden on 12-3-1823
          1. Ann Elizabeth Carden b. 1830
          2. Henry Carden b. 1832

---

25    Henry Hyde owned the largest plantation near Nashville, Tennessee on the Cumberland River. He had moved there around 1798 and owned a ferry that went across the River. The main road through Nashville today is called Hyde's Pike Ferry Road. Some people considered Henry the richest man on the Cumberland River.

    3. Sarah Carden (twin) b. 1838
    4. Susan Carden (twin) b. 1838
  5. John J. Hyde
  6. Jordan W. Hyde
Married Susan Drake
  7. Edmond Hyde d. 3-15-1849
Married Christianna Rains
  8. Charelita G. Hyde
Married Henry Cumming
3. Rebecca Hyde
Married John Stump on 5-16-1801 d. before 1829
  1. Pamelia Stump
  2. Christopher Stump
4. Richard Hyde b. 1785
Married Elizabeth Hooper on 3-11-1815
  1. James Hyde
  2. Richard Hyde b. 1825
  3. Thomas J. Hyde b. 1830
Married Lizzie _____
    1. Walter Hyde b. 1863
    2. Tom Hyde b. 1863
    3. James Hyde b. 1865
    4. Effie Hyde b. 1868
  4. Hooper Hyde b. 1831 d. 1871
    (no children)
5. Edmund Hyde d. before 1850
1st Married Rhonda William on 2-7-1815
2nd Married Christiana Rains
  1. Wellington H. Hyde b. 4-8-1830
Married Susan Manlove
  2. Edmund Hyde Jr. b. 7-28-1832
Married Mary Young
  3. Richard Hyde b. 8-22-1835 d. 8-11-1864
  4. J.B. Hyde b. 3-16-1837 d. 7-2-1864
6. Benjamin W. Hyde b. about 1786
Married Emily "Milly" Cherry in 1807
  1. William Hyde b. 1810
  2. Wesley Hyde b. 1812
  3. Carroll W. Hyde b. 1-6-1815

Married Arianna Alice Manlove (b. 3-13-1819 d. 3-30-1881), divorced 1859

1. William H. Hyde b. 1842 D.Y.
2. Susan Hyde b. 1845
3. Udara Hyde b. 1846
4. Arra Ann Hyde b. 1850
Married _____ Moudy
5. Carroll F. Hyde b. 1852
Married Lillie Baggett (b. 1862 d. 1910)
 1. Ermine Hyde b. 1882 in Tennessee
 Married James O. Hooker
  1. Hazel Hooker
  Married Jack Grant
   1. Linna Marie Grant
   Married Jim McCollough
   2. Winona Marie Grant
   Married Jack Neal
   3. Gordon Grant
   Married Mary Lee Green
  2. Linna Hooker b. 2-1904
  Married S.B. McIlroy
  *(See McIlroys)*
  3. Harold Hooker
  Married Lucille Henderson
   1. Betty Ann Hooker
   Married _____ Stellman
   2. Harolyn Hooker
   Married Andy Anderson
 2. Robert T. Hyde b. 1884
  1. Robert Hyde Jr.
 3. George "Bill" Wellington Hyde b. 3-2-1889
 Married Erma Wallace on 12-6-1927
  1. Joe Ann Hyde
  Married Terrell Hinds
   1. Bill Hinds b. 2-20-1952
   2. Holly Hinds b. 8-8-1954
   Married _____ Kepner
   3. Laura Hinds b. 9-20-1958
   Married _____ Jones

2. Roger (Buddy) Hyde
3. Frank Hyde
4. Hayden Hyde
4. Joseph F. Hyde b. 1889?
Married Kate _____ (b. 1896)
   1. Lois Hyde b. 1915
   2. Joe Forest Hyde b. 1919
   2. Jewel Hyde b. 1920
5. Ernest Earl Hyde b. 1892
Married _____
   1. Carroll Earl Hyde
   2. Hazel Earl Hyde
4. Charlotte Hyde
5. Benjamin Hyde b. 1822
6. Ledville Hyde b. 1828
7. Robert Hyde b. 1832
8. Jane Hyde b. 1835
7. Jordan Hyde b. 1-1795 d. 12-10-1827
Married Susan S. Drake (d. 12-24-1825) on 3-3-1825
8. Tazwell Hyde b. 3-17-1796 d. 5-3-1838
Married Susan Drake on 11-15-1815
   1. Sallie Hyde
   Married _____ Young
   2. Ellen Hyde
   Married _____ Green
   3. Felix Hyde b. 2-6-1817 d. 1832
   4. Tazwell Hyde Jr.
   Married Ella _____
      1. Sallie Hyde b. 1839
      2. N.B. Hyde[26] b. 1844 d. 4-6-1862
      Married Mollie Rayan on 9-6-1857
      3. Ann Hyde b. 1846
      4. Lizzie Hyde b. 1849

---

26    After N.B. Hyde was killed in the Civil War, his wife, Molly, became a spy for the Confederates. The line was pretty close to where they lived, and she went across and got messages and came back to give them to her sister, who turned them over to the Confederates. They were both caught before the war was over and put in prison, but were not killed, which was the usual punishment for spies.

6. Hartwell Hyde[27] b. 1-12-1760 d. 6-17-1833
Married Mary Revis (b. 9-29-1758 d. 5-2-1828)
   1. Latisha Hyde b. 7-19-1778
   2. Polly Hyde b. 1-101780
   Married Enoch Heaton
   3. Richard W. Hyde b. 10-24-1781 d. 11-5-1835
   4. Milly J. Hyde
   Married _____ Jordan (b. 5-1-1783 d. 8-19-1866)
   5. Sally L. Hyde b. 4-13-1785
   6. Sophia R. Hyde b. 3-17-1787
   Married _____ Jordan
   7. Priscilla H. Hyde b. 12-5-1789
   Married _____ Fulks
   8. Ann "Jincy" Hyde b. 7-11-1792
   Married _____ Avant
   9. Hartwell B. Hyde b. 11-26-1794
   Married Elizabeth Alston (b. 1803 d. 3-15-1884)
       1. Mildred Hyde
   10. Fariby Hyde b. 1797 D.Y.
   11. Elizabeth Hyde b. 6-24-1799
7. Cheney Hyde
8. Lucas Hyde

---

27    Hartwell Hyde moved from Halifax, North Carolina to Williamson County, Tennessee before his brother arrived in 1800. He had a large plantation called Solitude and many buildings necessary to plantation life including a gin, cobbler's shop, cooper's shed, and tread mill. The family suffered a tremendous loss during the Civil War, but his wife Mildred said it wasn't all bad. She said it may have freed the slaves, but it also freed her.

# The Baggetts

George Baggett, born, 1839, was the son of Eli Baggett and Sally. He married Amanda Dozier, born 1842, the daughter of Leonard Dozier and Jackie Thompson, on October 14, 1858. Leonard was the son of Richard M. Dozier and Polly Gayle.

The Baggetts lived near the Hydes in Roberston County, Tennessee—it was called the Baggett Community.

Carroll Hyde married Lillie Baggett (daughter of the above) about 1880—he moved after 1881 to Texas. For awhile, they lived at Haskell in Haskell County where he had a meat market. Some of his children were born there, and my grandmother Ermine went to school and said that one of her classmates was a Post. He went on to Michigan and became the owner of Post cereals. George Baggett and Amanda Dozier Baggett soon moved to Johnson County, Texas. They both lived to an advanced age. I remember Amanda—she must have died about 1932.

Lillie died young, soon after 1900. Carroll and Lillie lived in Hill County, Texas near James Schoolhouse and lived at the farm next to the Hooker family.

# The Hookers

William Hooker b. 1815 in Tennessee (came to Texas in the late 1850s from
Rutherford, Tennessee)
Married Malinda _____ b. 1823
1. James F. Hooker b. 1842 in Tennessee
Married Nancy _____
   1. Robert Hooker
   2. Mary Hooker
   3. Jennie B. Hooker
   4. James F. Hooker
2. John Carson Hooker b. 1847 in Tennessee
Married Sarah Odella Anderson (daughter of Levon Anderson)
   (Some of the children may be out of order/have incorrect birth dates)
   1. James Otis Hooker b. 1878 in Hill County, Texas
   Married Irmine Hyde (b. 1882)
      1. Hazel Hooker b. 1902
      Married Jack Grant
         1. Linna Marie Grant
         Married Jim McCullough
         2. Winona Grant
         Married Jack Neal
         3. Gordon Grant
         Married _____
      2. Linna Lorena Hooker b. 2-28-1904 in Texas
      Married S.B. McIlroy in 1923
         1. James R. McIlroy b. 1924
         2. Barbara McIlroy b. 1926
         3. Ralph Earl McIlroy b. 1931
         *(See McIlroys)*
      3. Harold Hooker
      Married Lucille Henderson
         1. Betty Ann Hooker
         2. Harolyn Hooker
   2. Edna Hooker

Married Tom Sanders on 12-24-1893
   1. Hooper Sanders
Married Flossie _____
      1. Hooper Sanders Jr.
   2. J.D. Sanders
Married Lucille _____
      1. Janice Sanders
      2. Elizabeth Sanders
      3. Billy Tom Sanders
   3. William "Will" Hooker b. 1880
Married Bessie _____
   1. Thelma Hooker
Married _____ Bridges
   2. Bessie Hooker
   3. Helen Hooker
   4. Wilburn Hooker
   5. Ralph Hooker
4. Francis "Frank" Hooker (female) b. 1885
Married Fred Bilbrey
(no children)
5. Samuel Alex Hooker b. 1888
Married Edna Cliet
   1. Margaret Hooker b. 1911
   2. Cliet Hooker b. 1913
   3. John Hugh Hooker b. 1915
   4. Leonard Hooker b. 1917
   5. Billy Charles Hooker b. 1925
6. Olivia Lorene Hooker b. 1891
Married Cooper Johnson
   1. James Johnson b. 1910
7. Hugh "Roy" Hooker b. 1883
Married Goldie _____
   1. Mozell Hooker b. 1923
   2. Bernie Hooker b. 1924
   3. Doris Hooker b. 1926
   4. LeRoy Hooker b. 1928
8. Gladys Hooker b. 1895
Married Neil Crowell
   1. Garland Crowell b. 1922
   2. Granville Crowell b. 1925

3. Billy Bob Crowell b. 1930
9. Sadie Hooker b. 1897
Married Horace Preston
   1. Daughter
3. Hugh Hooker b. 1856
4. Charles Hooker b. 1863

# The McLeans

The McLean line of our family comes down from Alexander McLean Sr. who was born on the Isle of Mull in 1709. His father had moved from Mull to County Antrim, Ireland. Alexander's mother died the night he was born and his father soon married again. As soon as Alexander was old enough, he hired himself to a man named Ratchford, who paid his way to America. They sailed from County Antrim and landed in Philadelphia. Alex worked for this man until his debt was paid. By the time he was thirty, he was out of debt and had saved several hundred dollars. At that time, he married Elizabeth Ratchford, the daughter of his former benefactor. Alexander and Elizabeth remained in Pennsylvania several years, where the first of their children were born. About the year 1748, they moved to Rowan County, North Carolina on a place about eight miles from Salisburg. In 1758, they moved to a tract of land near the junction of the South Fork and the Catawba River (now Gaston County, North Carolina). This was to be his permanent home. They had one daughter that lived (two more that died) in Pennsylvania. Afterwards, they had John in 1749, William on April 2, 1757, and then Alexander, George, and Thomas all born in North Carolina.

**Alexander and Elizabeth McLean**
 1. Jane McLean D.Y. (smallpox)
 2. Margaret McLean D.Y. (smallpox)
 3. Agnes McLean b. in Pennsylvania
 Married William McGill
 4. John McLean b. about 1749 in Raven County, North Carolina d. during the Revolutionary War at Buford's Bridge
 5. Alexander McLean b. 5-10-1755 in Gaston County, North Carolina d. 12-28-1849 in St. Clair County, Missouri
 Married Anna Haas (daughter of Simon Haas, who was killed by Tories during the Revolutionary War) on 4-1-1782
  1. Elizabeth McLean
  Married Sam McIlroy *(See McIlroy section for details)*
  2. William McLean b. 1794 in South Carolina d. 10-11-1853 in Randolph County, Arkansas

Married Elizabeth Byrd Cochran on 1-13-1820 in Cape Giradeau, Missouri.

    1. Mary McLean b. 1821
    Married William Thompson on 1-29-1837
    2. Sarah McLean b. 1823
    Married Sam Williams on 8-10-1848
    3. Amos McLean b. 1825
    Married Elizabeth Ann Garrett on 8-9-1849
    4. Margaret McLean b. 1828
      (Never married)
    5. Emily McLean b. 1830
    Married Moses W.
    6. John R. McLean b. 1832 in Arkansas
    Married Amanda M. Dodson on 11-16-1862
    7. Martha McLean b. 1834
    Married William Bates in 1853
    8. Stephen McLean b. 1836
      (Never married)
    9. Thalia McLean b. 1838 m. John England on 1-29-1871

6. William McLean b. 4-2-1757 in Lincoln County, North Carolina d. 10-25-1828
Married Mary "Polly" Davidson (b. 12-13-1766, daughter of Major John Davidson and Violet (Wilson) Davidson)

7. George McLean b. 10-14-1760 in Lincoln County, North Carolina d. 10-30-1854 in Bedford County, Tennessee
Married Rebecca Alexander (d. 12-31-1858 in Bond County, Illinois, daughter of Francis and Letitia (Braden) Alexander)

    1. John Alexander McLean b. 7-27-1790 in North Carolina d. 7-20-1859 in Illinois
    2. Matilda B. McLean b. 1793 in North Carolina
    Married James Scott Alexander in 1814
    3. Josiah Thomas McLean b. 11-12-1797 in North Carolina d. 10-12-1887 in Bond County, Illinois
    Married Nancy Sims on 5-30-1822
    4. Elizabeth McLean b. in North Carolina
    Married Cannon Harrison
    5. Jediah Alexander McLean b. 11-30-1802 in North Carolina d. 9-10-1895 in Bedford County, Tennessee
    6. Polly McLean b. 1804 in North Carolina

Married Jonathon Gentry
8. Thomas b. 1763 in Lincoln County d. 8-4-1856
Married Margaret "Peggy" Lewis on 10-10-1796

All of Alexander McLean's boys fought in the Revolutionary War (though Thomas may have been too young). John was captured one time but was exchanged and soon joined the army again. He was killed in a battle at Buford Bridge. America's first major victory was fought just a few miles from the McLean's home place and all of the boys were there. A few years after the battle, the McLean boys buried the bones of the dead and hauled a large rock monument to the top. This site at the Battle of King's Mountain is now a federal park, but that rock monument still stands. I have been there a couple of times and while visiting, also found the home place and the Smith graveyard. Many McLeans live in that section of North Carolina today.

Alexander and Anna Haas moved fairly soon after they married. They lived a short time in western Kentucky before settling in their permanent home near Cape Giradeau, Missouri. They had several children. Their daughter Elizabeth married Sam McIlroy in 1808 at Smithland, Kentucky. This story and a list of their children can be found in the McIlroy section.

William McLean (brother of Elizabeth) soon removed to Randolph County, Arkansas near his sister and raised a large family. William was well-known and served several terms of office in the county government.

# Early Immigrants that Could be Kin as Far Back as County Down

James McIlroy and wife, Sarah McCue, came to America about 1729-1730. They had one son, one year old, with them and later they had five boys and two girls. They stopped for awhile in Bucks County, where they had McElroy relations, then moved west to Cumberland County, Pennsylvania, where they remained until about 1755, then moved down the Valley of Virginia to Prince Edward County, Virginia where they remained several years after the death of James in 1770. Sometime near 1800, the brothers Hugh, Samuel, and James Jr. removed to Kentucky. Hugh had been an officer in the Revolutionary war and probably received land in Kentucky for his pay. These three have been well-documented and I will not include them in full in this undertaking. The two older ones, John and Archibald, I have tried hard to trace along with their descendants According to old Bible records by one of John's great-grandsons J.W. Bishop, records by their great-grandson James Madison "Matt" McElroy, and also records by Elizabeth Smith, widow of Archibald, son of John McElroy (she lived until December 20, 1863). Both of these men knew her well and received a lot of family history from her [Note that the first generation is not fully documented.]

# John McElroy (sometimes spelled *McLroy*)

**John McElroy**[28] b. 1728 in County Down, Ireland d. 1802 in North Carolina
Married Martha Moore
1. John McElroy Jr.[29] * moved to Caldwell County, Kentucky about 1800
1st Married Elizabeth Thompson?
   (All children by Elizabeth)
2nd Married Sarah Dunklin (widow) in 1809

---

28  Note that John McElroy's first two children were born in North Carolina. The younger ones were born in Greenville district, South Carolina.

29  John McElroy Jr.'s father and mother are not proven, but most of his descendants think he was the son of John and Martha. I am using this, but accept it with caution, because I do not have proof. John Jr. was born in Prince Edward County, Virginia about 1754. He married Elizabeth before 1772 in the Waxhaws of North Carolina and moved to the Greenville District of South Carolina before 1790. He lived near the Reedy River for at least sixteen years, then moved near Princeton, Kentucky, which was then Christian County but soon became Caldwell County. His first wife, Elizabeth, died about the time they moved to Kentucky. He then married Sarah Sullivan Dunklin. They had been neighbors back in South Carolina. Sarah's first husband was a wealthy man, so before they married, Sarah and Jr. entered into a pre-nuptial agreement. I have a copy that states that John gave one slave to Dunklin's estate plus other thingsand agreed to take care of and educate her Dunklin children. I guess that he did a good job on this, for his step-son Daniel Dunklin became the fifth governor of Missouri. All of John's children are not known, but the stated are close.

*  Many McIlroys came from this Caldwell County group. Some went to Franklin County, Arkansas; Weakley County, Tennessee; Robertson County, Texas; Erath County, Texas; Kerr County, Texas; Red River County, Texas; Grand County, Arkansas; and Nolan County, Texas. I have several records from the above, but not good enough to publish. I worked hard on these Caldwell County McIlroys, because my great-great grandfather lived next door to John, the head of this family, and married in a double wedding with Isaiah and his wife. About thirty years ago, I was looking at records in Princeton, the county seat of Caldwell County, Kentucky, and while there, I visited a woman named McIlroy who was listed in the phone book. When she came to the door, she said, "Come in. We are kin." I replied, "Probably, but not close." She said, "You look just like my brother Billy." We went downtown to see Billy at his shoe store and he looked exactly like my father. Coincidental? Probably. J.R.M.

1. John McElroy III b. 12-28-1771 in North Carolina d. 2-1-1853 in Weakley County, Tennessee
Married _____
  1. William McElroy
  2. Isham McElroy
  3. Aquilla McElroy b. before 1810
  Married _____
    1. Harriet McElroy b. 1843
    2. Thomas McElroy b. 1846 d. 1849
    3. Christopher McElroy b. 1848
    4. Pinkney A. McElroy b. 7-1850
  4. John McElroy
  1st Married _____
    1. Sarah Elizabeth McElroy
    Married George Dodge on 10-26-1853
  2nd Married Hetta Pennington on 5-19-1840
    2. Absolum McElroy b. 1842
    3. John N. McElroy b. 1846
    4. Rachel McElroy b. 1848
    5. Douglas McElroy b. 1852
  3rd Married Emaline Gaskin on 10-22-1854
    6. Jasper S. McElroy b. 12-5-1857 d. 10-6-1918 in Nolan County, Texas
    7. Thomas McElroy b. 1859
    8. Hetty McElroy b. 1862
  5. James McElroy b. 12-22-1811 d. 5-13-1892
  Married Nancy Goldsby
    1. Henry D. McElroy b. 12-16-1841 d. 3-31-1906
    Married Nancy McDonald
    2. John W. McElroy b. 7-1-1844 d. 2-4-1848
    3. Stephen Goldsby McElroy b. 1846 d. 8-10-1938 in Kerr County, Texas (served as a Texas Ranger and a rancher after the Civil War)
    Married Parthena Forbes
      1. Girl
      Married _____ Overall
      2. Ernest
      3. George
      4. Sid
      (probably more children)
      (more information available on Steven Golsby and James Lafayette families)

4. Sarah McElroy b. 5-13-1850 d. 8-13-1851
5. Mary Ann McElroy b. 1852
6. James Lafayette McElroy b. 1856 d. 1929 in Kerr County, Texas
Married _____ Kate Nowlin (also served as a Texas Ranger and was
in the mercantile business in Kerr County)
7. Margaret C. McElroy b. 1858
6. Nancy McElroy
7. Elizabeth McElroy
Married William Layton on 10-22-1827
2. James McElroy b. 3-30-1776 in North Carolina d. 6-10-1856 in
Greenville County, South Carolina
Married Elizabeth Ford
   1. Rachel McElroy
   2. Daniel F. McElroy
   3. John McElroy
   4. Harriet McElroy
   5. Permela McElroy
   6. Wilson B. McElroy
   7. Matilda McElroy b. 12-21-1828
Married J.H. Hopkins
   8. William Walker McElroy b. 12-21-1831
   9. Mary Isabella McElroy b. 1833 d. 9-5-1888
3. William McElroy b. 7-30-1782 d. 11-24-1857
Married Catherine Hiett (b. 9-16-1782 d. 5-9-1862) on 4-20-1803
   1. Jonathan McElroy b. 1-11-1804 d. 4-18-1876
Married Polly Cooper on 10-20-1825
      1. Catherine McElroy b. 1827
      2. James S. McElroy
Married Nancy Stark
         1. Lee Dennis McElroy b. 8-7-1872
Married Anne Dean
            1. Jean McElroy
            2. Katie McElroy
Married E.A. Block
         3. Alexander Y. McElroy
         4. John C. McElroy
         5. George H. McElroy b. 1838 d. 1914
         (Never married)
   2. Nancy McElroy b. 9-20-1805 in North Carolina d. 7-22-1844
Married James G. Glenn (b. 10-18-1799 d. 12-7-1857)

(9 children)
1. F.M. Glenn b. 9-14-1833
Married Susan Furley
  1. Laura Glenn
  2. Flora Glenn
  3. Albert Glenn
  4. Bedford Glenn
  5. Melville Glenn
3. Henry McElroy b. 10-28-1807 d. 3-5-1895
1st Married _____ Bennett
2nd Married M. Glenn
  1. James H. McElroy b. 8-9-1835 d. 6-28-1839
  2. Francis McElroy b. 5-15-1837 d. 9-8-1919
    1. William H. McElroy b. 1867
    2. Elizabeth McElroy b. 1868
    3. Sarah McElroy b. 1872
    4. Henry McElroy b. 1873
    5. Sussie McElroy b. 1876
    6. Mary McElroy b. 1878
  3. William H. McElroy b. 1842
  4. Samuel C. McElroy b. 7-18-1845 d. 2-23-1917
  5. Sarah McElroy b. 1849
Married William Martin on 12-24-1872
4. Harriet McElroy b. 11-28-1807 d. 1-28-1808
5. Elizabeth "Betty" McElroy b. 7-31-1811 d. 7-19-1832
Married William Layton on 11-1-1828
6. Abram T. McElroy b. 8-18-1812 d. 9-5-1832
7. William B. McElroy b. 10-18-1826 d. 10-10-1904
Married Dicey Young (d. 2-14-1877)
  1. Nancy E. McElroy b. 10-30-1849
  2. John R. McElroy b. 10-17-1851
  3. Buena Vista McElroy b. 8-12-1854
Married James B. Cash on 9-1-1970
  4. James William McElroy b. 12-16-1856
  5. Thomas J. McElroy b. 8-20-1859
  6. Mary B. McElroy b. 1862
  7. Ida L. McElroy b. 1864
  8. Charles E. McElroy b. 1866
  9. Edward H. McElroy b. 9-6-1872

4. Aquilla McElroy b. 7-30-1782 in North Carolina
Married Rodah Jones on 11-21-1808
  1. John McElroy b. 8-14-1814 d. 1860 in Saline County, Arkansas
  2. Sally McElroy b. 11-15-1816
  3. Elizabeth McElroy
  Married J. Jennings
  4. Chapley Wilburn McElroy b. 1819 in Kentucky d. 1-6-1875 in Arkansas
  5. Louisa G. McElroy
  6. Melinda McElroy
  7. Milley C. McElroy
  8. James Irvin McElroy
  9. Harriet McElroy
  10. William Joseph b. 12-20-1839
  11. Martha A. McElroy
  Married Jesse R. Clements on 2-2-1859
  12. Daughter (born dead)
5. Isaac Benjamin McElroy b. 1784 d. 1846
1st Married Polly Sullivant (d. at childbirth) on 2-15-1808
2nd Married Elizabeth Bennett (d. 1840) on 2-4-1810
  1. Stephen B. McElroy[30] b. 1814 d. 1862 in Illinois
  Married Elizabeth Hughey on 3-26-1839
    1. Emily Elizabeth McElroy
    2. Gillis Susan McElroy
    Married John Crow on 10-9-1865
  2. Mary McElroy
  3. John F. McElroy b. 1820
  4. Elizabeth B. McElroy b. 7-14-1824
  Married L. McElroy Duvall
  5. Lucy McElroy b. 1830
  Married Joshua Ford
  6. Emily McElroy b. 1832
  7. Aquilla McElroy b. 1836 d. 1860
3rd Married Celia Crouch on 12-9-1840
  8. Sarah McElroy b. 1842
  Married John L. O'Brien

---

30  Stephen B. McElroy was born in Crittenden County, Kentucky. As a young man, he devoted himself to agricultural pursuits, then moved to Johnson County Illinois in 1854 and lived there until his death in 1862.

6. David McElroy b. 1775 in Greenville County, South Carolina
7. Mary McElroy b. 1789 in Greenville County, South Carolina
Married William Tisdale
2. Samuel McElroy b. 1745 d. in Kentucky
3. George McElroy
4. Hugh McElroy (not traced)
5. David McElroy(not traced)
6. James McElroy(not traced)
7. William McElroy d. 1820
Married _____ Davis
   1. John McElroy
   2. Martha McElroy
   3. Hannah McElroy
   Married James Belt
   4. Rachel McElroy
   5. Nancy McElroy
   6. Elizabeth McElroy
8. Cowan McElroy
9. Wilkerson McElroy
10. Betsy McElroy
Married George Calhoun
11. Ann Elizabeth McElroy [31]
Married George McWhorter
12. Archibald McElroy b. 1-25-1772 in Waxhaw, North Carolina d. 4-6-1826
Married Elizabeth Smith (b. 5-26-1779 d. 1863)
   1. John McElroy b. 11-4-1798 d. 1883
   Married Linda Blakinship
      1. Arthur J.B. McElroy b. 1820
      Married Elizabeth Orr
         1. Rhoda McElroy b. 1848

---

31   Ann Elizabeth McElroy was married to George McWhorter and lived in the Waxhaws, almost on the line between North and South Carolina. She gave a disposition years later that she knew where Andrew Jackson was born. There had been an argument and each state tried to claim him. She said she knew where he was born across the road from where she lived. They went across the road to Camey's (the family's store) one morning and went to see the baby, and it was Andrew Jackson, who became President of the United States years later. The Jacksons actually lived a few miles from the Waxhaw settlement, but Andrew Jackson's mom was ill and baby Andrew Jackson was born at Camey's, not at the family home.

2. Martha McElroy b. 1854
3. Lavina McElroy b. 1855
4. Samuel McElroy b. 1857
5. David McElroy b. 1859
2. Sarah McElroy b. 1822 d, 10-25-1885
Married John McNeely
3. William McElroy b. 1824
Married Laurence Orr
4. Lavina McElroy b. 1828
Married Elijah Turner in 8-1877
5. Wilkinson S. McElroy b. 2-13-1831 d. 8-22-1867
6. George C. McElroy d. 12-1860
7. Lydia McElroy b. about 1834 (no records)
2. George W. McElroy b. 4-1800 d. 7-4-1833
Married Polly Noe
  1. Nimrod McElroy b. 10-26-1825 d. 4-19-1903
Married Elizabeth Newby on 6-16-1845
    1. Sarah E. McElroy b. 7-8-1846 d. 4-1-1866
    2. George Washington McElroy b. 1848 d. 4-1-1866
    3. Penina Jane McElroy[32] b. 9-12-1849 d. 8-14-1927
Married James Van Tuyl in 1868
      1. Cora Jane Van Tuyl b. 12-16-1870
Married _____ Coffman
      2. James F. Van Tuyl b. 3-18-1873 d. 1950
        1. Nina Hobbs Van Tuyl
        2. Laurie Florence Van Tuyl
      3. William E. Van Tuyl b. 2-10-1875 d. 9-7-1936
      4. Ora L. Van Tuyl b. 7-24-1878 d. 6-12-1932
      5. Myra Van Tuyl b. 9-13-1881 d. 9-12-1942
Married _____ Doty
        1. Olive Doty
Married _____ Miller
        2. Edwin Doty
        3. Ruby Doty
Married _____ Uvilla

---

32  At the age of ten years, Penina Jane came west with her parents, who settled in Burlington, Kansas until the spring of 1861 when they moved to the vicinity of Hillsboro, Illinois. This is the location where she married James Van Tuyl, but they soon moved back to Kansas and settled on a farm near Newton. Later that year, they moved to a farm near Potwin. She lived the rest of her life out there.

4. Leo Doty d. 1974
   1. Gean Kuranko
   2. Harry Doty
5. Wilbur Doty
6. Albert G. Doty
7. Clarence Doty d. 1876
   1. Ruth Doty
   Married _____ Blankley
   2. Diane Doty
   Married _____ Findlay
   3. Leslie Doty
   4. Doris Doty
8. Raymond Doty
9. Roy Doty
10. Chester Doty
11. Ralph Doty

6. Maggie Van Tuyl b. 5-11-1884 d. 1958
Married _____ Dunn
   1. Roberta Dunn
   Married _____ Corfman
7. Walter Guy Van Tuyl b. 3-5-1887
8. Ralph Van Tuyl b. 10-23-1888 d. 1973
9. Elvira Van Tuyl b. 4-15-1891

4. Samuel W. McElroy b. 10-31-1851 d. 11-4-1901
   1. Frank McElroy d. 1937
   2. Caroll McElroy d. 1948
   3. Harold McElroy d. 1960
      1. Harold McElroy d. 1960
   4. Athol McElroy d. 1962
   5. Mildred McElroy d. 1974
   Married _____ Bishop
      1. Rose Bishop
      Married _____ Bowen
      2. Burnett L. Bishop
      3. Frank C. Bishop
      4. Clifford Bishop

5. Mary Ann McElroy b. 1-17-1854 d. 4-17-1954
Married _____ Boyd
   1. Ollie Boyd d. 1895

2. Stella Boyd d. 1906
3. Frank Boyd d. 1978
6. Emily McElroy b. 10-2-1855 d. 12-18-1884
Married _____ Wells
   1. Malinda Wells
   Married _____ Tasker
      1. Olive Tasker d. 1873
      Married _____ Weaver
         1. Marie Weaver
         Married _____ Hardy
         2. Vivian Rose Weaver
         Married _____ Denton
         3. Dorothy Mae Weaver
         Married _____ Stephens
         4. Jimmie Weaver
         Married _____ Barbosa
7. Charles R. McElroy b. 7-14-1857
   (no children)
8. Irving McElroy b. 7-3-1859 D.Y.
9. Adam Pascal McElroy[33] b. 7-1-1860 d. 12-22-1951
Married Emma Alice Lowe on 11-4-1883
   1. Archibald Lowe McElroy b. 7-31-1884 d. 2-1-1941
   Married Jettie Plaxco on 9-16-1908
      1. Raymond Plaxco McElroy[34] b. 8-2-1909
      Married Junait A. McFarland (b. 6-6-1918) on 12-25-1935
         1. Raymond McElroy Jr. b. 8-26-1936 d. 9-27-1958
         2. Jettie Ann McElroy b. 9-1-1938
         Married William E. Barstow (b. 10-6-1936)
         on 4-2-1959
            1. Linda Ann Barstow b. 2-1-1961
            2. Susan J. Barstow b. 2-14-1965
         3. Phillip M. McElroy b. 10-7-1940 d. 1941

---

33   Dr. Adam Paschal McElroy was a native of Missouri and came to Fort Worth, Texas in 1895. He was a science teacher at Paschal High School, studied medicine at the old Fort Worth university and was licensed to practice in 1901. In 1909, he established a drug store in Fort Worth on Race Street, which was the first drug store on that side of the river.

34   Raymond Plaxco McElroy graduated from Texas A&M in the 1930s and was a friend of mine. He was captain of the M Company 393 Regiment 99th Division in World War II. This also was my regiment in World War II. He helped gather a lot of the information on this Lee County, Virginia group. (J.R.M.).

4. Juanita K. McElroy b. 7-21-1943
Married Oliver C. Crain on 6-17-1960
    1. Raymond L. Crain b. 2-25-1962
5. James Pascal McElroy b. 12-6-1943
Married Peggy Lyde (d. 1974) in 1967
    1. Michael J. McElroy b. 12-12-1869
    2. Patrick K. McElroy b. 2-21-1971
2. Walter McElroy d. 1979
3. Mildred McElroy b. 4-2-1917
Married E.G. Clapp in 1937
(no children)
4. Marie McElroy b. 10-13-1918
1st Married W.B. Messick
2nd Married H.T. Sourman
    1. H.T. Sourman Jr. b. 1946
    2. T.C. Sourman b. 7-13-1949
    3. Cunta Sourman b. 5-14-1952
    4. Pamela Sourman b. 2-16-1954
5. A.L. McElroy b. 8-2-1923
(Never married)
10. Amanda McElroy d. 1875
(no children)
11. Margaret McElroy d. 1864
(no children)
12. Walter Scott McElroy
13. William McElroy d. 1968
(no children)
14. Archibald McElroy d. 1874
(no children)
15. Oliver McElroy d. 1874
(no children)
16. Naomi McElroy
Married _____ Goodfellow
    1. Charles Card Goodfellow d. 1959
    2. Eva Goodfellow
2. Betsy McElroy b. 1827
3. Archibald McElroy

4. John McElroy [35] b. 4-11-1829 d. 3-10-1929
Married Nancy Gilstrap (d. 4-15-1915) on 1-19-1851
(7 children)
   1. J.P. McElroy
   2. Polly A. McElroy
   Married Van Valkenburg
   3. George E. McElroy
5. Emily McElroy
3. Martha McElroy b. 4-13-1802 d. 10-8-1803
4. Sarah McElroy (twin) b. 12-1-1803
Married William Davis
5. Amelia McElroy(twin) b. 12-1-1803 d. in Black Water, Virginia
Married Joseph M. Hackney
6. Cowan McElroy b. 11-6-1805
Married Elizabeth Anderson on 9-10-1833
   1. T.A.L. McElroy
   2. Hester McElroy b. 1839
   3. Elizabeth McElroy b. 1842
   4. John C. McElroy b. 1843
   5. Sarah McElroy
   6. Charles W. McElroy b. 1844 d. 1907
   Married Rosa Bell Poteet
      1. Loren McElroy b. 4-10-1902 d. 11-19-1927
      2. Houston McElroy b. 5-29-1903
      Married Estella King on 8-19-1929
         1. Houston McElroy Jr. b. 4-16-1930 d. 4-25-1932
         2. Harold L. McElroy b. 6-12-1931
         1st Married Pearl Myler
            1. Connie McElroy
         2nd Married Peggy Flannery
         3rd Married Edye North
         3. James R. McElroy b. 10-8-1933
         Married Lois Kleineick
            1. Patrick McElroy b. 9-4-1955
         4. Betty Ann McElroy b. 9-6-1936
         Married Earl Keisling

---

35   John McElroy was a soldier in the Confederate Army. He was a well-known and valuable citizen in Atchison County, Kansas. He lived for 99 years, eleven months, and two days, and if he had not met with an accident three or four years previous to that, he might have reached a much greater age.

1. Teresa
3. Lillie McElroy b. 12-25-1904
1st Married Jim Hall
2nd Married May Salley
3rd Married Robert Knowles
(No children)
4. Herbert McElroy b. 4-7-1907 d. 1977
Married Hazel Hammonds
(5 children)
5. Ollie McElroy(twin) b. 11-7-1909
Married Emmett Riley
1. Bob Riley
6. Emma McElroy(twin) b. 11-7-1909
Married Rufus Dougherty
1. R.L. Dougherty
2. Wilma Dougherty
7. W. Wilkerson McElroy b. 1844
8. Mary McElroy
9. George C. McElroy b. 1849
Married Alice Roop (b. 1865 d. 1880)
1. William McElroy
2. Emmet McElroy
Married Ethel Miles
1. Katherine McElroy
Married Carlton Apperson
3. Orphia McElroy
Married Bradley Orr
4. Fieldon McElroy
Married _____ Williamson
5. Katherine McElroy
Married Hash Walter
1. Fulton T. McElroy b. 12-2-1921
Married Arietta Wyand on 9-2-1944
10. Lydia McElroy b. 1851
11. Francis M. McElroy b. 1854
7. Archibald McElroy Jr. b. 11-16-1803
Married Hester Anderson

1. James Madison "Matt" McElroy[36] b. 1-30-1839 d. 6-6-1920 in Greenville, TX
Married Joanna F. Barron (b. 1-20-1852 d. 4-3-1940)
  1. Ida Mays McElroy b. 2-14-1872 d. 8-15-1905
  Married Jeff Marion
  (not traced)
  2. William George McElroy b. 8-3-1873 d. 8-3-1873
  3. Lily Rose McElroy b. 8-29-1874 in Lee County, Virginia d. 11-2-1962 in Dallas, Texas
  Married Jess Pugh on 10-3-1897
    1. Fauler Gertrude Pugh b. 1-11-1899 d. 7-4-1970
    Married Glenn Prebble
    2. Nola Belle Pugh b. 3-20-1903
    Married Robert English

---

36    James Madison "Matt," McElroy, son of Archibald, was born January 30, 1839 in Lee County, Virginia. He grew up in this county. He went to the University at Nashville, Tennessee to study for the ministry. He was interrupted in his studies by the outbreak of the Civil War. He and another student went to Abingdon, Virginia and on May 27, 1861 enlisted in Captain Daniel S. Dickinson's Company (Lee Grays), Cavalry Battalion, 50th Regiment, Virginia Infantry, Confederate States Army as First Sergeant. This Company was subsequently engaged in battle with the Union Army at Shiloh. When the battle was over, the General said "Orderly, call the roll." J.M. McElroy was the orderly. Roll call showed all but 25 men had been killed, including Captain Dickinson. The others had been wounded. On September 26, 1861 the entire Company was mustered out of service. He reenlisted in Company A, same Regiment on April 1, 1862, and was discharged July 29, 1863 by reason of having been elected as a delegate to the House of Delegates of Virginia. He served one term and refused to stand for reelection. He said, "An honest man cannot stay in politics." He later moved to Texas and settled near the Barron Cemetery in Grayson County. He moved to Hunt County, near Greenville, Texas where he reared his family. His honesty, steadfastness and willingness to help the underdog soon made him a pillar in the Salem Community where he lived. Each election year men in the community would come to the house and sit n the porch to discuss the election and try to find out how "Uncle Mat" was going to vote … he would not commit himself. He wanted the men to make up their own minds. He would analyze the merits and short comings of the candidates and leave the choice to the visitor. Every new preacher assigned to the Salem Church would pay "Uncle Mat" a visit and sit for hours discussing the Bible. He had a keen insight and was a good analyst of most subjects. He said to me one day as we stood on the porch watching a model of the Wright Brother's airplane trying to fly over the city of Greenville, "Chap, one day those things will be flying to Europe." I said, "Dad, they can't … that thing couldn't get off the ground yesterday." I had been to the County Fair and watched them try to fly the plan and they couldn't make it. J.M. McElroy was a calm, serene person. Seemingly, tragedies never touched him, but the expression of his eyes told how deeply he was affected. He died sitting in his rocking chair on the porch where he spent his summers.
*Above written by Vera Belle Neal, his daughter*

3. Jessie Otho Pugh b. 6-30-1906
Married Leslie D. Gray
4. James Madison Pugh b. 6-27-1911 d. 1970
4. Margaret McElroy b. 1-8-1877 d. 1-26-1968 in Lubbock, Texas
Married Ephraim H. Pugh on 1-2-1898 in Hunt County, Texas
   1. Effie E. Pugh b. 1-20-1898
   1st Married James Mercer
   2nd Married Clarence Moore
   2. Frances E. Pugh b. 1-15-1911
   Married Dr. W.A. Maddox on 9-26-1944
   3. Inez M. Pugh b. 10-11-1914
   1st Married Emory Turner
   2nd Married Winston Trostle
5. Penola F. McElroy b. 7-21-1878 d. 7-21-1878
6. Hester L. McElroy b. 6-9-1880 in Grayson Country, Texas d. 9-26-1971 in Greenville, Texas
Married John Dennis on 3-15-1936
7. Cecil I. McElroy b. 3-23-1882 in Grayson County, Texas
1st Married John Hancock in 1902
   1. Vashti L. Hancock b. 8-13-1905 in Hunt County, Texas
   Married John Waddell
2nd Married Robert Smith in 1911
8. Archibald McElroy b. 6-26-1884 in Grayson County Texas d. 1-28-1928 in Parsons, Kansas
Married Maude Pickle on 6-4-1905
   1. Bessie Maude McElroy b. 11-10-1905 d. 11-11-1967
   Married David A. Cushman on 8-4-1928
   2. Anna Lorene McElroy b. 4-24-1907
   Married Arthur Souter on 2-16-1925
      1. Dorothy May Souter
      1st Married _____ Bradley
      2nd Married _____ Wirth
         1. Leanna
         Married _____ Phillips
      2. Anna Souter
   3. Claudia Lucille McElroy b. 11-28-1908 d. 8-6-1972
   1st Married Henry O. Souter on 8-23-____
   2nd Married _____ Cline
   4. James Weldon McElroy b. 6-16-1911 d. 3-13-1967

Married Anna Journot in 1923
(no children)
5. Eleanor Lee McElroy b. 3-23-1913
Married Lewis Morarity in 1924
(no children)
9. Fay McElroy b. 7-30-1886 in Collinsville, Texas d. 11-26-1963 in Yuna, Arizona
1st Married Granville Phipps
1. James Barron Phipps b. 6-23-1906 d. 9-12-1970
Married Margaret Belle Blackburn on 6-5-1937
2. Martha Viola Phipps b. 10-15-1907
Married Charlie Elmer Doran on 9-2-1925
3. R.M. Phipps b. 6-30-1910 d. 1-3-1911
4. Richard Franklin Phipps b. 6-30-1910 d. 1-3-1911
Married Florence Pearl Launder
5. Alice Pauline Phipps b. 1-4-1918 D.Y.
2nd Married _____ Edwards
10. Richard C. McElroy b. 12-9-1888 in Grayson County, Texas
Married Verna Brunson in 1920
1. Chester Leon McElroy b. 8-8-1923 d. 5-22-1970
Married Jennie Lekson on 8-23-1947
1. Richard Charles McElroy b. 9-12-1949 d. 12-19-1970
Married Mary Gerbasha
2. Janice McElroy b. 2-26-1956
2. Carl Richard McElroy b. 2-26-1956
11. Vera Belle McElroy b. 9-23-1891 in Grayson County, Texas
Married James Roy Neal
1. James F. Neal b. 12-19-1920 in Sonora, Texas
Married Shirley L. Barclay on 12-20-1946
1. Dennis Edwin Neal b. 10-23-1947
Married Cynthia Whitaker (b. 3-7-1950) on 5-22-1971
2. James Ray Neal b. 2-25-1949
Married Susan Palmer in 6-1969
3. Patrick Allen Neal b. 7-22-1950
4. Sharon Kay Neal b. 6-17-1952
Married Arthur Magnum in 3-1970
5. Kathleen Sue Neal b. 10-14-1953.
6. Terrie Colleen Neal b. 6-24-1956
7. Brian Dean Neal (twin) b. 12-7-1957
8. Darrel Gene Neal (twin) b. 12-7-1957 d. 12-8-1957

9. Robert Bruce Neal b. 8-13-1959

2. William S. Neal b. 8-7-1922 in Ft. Stockton, Texas

1st Married Adella Lozona

    1. Billy Marie Neal b. 8-8-1945)

2nd Married Merna Ephrata (Peelman)

    1. James W. Neal b. 2-17-1957

3. Maurice R. Neal b. 7-15-1924 in Ozona, Texas

Married Nettie Lee Richards (b. 6-20-1920) on 3-2-1948

    1. Bruce E. Neal b. 12-2-1948

    2. Patrick E. Neal b. 4-7-1854

    3. Vera A. Neal b. 9-17-1957

4. Jackie V. Neal b. 9-14-1926 in Ozona, Texas

Married Ida Renn (b. 10-2-1927) on 9-13-1952

    1. John Barron Neal b. 1-2-1954

    2. Amy Jo Neal b. 10-25-1954

12. Nola B. McElroy b. 3-27-1894 in Grayson County, Texas

Married A.G. Curnutt

(no children)

2. Margaret Evaline McElroy b. 1843 d. 3-19-1891

Married John G. Barron (d. 10-5-1887) on 9-13-1866 in Lee County, Virginia

1. Rose Barron b. 1867 in Lee County, Virginia d. 7-15-1905 in Cook County, Texas

Married James N. Roach

    1. Mary Roach b. 6-4-1894

    1. Mary A. Roach

    Married Claud Betts

    (3 children)

    2. Homer Roach

    (Never married)

    3. Robert Roach

    Married Stella Bailey

    (2 children)

    4. Celia R. Roach

    Married Mack Carr

    (6 children)

2. Marie "Nettie" Barron b. 1-15-1868 in Big Stone Gap, Virginia d. 2-1955 in Lubbock, Texas

Married Albert G. Harrison

1. Mary Rose Harrison b. 1897 d. 8-16-1937
2. John B. Harrison b. 1898
3. Ruth Harrison b. 1900 d. 8-29-1964
Married C.V. Grass
4. Henry H. Harrison b. 5-5-1901
Married Henrietta Winslow
5. Sam W. Harrison b. 1904
6. Sue K. Harrison b. 12-19-1907
Married Max D. Menzies
   (3 children)
3. Wade Barron b. 1870 d. 1891 in Cook County, Texas
4. Robert Lee Barron b. 5-28-1872 in Collinsville, Texas d. 6-20-1934 in
Van Alstyne, Texas
Married Rebecca Reasor in 1893
   1. Rosa Barron b. 1894 d. 4-13-1970
   2. E. Barron b. 1895 d. 6-12-1951
   Married Claud A. Wall
   3. James J. Barron b. 1897 d. 1947
   Married Dora Presley
   4. Joseph W. Barron b. 1901
   Married Mary E. Small
   5. John D. Barron b. 9-13-1903
   Married Minnie E. Crews
   6. Robert Duke Barron b. 1909 d. 1968
   Married Flora E. Meeker
   7. Lillie Belle Barron b. 1911
   Married George Duke
      (no children)
   8. Paulene Barron b. 1913
   Married Lonnie S. McCord
      (no children)
   9. Ora L. Barron b. 1915
   Married George Dodson
      (no children)
   10. Jeanette Barron b. 1917
   Married Frank Fyke
   11. Archibald Barron b. 1918
   Married Fannie Howell
5. Nora Belle Barron b. 8-25-1874 in Tioga, Texas d. 4-15-1953 in Dallas,
Texas

Married Bevis Davis on 9-2-1894
1. Lillie C. Davis b. 9-26-1895
Married Cecil Bell (d. 8-1915)
  1. Geneva Bell b. 1916
  Married C.T. Teague
    1. Linda Teague b. 11-10-1937
    2. Patrick Teague b. 3-3-1946
  2. Gladys Bell b. 10-17-1911 in Tioga, Texas
  Married James Bledsoe
  (no children)
  3. Charyn Bell b. 2-15-1924
  Married Walter Schidt
  4. Cecelia Bell b. 1-6-1926
  Married John L. Jenkins
  5. Cecil C. Bell Jr. b., 5-28-1927
  Married Margaret Lair
  6. Child b. 1932 (born dead)
  7. James E. Bell b. 3-26-1933
  Married Mary L. Manning
  8. Jerry D. Bell b. 8-7-1937 d. 12-24-1937
2. Grady H. Davis b. 8-24-1897 d. 7-29-1971
1st Married Audrey Worsham
2nd married Rhetta _____
3. Iola Mae Davis b. 10-1899 d. 7-1965
Married Thomas M. Sunner
  1. Glenn Sunner
4. Fulton Davis b. 11-29-1901 d. 12-19-1902
5. Lonnie Lee Davis b. 12-9-1903 d. 4-27-1904
6. Winnifield Davis b. 7-12-1905
7. Bishop Davis b. 1-10-1908
Married Vera Jane Jenkins on 12-24-1930
8. William J. Davis b. 2-5-1910
Married Vera L. Myers
9. Lola Cerene Davis b. 5-15-1915
Married Arnold J. Nicholson
6. Maggie May Barron b. 11-29-1876 d. 12-24-1966 in Oklahoma
Married Benjamin Duke Smith
7. Lou Emma Barron b. 1877 d. 1898
(Never married)

8. Archibald McElroy Barron b. 1880 d. 1935
Married Ann Mitchell
9. Dollie Barron b. 11-7-1882 in Collinsville, Texas d. 1-25-1928 in Clovis,
New Mexico
Married Insley Leroy Strange on 4-19-1901
3. Elizabeth "Lizzy" McElroy b. 3-27-1845 d. 6-15-1934
Married George Bishop on 6-26-1871
4. La Vina McElroy b. 1855
Married Dall Kinser
5. George Cowan McElroy b. 12-13-1857
Married Mary Elizabeth Lawson on 12-14-1882
   1. Ralleigh McElroy b. 12-28-1883 d. 4-21-1946
   2. Rose Ellen McElroy b. 7-12-1885
   Married Harvey Lambert on 2-19-1910
   3. Margaret Emmer McElroy b. 9-8-1887
   Married Ova Heflin on 5-8-1912
      1. Cowen Allen Heflin b. 4-6-1913
      Married Darlene Hunt
         1. Cheryl Heflin b. 9-28-1945
         2. Dott Claudell Heflin b. 10-2-1915
         Married Verle Wilburn Spoonemore
            1. Arlish Martin Spoonemore b. 3-4-1941
            2. Joyce Oatel Spoonemore b. 3-4-1943
            3. Joanna Margaret Spoonemore b. 3-2-1945
            4. Marlin Edgar Spoonemore b. 11-13-1947
         3. Mary Ellen Heflin b. 2-4-1918
         Married Floyd Dallas Barton on 10-22-1938
            1. Floyd Allen Barton b. 8-25-1939
         4. Newton David Heflin b. 12-1-1920
   4. Dollie McElroy b. 2-18-1889 D.Y.
   5. Willie Oscar McElroy b. 4-1-1890 d. 1-6-1945
(Never married)
   6. Archibald McElroy b. 9-21-1892
Married Martha A. Cox in 1926
      1. Etta Beth McElroy b. 12-17-1926
      Married Robert Allen Carlson
      2. Billie Cowan McElroy b. 7-11-1928
         1. William Marshall McElroy
         2. Matthew Wayne McElroy
         3. Russell Lewis McElroy

3. Roy Burton McElroy b. 11-4-1929
4. Rita Dorene McElroy
5. Bobby Gene McElroy b. 7-29-1931
Married Frances Figeuroa
   1. Barbara Jean McElroy
   2. Michael McElroy
   3. Timothy McElroy
   4. Patrick McElroy
7. Lucy McElroy b. 8-13-1894 d. 11-12-1948
8. Elizabeth S. McElroy b. 12-14-1809
Married David Noe Jr.
9. Samuel McElroy b. 2-12-1812 d. 3-1-1847
(Never married)
10. Jane McElroy (twin) (died at birth)
11. Violet McElroy b. 3-1-1815 d. 3-13-1848
Married Joseph C. Bishop
12. Wilkerson McElroy b. 6-10-1818
(Never married)
13. Lydia McElroy b. 8-8-1820
Married Alexander Bishop on 11-1836
   1. Francis Preston Bishop b. 8-27-1837 d. 9-25-1894
   Married Angie Rayle (Shepard) (widow) on 11-2-1871
      1. Oscar S. Bishop b. 9-22-1872 d. 1901
      Married Fannie Holston
      2. Charles F. Bishop b. 10-14-1875 d. 1957
      3. Elizabeth Bishop b. 12-13-1877 d. 1903
      Married Virgil Rymer
      4. Lucretia G. Bishop b. 8-19-1884
      5. William Alexander Bishop b. 4-16-1884
      Married Elizabeth Pangle
         1. Charles W. Bishop b. 9-10-1927
         Married Evelyn Tolvson in 1950
   2. James Madison Bishop b. 1839 d. 11-19-1913
1st Married Margaret E. Wood in 1859
      1. Carson Bishop
      2. Lesley Bishop
      3. Edward Bishop
      4. Alfred Bishop
      5. Lillie Bishop

2<sup>nd</sup> Married Mamie _____

3. not traced

4. not traced

5. not traced

6. William Wilson Bishop b. 6-14-1844 d. 9-22-1898

Married Sarah L. Karns

   (several children)

7. not traced

8. John McElroy Bishop b. 1848 d. 10-9-1933

1<sup>st</sup> Married Margaret M. Wood

2<sup>nd</sup> Married Nancy Sevier Jones in 1885

   1. Bertha I. Bishop b. 5-5-1875 d. 5-23-1965

   Married J.M. Tillery in 1896

      1. Mildred Tillery

      2. Eula Tillery

      3. Margaret Tillery

   2. Percy Poe Bishop—Maj. General U.S. Army b. 5-27-1877 d. 4-8-1967

   Married Grace Calvert

      1. Dorothy E. Bishop b. 1-21-1912

      Married Harold C. Donnelly Lt. General U.S. Air Force

         1. Margaret Donnelly

         2. Judith Donnelly

   3. Eva Bishop b. 1880 d. 1-3-1967

   Married Zed Conver

9. Child

10. Child

11. Mary Lavinie Bishop b. 3-20-1856 d. 1-14-1943

Married John F. Dickerson (b. 1840 d. 1910) on 1215-1881

   1. Ernest Dickerson b. 9-18-1882

   Married Mamie Davis

      1. Ernest Dickerson Jr. b. 9-20-1922

      2. Lynn Dickerson b. 3-10-1924

   2. Robert W. Dickerson b. 1-16-1864 d. 12-25-1899

   3. Annie Dickerson

   Married William Wells

      1. John D. Wells b. 3-8-1911

      Married Francis Bates

         1. Marinne Wells b. 9-13-1950

         2. Katherine Wells b. 8-20-1952

3. William H. Wells b. 5-1-1916
Married Barbara Cuffman in 1949
  1. William R. Wells b. 1959
  Married _____ on 9-24-1921
  2. John D. Wells lb. 1963
4. Ada Wells b. 1887
Married Robert D. Craig
5. Sarah "Sally" Wells b. 1890
6. George C. Dickerson Wells b. 1892 d. 7-9-1938
Married Francis P. Russ on 7-15-1920
12. S.D. Bishop b. 1-29-1859 d. 9-1909
1st Married Minnie Graves
  1. Lydia Bishop b. 6-2-1894 d. 6-2-1894
  2. Paul D. Bishop b. 6-2-1894
  Married Beatrice Hallmark in 1920
  3. Preston W. Bishop b. 9-12-1896
  1st Married Mary Lenox in 1921
  2nd Married Bessie Mae Ingle (b. 1880)
  4. Hernice W. Bishop b. 7-10-1902
  5. Bula B. Bishop b. 1904 d. 1904
  6. Lee Ray Clifton Bishop b. 1905
  Married Lorene Gardner
  7. Baby (born dead)
  8. Fredrick A. Bishop b. 11-25-1908
  Married Lucille Gore in 1933
13. Thomas C. Bishop b. 12-9-1862 d. 12-31-1891
Married Nannie Haggard
  1. Clifton C. Bishop b. 1-29-1896
  Married Dora Witherspoon in 1923
  2. Gladys Haggard Bishop b. 5-29-1901
  Married Fred Harrington
  3. Mary Elizabeth Bishop b. 5-3-1903
  Married Edgar Bush in 1923
14. Patsy McElroy b. 2-5-1823
Married Charles Chrisman

# Archibald McElroy (or *McLroy*), brother to previously mentioned John)

Archibald McElroy b. about 1730 d. 10-7-1780 (probably at Battle of King's Mountain—some report that he was killed a little later at the Battle of Cowpens)

1st Married Ann Aston (b. about 1835 d. 1783)

  1. Thomas S. McElroy b. 1755 (not traced)

  2. John McElroy b. 1757 d. 1781

    1. John W. McElroy (became a prominent citizen and general of the local militia during the Civil War)

    Married _____

      1. Daughter

      Married R.B. Vance (member of Congress for 16 years)

      2. John Smith McElroy (colonel during the Civil War and later became a prominent lawyer in Madison County, North Carolina)

      Married Mary Carter

      3. James McElroy

      4. Nicholas McElroy

      5. Robert McElroy

  3. James McElroy b. about 1759

  Married Vilot Davis Calhoun (daughter of Adam Calhoun)

    1. Adam Calhoun McElroy[37] b. 4-8-1779 d. 6-26-1846

    Married Jane Cunningham (b. 1788 d. 8-2-1846)

      1. Adam Calhoun McElroy Jr. b. 10-4-1812 d. 9-13-1889 in Rutherford County, Tennessee

      Married Margaret Youree (b. 3-25-1819 d. 2-29-1894)

        1. Samuel F. McElroy d. in Civil War

        2. James McElroy b. 1848

        3. Adam C. McElroy b. 1848 d. 7-24-1898

---

37   This should be used with caution as there are some doubts about which McElroy was the father of Adam Calhoun McElroy.

4. Silas Newton McElroy
Married Susan McKnight
  1. John McElroy
  Married M. Hilda Hair
  2. Samuel McElroy
  Married Birdie Barker
  3. Virginia McElroy
  Married Vance Barker
  4. Sallie McElroy
  Married Dave Hair
  5. H. McElroy
  Married Lois Shelton
5. Nancy Elizabeth McElroy
1st Married Eddie Carter
  1. Eddie Carter
  Married Charley Elrod
    1. Bruce
    Married Mable Dement
    2. Scott
    Married Christine Fann
    3. Hoyt
    Married Louise Brandon
    4. Edward
    Married Pauline Harris
2nd Married Dennis Creson
  1. Walter Creson
  Married Anna Boon
    1. Carolyn Creson
    2. Walter Creson
    3. David Creson
6. Mary Jane McElroy b. 1851 d. 1915
Married David Dement on 12-2-1875
  1. Mary Idella Dement
  Married Daniel Hill Sneed on 12-21-1898
    1. Guy Wilson Sneed
    Married Alice Hunt on 12-21-1925
      1. Charles Dawson Sneed
      Married Audry _____
        1. Kim Sneed

2. Robin Sneed
3. Kelly Sneed
4. Renee Sneed
2. Jodie Sneed
Married Wilford Helsley on 12-21-1934
  1. Patricia Diane Helsley
  Married David Anthony
    1. Donna Lynn Anthony
3. William David Sneed
Married Ruby Harrison
  1. William Ray Sneed
  Married Barbara _____
    1. Cheryl Sneed
4. Daniel Hill Sneed
Married Mae More
  1. Daniel Hill Sneed Jr.
5. Della Louise Sneed
(Never married)
6. Arthur Sharber Sneed
(Never married)
7. William A. McElroy
1st Married Rebecca Hogwood
2nd Married Mary McKnight
3rd Married Adrian McKnight
8. A.B. McElroy b. 1854 d. 1926
Married Emma Knoy
2. Matthew Lile McElroy b. 10-10-1814 (moved to Ellis County, Texas several years before the Civil War)
Married Jane Witherspoon (b. 12-25-1818 d. 1899)
  1. Mary H. McElroy b. 10-30-1836
  1st Married _____ Lange
  2nd Married John M. Andrews
  2. Martha Jane McElroy b. 10-10-1838
  1st Married Robert Chapman
  2nd Married Matthew A. Lang
  3. Joseph A. McElroy b. 11-27-1839 d. 12-11-1866
  Married Edna Laughlin in 1866
  4. William David McElroy b. 9-20-1841 d. 11-11-1927
  1st Married Harriett Culbertson in 1866
    (five children)

2nd Married Mollie Meredith (d. 4-25-1910) in 1880
   1. Georgiana McElroy b. 8-4-1867
   2. James O. McElroy b. 7-23-1870
   3. Violet McElroy b. 5-14-1872
   4. Sarah McElroy b. 12-17-1874
   5. William M. McElroy b. 3-27-1877
   6. Charles R. McElroy b. 9-10-1881
   7. Cora Ella McElroy b. 3-29-1883
   8. Jennice McElroy b. 9-15-1885
   9. Collette McElroy b. 1-13-1888
   10. Rodney McElroy b. 1-3-1890
   11. Leola McElroy b. 2-23-1898
   12. Allie McElroy b. 12-6-1901 d. 11-26-1905
5. James W. McElroy b. 11-28-1843 d. 1921
Married Henrietta Summers
6. George Calhoun McElroy b. 8-21-1845 d. 12-24-1925
1st Married Elizabeth Chapman
2nd Married Lula Sawyer
7. Matilda McElroy b. 1-21-1847
Married Thomas Moore in 1872
8. Thomas C. McElroy
Married Laura Slaton
9. Violet Ann. McElroy b. 3-15-1851 d. 9-11-1874
Married G. Vance in 1873
10. Matthew S. McElroy b. 11-23-1853 d. 9-20-1938
1st Married _____ Knight in 1875
2nd Married M. Dickerson in 1887
11. John Newton McElroy b. 3-21-1856 d. 12-28-1892
Married Leila Hood
   1. Ed McElroy b. 9-13-1893
   Married Myrle Anderson on 6-1-1916
      1. John Edwin McElroy
      2. Jeanne McElroy
      3. Ed McElroy Jr.
      4. Tom McElroy
      5. Pat McElroy
12. Fenis M. McElroy b. 11-19-1859 d.1867
(Never married)
13. Jefferson E. McElroy b. 7-26-1861

Married Lillie Gilliam in 1883
3. George McElroy
4. Newton McElroy
5. John C. McElroy
6. William E. McElroy
7. James McElroy
8. Elizabeth McElroy
9. Matilda McElroy
Married Eli Thompson on 8-16-1844
10. Violet McElroy
(Never married)
11. Margaret McElroy
Married Robert Hood on 7-23-1839
12. Martha McElroy
Married Thomas McDaniel on 8-16-1844
4. Ruth McElroy b. 1761
Married _____ Bowen
5. William Christopher McElroy b. 1763 d. 1831
Married Sarah Hopkins in 1785
   1. James McElroy b. 7-24-1789
   1$^{st}$ Married Mary Small
      1. John McElroy d. in Franklin County
      2. William McElroy[38] b. 7-24-1812
      1$^{st}$ Married Missouri V.
         1. Andrew Jackson McElroy b. 1834 d. 1863
         2. Milinda H. McElroy
         Married James H. Vavhoose
      2$^{nd}$ Married Elizabeth Russell d. 1864
      3$^{rd}$ Married Martha Brooks in 1865
         1. William R. McElroy
         2. James H. McElroy
         3. Charles W. McElroy

---

38   After moving to Madison County, Arkansas, William McElroy operated a merchandising business along with farming. After the Civil War, he started a bank in Fayetteville, Arkansas. The bank did well and became the leading bank of Fayetteville; also, for 100 years, it was a private bank until it was sold to Wal-Mart. His habits were always good he amused himself by going to the country dances, never belonged to any secret organization, cast his vote for the Democrats, was discreet in all things, and was precise in all business transactions and accurate even to a penny. He leaned too much on certainties not to be a success. His farm at Fayetteville is now occupied by the University of Arkansas.

    4. Anna May McElroy
    5. Kate McElroy
3. Robert McElroy b. 7-13-1815 d. 1878 in Franklin County, Arkansas
Married Phoebe Stokes (b. 1818)
    1. John R. McElroy b. 1837 d. 6-13-1887
    2. Sarah Elizabeth McElroy b. 1839 d. 2-17-1880
    Married William H. Russell on 11-11-1859
        1. Mary V. Russell
        2. Mary J. McLane Russell
        3. Maggie Russell
        4. Married Jesse H. Hobbs
        5. Willie Bell Russell
        6. Fannie Russell
        7. Ida Russell
        8. Dora Russell
    3. William Christopher McElroy b. 3-25-1842 d. 4-5-1893
    1st Married Mary Catherine Hamm
    2nd Married Rebecca Stokes
        1. Robert Lee McElroy b. 6-13-1862 d. 1935
        Married Linda McNally
            1. Gladys McElroy
            Married John Bolinger
            2. Bayard McElroy
            3. Paul McElroy
            4. Ferris McElroy
        2. Gertrude Leslie McElroy b. 1-21-1864
        Married Samuel Winkleman
        3. Walter Alexander McElroy b. 3-4-1866 d. 9-5-1920
        1st Married Sarah Elizabeth Carpenter
        2nd Married Nettie Marcum
        4. James Hayden McElroy b. 9-16-1867 d. 1-23-1977
        Married Martha Davis
            1. Florence Ellen McElroy b. 7-29-1895
            Married Nelson Hale
            2. Jessie Myrtle McElroy b. 11-20-1897
            3. William Christopher McElroy b. 6-1899 d. 7-9-1971
            Married Ida Faye Weaver
            4. George Hopkins McElroy b. 1-17-1902 d. 11-3-1983

Married Jewell Elsie Johnston
   1. James Rudolph McElroy b. 8-13-1929 d. 4-27-1956
   Married Bertha Odell Craig (b. 12-25-1929)
      1. James Craig McElroy b. 9-9-1953
      Married Bertha Lou Hiskey on 2-18-1977
   2. Martha Ann McElroy b. 9-10-1930 d. 11-4-1930
   3. George Hopkins Jr. McElroy b. 1-19-1932
   4. Dena Loye McElroy b. 12-2-1939
   5. Bonnie Lee McElroy b. 5-29-1904 d. 1-14-1988
5. John Russell McElroy b. 1872 d. 1933
6. Lillian D. McElroy d. 1920
Married William Miller
7. George Stokes McElroy b. 4-20-1875 d. 8-29-1913
Married Martha Elizabeth Tompkins
   1. William Andrew McElroy b. 1-15-1897 d. 3-26-1970
   Married Vesta Gillespie (b. 10-15-1903 d. 5-7-1973)
      1. Billie June McElroy b. 3-26-1923
      1st Married Claude Northcutt
         1. Roberta Ann Northcutt b. 3-29-1940
         Married Charles A. Bayless on 1-6-1958
            1. Darrell Wayne Bayless b. 3-24-1960
      2nd Married James E. Burch
      2. Sandra Lee Burch b. 11-11-1946
      3. Howard James Burch b. 7-10-1950
      Married Janice Kay Wolfe in 1970
      4. Victoria Lynn Burch b. 9-11-1956
      Married Michael Thompson
      2. Jack Paul McElroy b. 3-21-1925
      1st Married Willa Dean Schneider
      2nd Married Gertrude Steffy
         1. Jackie Paul McElroy Jr. b. 1-26-1944
         2. Michael William McElroy b. 7-27-1946
      3. Glenn Howard McElroy b. 8-10-1927
      Married Laura Lou Wyche on 3-11-1947
         1. Eddie Keith McElroy b. 5-10-1952
         Married Debbie Kennamer
         2. Laura Susan McElroy b. 1-19-1960
      4. Georgia Jewel McElroy b. 10-30-1929
      Married Gerald Don Stewart on 8-31-1948
         1. Bruce Gordan Stewart b. 7-21-1952

Married Camisa Jean Lobaugh
2. Brent D. Stewart b. 7-5-1958
5. Kenneth Ray McElroy b. 2-27-1934
1st Married Marlene Myra Bohnert
  1. Catherine Marie McElroy b. 8-11-1960
2nd Married Elsie Virginia Johnson
  2. Kenneth McElroy b. 2-27-1968
6. Charles Edward McElroy b. 12-13-1937
Married Nora Jean Hunt on 9-21-1956
  1. Charles Edward McElroy b. 10-5-1957
  Married Deborah Glenn Tipken on 12-19-1975
  2. Eliza June McElroy b. 1-15-1959
7. Nancy Elizabeth McElroy b. 6-1-1946
Married Wesley C. Moore
  1. Derek Jason Moore b. 1-26-1971
2. Oral H. McElroy d. 1970
Married Iva Gardner
3. Molly McElroy
Married Leonard J. Barham
4. Myrtee McElroy
Married Mark Woolsey
5. Bertie McElroy b. 1-16-1906
1st Married Clyde Faubus
2nd Married Jim Walker
6. Vivian McElroy
Married Euless Ketchem
7. Garland McElroy d. 3-1971
8. Georgia Lillie McElroy b. 12-24-1913
8. Charles Scott McElroy b. 8-1878 d. 1949
Married Mary Childers in 1905
9. Phoebe Effie McElroy b. 12-30-1880
Married David Cluck
10. William Edgar McElroy b. 6-1883
1st Married Martha Smith
2nd Married Alice Witt
4. Elizabeth Jane McElroy b. 1844 d. 4-6-1934
4. Edward Stokes McElroy b. 6-6-1823
Married Ann Rumsfelt
5. Nancy McElroy

Married Sanfrod Gorin on 6-1-1842
6. M. McElroy b. 3-11-1827
7. John Huts McElroy b. 1828
Married Elvina Rumsfelt
8. Larkin McElroy b. 1829
Married Silvinia Buchannon
9. George Washington McElroy
Married Luticia Stokes
10. Pinkney McElroy b. 1843
11. Martha McElroy b. 12-17-1837
Married William Hilliard
12. Robert Allen McElroy b. 3-12-1840
Married Martha Jane Whilford
6. Archibald McElroy b. 9-6-1765
Married Martha Craig
  1. William McElroy
  2. James McElroy
  3. Susan McElroy
  4. Jane McElroy
  Married S. McCully
  5. Margaret McElroy
  Married W. Steele
  6. Archibald McElroy
  Married R. Bellotte
  7. Samuel McElroy
  Married Mary Montgomery Dickson
    1. William McElroy (moved west)
    2. James D. McElroy
    Married Carolina Watkins
      (no children)
    3. Antoinette McElroy
    Married John Gilkerson
    4. Martha E. McElroy
    Married William Milan
    5. Samuel M. McElroy (moved to Oregon)
  8. Martha McElroy
  Married Thomas Wilkes

# Alfred McElroy & Son James

Alfred McElroy b. soon after 1700 in Northern Ireland, lived and raised family at Cape Fear (Cape Fear is near Wilmington, which had a great port—it is likely that he landed here for most of the early McIlroys did not migrate near the coast North Carolina)
Married _____

1. James McElroy[39] b. 9-1-1759 in Cape Fear, North Carolina d. 1848 in Allen County (first Warren County), Kentucky
Married Fannie Langston (b. 4-26-1759)on 4-16-1782
    1. Ruth McElroy b. 11-7-1783 d. 9-30-1870
    Married Langston Williams (b. 7-11-1772 d. 9-10-1840) on 12-24-1801
        1. Rebecca Williams
        Married _____ Ragland
        2. Fannie Williams
        Married _____ Williams
        3. Sarah Williams
        Married _____ Thompson
        4. George W. Williams b. 4-28-1808 d. 12-16-1875
        Married Matilda Layle
            1. Nancy
            Married J.H. Francis in Dec. 1869
        5. Benjamin H. Williams
        6. John M. Williams
        7. Richard H. Williams
        8. Nancy Williams
        Married _____ Wright
        9. Elizabeth Williams d. 1-13-1857

---

39    James McElroy lived near Greenville County, South Carolina for several years after he married Fannie Langston. I found records that he and John McElroy witnessed several documents together. This probably was the John that moved to Caldwell County, Kentucky, for he had moved from Greenville to Caldwell County about the same time James moved to Kentucky. James was a Revolutionary War soldier and at one time was a courier for General George Washington.

(Never married)
10. Isaac N. Williams b. 12-3-1822
Married Elizabeth Griffin on 6-6-1871
11. James F. Williams
12. Irene J. Williams
Married _____ Hinton
2. John McElroy b. 2-27-1786
3. Betty McElroy b. 2-12-1788
4. Sarah McElroy b. 6-24-1790
Married Balam Thompson (d. 3-1838) on 6-15-1807
5. Caswell McElroy b. 12-30-1791
6. Samuel M. McElroy b. 7-5-1793
Married Mary Williams on 4-1-1713
7. Foster McElroy b. 12-25-1794
8. Alfred McElroy b. 12-25-1796
9. James McElroy Jr. b. 3-19-1799
Married Alice Ham in 1819
    1. Alfred McElroy b. 7-11-1823 d. 12-17-1897
    Married Sarah Blackburn (b. 1823 d. 10-16-1901) on 1-26-1845
        1. William M. Mordicia McElroy b. 5-18-1847
        Married Drucilla Russell (d. 9-1905) on 12-25-1867
            1. Emma McElroy b. 10-31-1868
            Married J.W. Perry on 12-25-1889
                1. Myrtie Perry
                Married Leslie Pope on 1-10-1910
            2. Victoria McElroy b. 12-29-1870
            3. Cornelia McElroy b. 5-10-1874 d. 12-27-1880
            4. Effie McElroy b. 6-4-1876
            Married Pink Holiman (d. 10-23-1907) on 5-22-1902
            5. Fletcher McElroy b. 10-11-1879 d. 7-2-1911
            6. Lillie McElroy b. 12-18-1881
            Married Everett Guy on 2-19-1905
                1. James Blackburn Guy b. 12-25-1905
                2. Leonard Guy b. 6-6-1907
            7. Blackburn McElroy b. 10-9-1887
        2. S. Bruce McElroy b. 2-18-1851 d. 10-7-1929
        3. Louisa McElroy b. 3-6-1854
        Married W. R. Fryer
        4. Mary C. McElroy b. 6-17-1851 d. 1943
        (Never married)

2. Rebecca McElroy
Married _____ Williams
3. William J. McElroy [40] b. 7-10-1825
Married Mahala Dodson
   1. James McElroy Jr. b. 1850 d. 1924
   2. Rebecca M. McElroy b. 5-13-1852 d. 11-17-1852
   3. Sarah A. McElroy b. 2-22-1853 d. 8-23-1914
   4. Thomas J. McElroy b. 8-20-1854 d. 9-26-1927
   5. Marsalete McElroy b. 1856
   6. Albert F. McElroy b. 8-31-1858 d. 1925
   7. Martha J. McElroy b. 12-16-1859 d. 3-29-1934
   (Never married)
   8. Mary F. McElroy
   9. Mahala R. McElroy
   Married _____ Hinton
   10. Eunice McElroy b. 3-24-1964 d. 1-24-1923
4. Moses H. McElroy b. 1828 d. 1895
Married Kareen Hunt (b. 1831 d. 1872)
   1. Ellen McElroy
   Married John Whitney
   2. Ollie McElroy
   Married T.J. Ham
   3. James K. McElroy b. 4-30-1857
   4. A.C. McElroy d. 1907
   5. H.A. McElroy[41] b. 6-13-1869
   1st Married Ethel Claypool in 1906
   2nd Married Hawley Payne
      1. Francis McElroy b. 5-15-1914
      2. Ruth McElroy b. 10-14-1916
      3. H.A. Payne Jr. b. 2-25-1918
      4. John Robert Payne McElroy b. 8-7-1920
5. Jane F. McElroy
Married _____ Jent
6. Hartwell McElroy Jr. b. 3-10-1835 d. 1-12-1916

---

40   William J. McElroy was a sergeant, captain, lieutenant-colonel, deputy, and county surveyor. He was a member of the legislature of his native state for three terms. He is num-
bered among the most influential men of the county.

41   H.A. McElroy was a good businessman and in the 1920s, he farmed a chain of five and ten
cent stores that became very popular in Tennessee and Kentucky.

1st Married Adeline Shields (b. 10-16-1842 d. 3-15-1884)
1. Eugene McElroy b. 7-6-1866
Married F. Worsham
　　1. Paul Lee McElroy
　　2. Homer Glenn McElroy
　　Married Macie Eugena Smith
　　　　1. Clinton E. McElroy b. 1-5-1938
　　　　Married Julia E Nance
　　　　　　1. Clinton McElroy Jr.
　　　　　　2. Homer Glenn McElroy Jr. b. 11-19-1939
　　　　　　Married Gail Stockhouse
　　　　　　　　1. Paula Leigh McElroy
　　　　　　　　2. Shannon Glenn McElroy
2. Mary Alice McElroy b. 1868
3. Alfonso McElroy b. 1871
(Never married)
4. William A. McElroy b. 1873
Married Nellie Reeder
　　1. Gladys McElroy
5. Mordicai Washington McElroy b. 1877
　　1. Oscar Lee McElroy
　　1st Married Katie Rice
　　　　1. John Lee McElroy
　　　　Married Regina Marshall
　　　　　　1. Russell McElroy
　　　　　　2. Mary McElroy
　　　　　　3. Linda McElroy
　　2nd Married Gladys Vance
　　2. Orval McElroy
　　3. Other McElroy
　　4. Juanita McElroy
　　5. Cartha McElroy
　　Married Charlie Thomas
　　　　1. Evelyn Thomas
6. Andrew Jackson McElroy b. 1879 d. 1944
Married Nellie Webster
　　1. Douglas McElroy
　　2. Donald McElroy
2nd Married Nancy Fishborne
7. Ora McElroy b. 6-15-1887 d. 1969

(Never married)
8. Dosiah McElroy
Married Loren Travelstead
  1. Bradford Travelstead
  2. Roy Glenn Travelstead
  3. Wilma Travelstead
  Married Harry Lewis
    1. Steven Lewis
    2. Mark Lewis
    3. Candice Lewis
9. Granson Fletcher McElroy
  1. George McElroy
  2. James McElroy
  3. Ray McElroy
  4. Virginia McElroy
  5. William McElroy
7. Nancy McElroy b. 1837
Married _____ Jackson
8. Mary E. McElroy b. 1840
Married _____ Hunt
10. Francis "Fannie" McElroy b. 10-24-1800 d. 10-29-1886
Married Ralph Waling (b. 11-3-1793 d. 8-22-1871) on 9-27-1818
11. William B. McElroy b. 6-10-1802 d. 1869
Married Lydia Spann in 1822
  1. Unknown
  2. Francis McElroy b. 7-16-1823 d. 12-3-1863
  Married John Hinton
  3. George B. McElroy b. 4-8-1825 d. 6-7-1863
  4. Nathan D. McElroy[42] b. 5-6-1827 d. 2-22-1901
  Married Armarinda Cornwall on 7-16-1869
    1. William J. McElroy b. 1-16-1870 d. 7-20-1927
    Married Fannie (b. 2-26-1870 d. 9-11-1957)
    2. Lether Pierce McElroy b. 9-5-1871 d. 5-2-1931
  5. Barney McElroy b. 1830

---

42   Nathan D. McElroy was constable of Allen County, Kentucky for about fifteen years and also land commissioner and deputy clerk.

# History of Another Daniel McIlroy

*Written by John Wisely McIlroy and Rewritten by John M. McIlroy, Sr.*

Daniel McIlroy was born in Ireland in 1778. He married Jane Wisely in 1800. She was born in Scotland. They were married in Belfast, Ireland. Soon after marriage, took a sail ship and were seventeen days on the ocean, landing in Quebec, Canada. Went from Canada to Maysville, Kentucky. Lived near there for thirteen years. My father, Thomas McIlroy, and several of the children were born there. Daniel McIlroy owned four little horses and a schooner wagon. Put the children and everything they owned in a wagon and started to Missouri. Crossed the river at St. Louis, came to Pike County and settled near Bowling Green on poor land in the woods and lived in a cabin. Grandfather rode a horse to Palmyra, Missouri and in entering his land told them his name but they wrote his name in the deed Daniel McElroy. He did not discover his mistake before he died, six years afterward. Grandmother was left with seven children. My father, Thomas, was sixteen yeas old. Then my father married my mother, Letitia Henry, of near Clarksville and moved there. My grandfather and family had spelled the name with an *I*, but the administrator discovered the mistake in spelling the name in the deed. He told my grandmother she should spell her name as it was written in the deed or it could cause trouble later. She and they younger children spelled it with an E. My father was seventeen at that time and decided to spell it as his father had—McIlroy. My father married Letitia Henry, daughter of Alexander and Elizabeth Ann Allison in November 1845—their children were John Wisely, Edna Alice, and George Clark. She died August 4, 1854.

May 19, 1855 married Lucretia Henry, first cousin of my mother. She died March 6, 1856. Married Jane Martin, Daughter of Judge Martin of Frankford, Missouri in March, 1867. She died in May 1858. Married Margaret Stark on February 3, 1859. I saw my father married to his second and fourth wives. When he married his third wife I was a small boy. My father thought twenty-five miles to Frankford, Missouri was too far to ride horseback. The children of Thomas and Margaret were Henry (Wilmer's father) and Ella—her children,

Elizabeth and McIlroy—called (Mack) Fry. William was born January 6, 1864, his children Mary, Thomas and Elizabeth born March 17, 1866. Her children, McIlroy (called Roy), Mary and Elizabeth.

My father, Thomas McIlroy, was born July 20, 1820. His sisters were Mary who married John Benning; Margaret married Henry Pettibone; Elizabeth married David McClure of Mexico, Mo.; Robert married Dagarine Eidson and John never married, he lived in Bowling Green. My father died November 27, 1909. When my father sold wood in Bowling Green, he drove a steer cow and horse to the wagon. George Clark McIlroy married Mary Shaw (called Mollie). Their children were Hardin of Tucson, Arizona; Elizabeth Letitia married Ed Mantiply, her second husband was Arthur Easley and the lived near Nashville, Tennessee.

Ina married a Texas man; Mable married Howard Hunter; cannot remember the fifth girl's name; Edna Alice McIlroy married Frank Mackey at 16 years of age. Their children were Minnie, who died in infancy; Margaret Letitia married Dr. Manning of Marshall, Mo.; Augusta married John Roberts of Clarksville, Mo.; Lucinda Jane, called Lulu, married Frank Naylor of Marshall Mo.; Maude married William Armentrout of Salisbury; Bernard died when a small boy.

William Goodman was born in Virginia and came to Kentucky when a small boy and then to Missouri. He married Delilah Boggess. He died at age fifty-six, his wife at fifty-eight years. Their children were Margaret, who married Nelson Tinsley. Margaret died at twenty-five years of age. John R. Goodman married Belle Finley and died at age fifty-nine. Their children were John Warren and William. William Nathan married Grace Robinson. William died at age sixty-eight. They had one child, Blanch.

Kate married George Hogue. She died at twenty-eight years. Their son was named William Milburn. Their fifth child was Almyra (Allie) born June 22, 1853, died October 30, 1931, who married John W. McIlroy. Their children were Lena Letitia, Ora Delilah and William Thomas. There was one daughter and one son in the Boggess family. Orpha Boggess married Parson Brown of near Eolia, Missouri. Their daughter, Betty, married John Thomas Mackey. They had three daughters and two sons. Orpha marred Webb Strange; Ella marred Lem Butts and Ada married William Wamsley; Parson (Parse) married Lou Wells. Tucker (Tuck) married Ora McBride; Naomi married a Mr. Gooch, moved to Shelby County, Missouri.; Susan married Henry Schooler and had two children, Henry Jr. And Katherine (Kitty). Kitty married James Stark and had two children, Margaret Stark Johns and William Stark, who marred a Miss Elgin, his first wife. His second wife was Lou Turner. Their children were Ruth

Stark Gillum and Harold Stark. Boseman Boggess, the son, married Eliza Stark, one of seventeen children. They had no children.

# A Brief History of the West
# Texas McIlroys

March 8, 1978

According to my father, as told to him by his father, the McElroys came to the United States from Ireland. Their original home, however, was Scotland.

My grandfather, John R. McElroy, moved his family, by covered wagon, from Kentucky to Texas in about 1856. They settled near the little town of Forrestburg, in Montague County, where my father, William Dora "Shinnery", was born on October 17, 1861.

My grandfather fought through the Civil War with a regiment of Texans commanded by Colonel Sam Maines. He was wounded once by a shot on the shoulder. He served nearly five years. My father was born while my grandfather was in the service and was four years old when my father saw him for the first time.

One year, my father, a brother (Natheniel J.) and a sister (Ellen) were captured by a small band of marauding Comanche Indians and carried into the Oklahoma Indian Territory where they were held for about 18 months before my grandfather could find them. He ransomed them with about $2,000.00 worth of flour and other supplies.

In 1874, the family moved to Wichita County near the present site of Wichita Falls to become one of the early residents of that area, eight years before the coming of the railroad.

My father had three brothers, Cal, George, and Nathaniel; and five sisters, Mary Jane, Ellen, Lydia, Frances, and a baby sister that died shortly after birth. Cal, who became an expert with a pistol, accidentally killed himself while performing as a trick shooter with an early wild west show. George had to daughters, Quinnie and Audie. Quinnie, now deceased, married Doc Newton and lived in Valentine, Texas. Audia married Henry Bochat and now resides in Del Rio, Texas. Nathaniel lived in Mangum, Okla. And raised a large family. All the McElroys that live or were born in that area are his descendants.

My father began working for the Waggoner Ranch in 1879. He worked for the Waggoners for most of his life, until his retirement in 1934. He married Carrie Delma Lorance on April 7, 1895. He passed away June 30, 1943.

During World War I, Price served in the army, Tolleson was in the Navy. During World War II, Robert was in the Army, A.B. and I were in the Air Force. We were lucky, no casualties.

A.B. has three children: Rodney, Reese, and Debra. Robert has three: Patricia, Glenda, and Robert. I have one, Joan.

I am a retired Texas school teacher, having taught 41 years. I am also a retired Air Force reservist. I graduated from Texas A&M in 1927; from Vernon (Texas) High School in 1922.

Yours Truly,
W.D. McElroy

# William Story McElroy
# Family Genealogy

McElroys are Scots-earliest of whom we have knowledge was John, who, with his wife, Jean, lived in Scotland near Glasgow. Their son, Hugh, and two brothers left Scotland at the time of the persecution, and settled in County Down, Ireland. One or more of these was among the defenders of Londonderry in 1089. Tradition says that all the McElroys in County Down, Ireland, were descendants of these three brothers. The earliest McElroy migrating to America was probably William who came to Bucks County, Pennsylvania in 1717. His daughter, Agnes, married John Scot from whom descended Mrs. Carrie Scot Harrison, wife of Benjamin Harrison. James M. McElroy was the grandson of William McElroy who came to America in 1717.

James M. McElroy was the ruling elder in the Associate Reformed and United Presbyterian churches for sixty years. Dry goods business. Member St. Clair church at Mt. Lebanon, Pennsylvania for thirty years. He, his first wife, Mary Story, his second wife, Mary Dunlap, and daughters, Mary Story and Margaret, are buried in burying grounds of St. Clair United Presbyterian church, Mt. Lebanon, Scot Township, Allegheny County, Pennsylvania

James M. McElroy b. 1811 at Turtle Creek, Pennsylvania d. 10-27-1900 at Hulton, Pennsylvania at home of daughter Agnes (Mrs. Orlando Metcalf McElroy)

1st Married Mary Story (b. 1805 d. 1-25—1838, daughter of John Story who died Dec. 25, 1838 at his residence in Zelianople, Pennsylvania)

    1. William Story McElroy b. 6-7-1834 in Bucks County, Pennsylvania d. 6-27-1834

    2. William Story McElroy b. 11-4-1835 d. 3-30-1901

2nd Married Mary Dunlap (b. 2-14-1807 d. 2-27-1883, daughter of Robert and Agnes Dunlap of Larne, Ireland, family came to America in 1818 and settled in Pittsburgh, Mr. Dunlap one of the founders of Associate Reformed Church (Second United Presbyterian) along with Reverend Joseph McElroy, DD., Mary raised thousands of dollars for sanitarium at Ramleh near Alexandria, Egypt.)

    1. Agnes b. Sept. 23, 1841

Married Orlando Metcalf on 11-5-1863 at Turtle Creek, Pennsylvania, invested in railroad in Colorado Springs, lost a fortune with railroad investment but could afford it.
1. Mary Cole b. 4-21—1850 d. 8-5-1851
2. Eliza (Leila) b. 1-22-1848 d. 9-6-1896
Married Charles Sylvester Fetterman (son of Wilfred B. Fetterman, grad. West Point)
3. Margaret b. Sept. 8, 1845
4. Mary Story b. Sept. 12, 1893 d. Jan. 4, 1896
5. William Story b. Nov. 4, 1835 d. Mar. 30, 1901 buried in family plot Linn
Grove Cemetery, Greeley, Colorado
Married: Mary Ann McCague (b. 8-35-1842 d. 5-19-1912, daughter of William H. McCague of Ripley, Ohio who was born Sept. 20, 1819 in Union, Ohio, son of Thomas and Katharine Platter McCague—flour mill and foundry owner. Family home in Ripley has monument identifying home as one of stops on underground railway on route to help escaping slaves.
1. Katharine Story McElroy Sr. b. 10-2-1869 d. 10-31-1950, started Katharine Jr. and William Charles on harp in Santa Barbara, California, very aristocratic looking and acting lady, state-vice-regent DAR in Colorado National Committee,
2. Orlando Metcalf McElroy b. 7-14—1871 d. 11-51916, one of the founders of famous Lost Soldiers Oil field in Wyoming, contracted typhoid fever after drinking bad water at the oil field
Married Bertha Davis on 5-9-1893 (daughter of Charles Davis and Florence Newby)

Charles Davis, the son of John R. Davis came from Wales when his wife was asked to nurse Queen Victoria's newborn son. John would not let his wife do so, and his wife and their newborn son came to America. Florence Newby's father, Joshua Newby was born in Schuylkill, Pennsylvania and married Anna Davis. The Newbys are prominent in Hartford, West Virginia. Charles was Weld County Clerk and recorder, State Representative, State Auditor, director of famous Denver Welsh Quoir which won festival in Central City. They had nine children Bertha, George, Anna, Charles, Dewey, twins Ida and Thomas, and Helen Louise. Bertha was in the second class of nurses to graduated from St. Joseph's hospital in Denver and in 1906 became a registered nurse. She was one of the first deaconesses of First Presbyterian Church in Greeley, Colorado—fine homemaker and mother.

Children of Orlando Metcalf McElroy and Bertha Davis:
1. William Charles McElroy b. 3-26-1916 d. 2-28-1977, was an electrical engineer with Westinghouse, a fine father, husband, son, and brother, served in New Guinea as degaussing officer in World War II, a Lieutenant in navy
Married Evelyn Day Hoffman—(daughter of Dr. and Mrs. Harry Hoffman)

Children of William Charles McElroy and Evelyn Day Hoffman:
1. William Charles McElroy, Jr. b. Feb. 3, 1945 Greenville, Ohio, nuclear engineer with Westinghouse-, graduate of Stanford University, won Westinghouse National Golf Tournament
Married Sharon Ann Ellis Tyree b. Aug. 22, 1943

Adopted children of William Charles McElroy, Jr. and Sharon Ann Ellis Tyree:
1. Stephen Michael McElroy b. Feb. 24, 1961
2. Leon Scott McElroy b. June 25, 1963
3. Ann Theresa McElroy b. Dec. 24, 1964

2. Mary Ann McElroy b. Feb. 14, 1947 Denver, Colo., graduated from Stephens College, University of Colorado, Delta Gamma, harpist
Married Billy Doran Sherley
1. Rikki Lynn Sherley b. 5-27-1971

3. Lynne Katharine McElroy b. 8-21 1951 in Denver, Colorado, graduated from Colorado State University, harpist, Kappa Alpha Theta Jr. 9 hole golf champion Colo.
Married: Thomas George Carter b. Oct. 2, 1950 descendant Daniel Boone, Detroit, Mich.

Children of Lynne Katharine McElroy and Thomas George Carter:
1. Corinne Katharine Carter b. April 16, 1976 Hereford, Tex.

4. Richard Hoffman McElroy b. October 25, 1956 Denver, Colo., graduated from University of Arizona 1977, business

Katherine Story McElroy, Jr., graduated from Stephens College, University of Colorado, University Northern Colorado MA, harpist, registered, professional parliamentarian, served two terms for Dorothy Elston who became treasurer of the United States, published McElroy Chart of Motions—poetry, short story, manager of the McElroy farm and business property, original family home of 1872 still in family as of May 1978.

# Bert McIlroy's Family Story

Record of John H. McElroy
Co. I Reg't 3<sup>rd</sup> Ark. C Vol's
Enrolled Dec. 27, 1863, Discharged June 30, 1865

John H. McElroy and Sarah Jane Conley were marred Feb. 6, 1865 at Lewisburg, in Conway Co. Ark. By Rev. Stocton.

John H. McElroy born Dec. 17, 1829 died May 30, 1907
Sarah Jane McElroy born Dec. 21, 1840 died June 10, 1925

1. Mary J. McElroy born April 2, 1854 died
2. Thomas J. McElroy born Aug. 1, 1856 died
3. Amos McElroy born Dec. 29, 1857 died May 6, 1921
4. Sarah I. McElroy born March 9, 1866 died Jan. 28, 1893
5. Lenora L. McElroy born June 10, 1868 died
6. Gashum McElroy born June 2, 1871 died
7. John R. McElroy born July 26, 1874 died.
8. Elot McElroy born Dec. 18, 1877 died Aug. 14, 1957
9. Anna McElroy born June 29, 1880 died June 29, 1880
10. Henry H. McElroy born Feb. 16, 1882 died Aug. 9, 1884

Information copied by Dale Barnett, May 16, 1969, from "Soldiers Family Record" of John E. McElroy. Original record is being kept by Mrs. Donnie Sherrill, Snowball, Ark.
December 1, 1978
Dear Mr. McIlroy:
    Based upon information given me by my cousin, Dale Barnett, the son of Mary McElroy Barnett, my Dad's sister, and upon information given to me by my Father, John Walter McElroy, I Will give you a little additional information on my branch of the McElroy family.
    My father was the son of Amos McElroy, one of several Amoses, particularly known as "Black Amos", because of his Indian characteristics inherited from his mother. Amos was the son of John Houston McElroy, who came to

Arkansas from Tennessee when he was a teenage boy. My best information is that John Houston McElroy was the son of John Riley McElroy, who had been a school teacher at Lebanon, Tennessee.

John Houston McElroy was married to Sally Dean, a half-blood Cherokee woman, who was the sister of Emanuel Dean and Bowman Dean. They lived on Silver Hill, between Marshall, Arkansas and the Buffalo River. Of this marriage three children were born, Mary J. McElroy, born April 2, 1854, and married into the Fox family. Fox, Arkansas was named for this family; Thomas J. McElroy, born April 1, 1856, and Amos McElroy, born December 29, 1857. Amos was the father of my father, John Walter McElroy, and my aunts, Lenora and Mary Ellen McElroy, later Burnett. Nora married Andrew Barnett and Mary married his brother Murphy Barnett.

After the Civil War, John Houston McElroy was married to Sarah Jane Conley, February 6, 1865, and the following were born to that marriage; Sarah I. McElroy, March 9, 1866; Lenora L. McElroy, June 10, 1868; Gasum McElroy, June 2, 1871; John R. McElroy, July 26, 1874: Elot McElroy, December 18, 1877; Anna McElroy, June 29, 1880 and Henry H. McElroy, February 16, 1882.

My grandfather, Amos McElroy, went to Seymour, Missouri, and in that county met and married Mirenda Rush, a tall woman with blond hair. Of that marriage was born my father, John Walter McElroy, November 9, 1884, Lunda Lenora (Nora), October 14, 1886, and Mary Ellen, February 14, 1888, and Freddie, who was born shortly before his mother died and he died two days later. After the death of Mirenda, "Black Amos" took his children back to Arkansas to the home of his father, John Houston McElroy. He married Mamie Duff and had a child who was named Fred McElroy. This marriage ended shortly. The children of the first marriage, including my father, lived with John Houston McElroy at Bur Oak on Silver Hill in Searcy County. In the meantime Amos McElroy married Susie Goldsmith and they had a son named Oscar who died in his youth.

My Aunt Mary says that her dad left home to find work. My father, Aunt Mary's brother, tells me his father left home after an incident in which a man had threatened his life with a Winchester rifle and his dad, who was cutting wood at the time, threw an axe against the fire of a Winchester rifle and hit his attacker in he temple. IT was immediately after that when he left Arkansas for the Indian Territory to look for work. Amos McElroy lived in central Oklahoma Territory for a number of years under the name of Charlie Johnson. He later moved to Coalgate, Oklahoma. My Aunt Mary says that my father, John Walter McElroy left Arkansas to go to the territory to search out his father and found him at a place called Nixon, Oklahoma. My father's version is that he was walking down the streets of Coalgate, Oklahoma in about 1912, going along the boardwalk, when he met a little man with a big white hat and a red banana around his neck. The man walked with a noticed limp, which was not characteristic of Amos McElroy, but my father thought he recognized the facial features and stopped the man to say, "I am looking for a man named Amos McElroy from Arkansas." The reply was, "What do you want, Whippersnapper." When my father, John Walter, McElroy, had identified himself, there was an emotional reunion between the two. Amos McElroy, who according to his sister, Mary, had changed his name to Albert McElroy, took my father to his home, where my father met two or three sisters and brothers, one of whom, Mrs. Frances Cogburn, still lives at Clayton, Oklahoma. Amos McElroy died May 6, 1921, at Jumbo, Oklahoma, near Clayton, and is buried in the Clayton Cemetery. His father, John Houston McElroy, died May 13, 1907, and was buried at Silver Hill Cemetery in Searcy County, Arkansas. At his grave is a government tombstone showing him as a Quartermaster Sergeant of the Arkansas Calvary, Volunteers. The date of his death, 1907, has the "7" carved backwards on the stone. This little cemetery was a part of the farm of John Houston McElroy which he dedicated to a cemetery. In this cemetery are many stones which indicate that the people of this community migrated from Buncombe County, North Carolina. This community was made up mostly of Scotch—Irish immigrants who came tout of Carolina and Tennessee to Arkansas. Many were intermarried with Cherokee people in Carolina and Tennessee and many more were intermarried with the Cherokees who first moved from Tennessee and Carolina in 1819 to West Arkansas.

The Dean family was apparently among the early removal from Carolina to West Arkansas.

The children of the first marriage of Amos McElroy, John Walter McElroy, Lunda Lenora McElroy (Barnett) and Mary Ellen McElroy (Barnett) married and had children as follows. 1. John Walter McElroy married Mary Alverson in 1906 and had a daughter, Vernie Blane McElroy, born March 19, 1907, who now lives in Tyler, Texas. That marriage ended and in 1916 he married Terra V. Harrison in Jackson County, Oklahoma and had four children; Bert McElroy, Fred Thomas McElroy, John Dale McElroy and Mary Juanita McElroy.

Bert McElroy lives in Tulsa, Oklahoma and is a lawyer. Fred T. McElroy lives in Purcell, Oklahoma and operates a general merchandising store. John McElroy lives in new York and is vice-president and general counsel for National Distillers Products Corporation. Mary Juanita McElroy lives in Altus, Oklahoma and is the manage of Viewmore Television System in that city.

The family of the two sisters who married Barnett brothers is scattered. Pearl Barnett Goodman lives in West Hollywood, Florida. Walter Barnett lives in

Lakeland, Florida. John Barnett lives at Walnut Hill, Illinois and Oleta Barnett Wallace lives at Lakeland, Florida. These are the children of Mary McElroy.

The children of Lenora (Nora) McElroy Barnett are Hugh Barnett of Harrison, Arkansas, May McClinton, Harrison, Arkansas, Edd Barnett, Harrison, Arkansas, John Barnett, Fowler, California, and Mabel Barnett Beard of Fayetteville, Arkansas, Jack Barnett of Laton, California. Grandchildren of this union include the Holder boys of Northwest Arkansas, Perry D. and Kenneth.

In my own family, as a son of John Walter McElroy, I have three children, Bert Colyar McElroy, a lawyer in Tulsa Oklahoma, age 35, Meredith McElroy, a library scientist of New Orleans, now enrolled in Denver University to work on her masters degree, and Martha Jane McElroy, who now lives at Knoxville, Tennessee where her husband, Henry Keeling, is working on a masters degree at the University of Tennessee.

Many of the kinfold of my father live in the community of Bixby, Oklahoma. I did not know of them until I moved to this community in 1941. My father's cousins, Gasum and Green McElroy, came to that community many years ago and have descendants across the countryside.

John Walter McElroy died at the age of 90 with his boots on in a car accident near Broken Arrow, Oklahoma. He came to Oklahoma in about 1904 as a horse trader, later moved to Texas and came back to western Oklahoma in 1914 where he married Terra Harrison, my mother, and where he lived until he moved to the Tulsa community in 1954.

In Tulsa, Oklahoma the first livery stable in operation, 1884, was opened by John McElroy. George McElroy was the first saddle maker in the City of Tulsa. His son, Oscar, has been reported to be the first white child born in Tulsa, then known as Tulsey Town. The Dean of Men at Oklahoma State University, former known as Oklahoma A&M College, was Dean Thomas McElroy. Most of these people migrated from Arkansas and are believed to have been related to the family of John Riley McElroy, which came out of Tennessee early in the 1800's.

The mixture of McElroy to which I belong came from maternal stock out of Tennessee. My mother was a Harrison. Her maternal grandparents were the family of Strains and her father's maternal family was Grant. Most of these people were descendants of immigrants from Ireland who came from the coventers stock of Scotland. Thus most of them were what we know as the "Scotch-Irish-Harrison, Grant, McElroy, Strain, McGillibray, etc." All of these people were shown as immigrants from Ireland, but were in fact Scottish people.

I have observed the McIlroy name from here to Inverness in Scotland and to my surprise I have found lawyers, doctors, and many preachers. I thought as I grew up in the west of Oklahoma that all McElroys were farmers, hillbillies, and cowpokes and I thought I might be one of the first to be a lawyer. In reading the history of the family I find that I am one of many in the generations of lawyers, doctors, preachers and professional people.

Very truly, yours,
Bert McElroy

# Additions to the Previous Information

John Riley McElroy
Married Sarah _____ in 1804 in Tennessee
1. Gasham McElroy b.1824
Married Armeta Jones (b. 1847 d. after 1900)
  1. William T. McElroy b. 1848
  2. Samuel C. McElroy b. 1850
  Married Mary _____
    1. John McElroy b. 1872
    2. Levi McElroy b. 1874
    3. Dora McElroy b. 1877
    4. Armeta McElroy
  3. Albertine McElroy b. 1854
  4. George McElroy b. 1855
  5. Jane McElroy b. 1856
  6. John McElroy b. 1859
  7. Sarah McElroy b. 1864
  8. Mary McElroy A.
  (Never married)
  9. Samantha
  Married H.J. Jackson
    1. Leander Jackson b. 1891
    2. Carey Jackson b. 1899
2. Nancy McElroy
  1. Greenberry H. McElroy b. 1854
  Married Rachel "Candy" Rambo
    1. Miranda McElroy
    Married John Ferguson
    2. Amos Greenberry McElroy b. 1884
    Married Myrtie Daniel
      1. Dorsey McElroy
      2. Dolph McElroy
      3. Coy McElroy
      4. Gertrude McElroy
      Married _____ Kelling
        1. Paul Kelling
      5. Lorene McElroy
  3. Nola McElroy b. 1891

4. Andrew McElroy b. 9-1894
   1. George McElroy
   2. Roger McElroy
   3. Howard McElroy
5. Dewey McElroy b. 8-1899
   1. Lee McElroy
   2. W.W. McElroy
   3. Frank McElroy
2. Amos R. McElroy
Married Jane Hinson
3. Sarah McElroy
Married George Battenfield
3. John Houston McElroy b. 12-17-1829 d. 5-3-1907
1st Married Sarah Deen (d. 1925)
   1. Mary J. McElroy b. 4-2-1854
   Married _____ Fox
   2. Thomas J. McElroy b. 8-1-1856
   3. Amos McElroy b. 12-29-1857 d. 5-6-1921
   1st Married Miranda Rush
      1. John Walter McElroy b. 11-9-1884
      1st Married Mary Alverson in 1906
         1. Vernie McElroy b. 1907
      2nd Married Terra Harrison
         1. Bert McElroy
            1. Bert C. McElroy
            2. Meredith McElroy
            Married Henry Keeling
         2. Fred T. McElroy
         3. John D. McElroy
         4. Mary McElroy
      2. Nora McElroy b. 1886
      Married _____ Barnett
         1. Hugh Barnett
         2. May Barnett
         3. Edd Barnett
         4. John Barnett
         5. Maple Barnett
         6. Jack Barnett
      3. Mary McElroy b. 1888
      Married _____ Barnett

    1. Pearl Barnett
    2. Walter Barnett
    3. John Barnett
    4. Oleta Barnett
2$^{nd}$ Married Sarah Conley
    4. Freddie McElroy D.Y.
    4. Sarah I. McElroy b. 3-9-1866 d. 1-28-1893
    5. Lenora L. McElroy b. 6-10-1868
    6. Gasum McElroy b. 6-2-1871
    7. John R. McElroy b. 7-26-1874
    8. Elot McElroy b. 12-18-1877 d. 8-14-1957
    9. Anna McElroy b. 6-29-1880 d. 6-29-1880
    10. Henry H. McElroy b. 2-16-1882 d. 8-9-1884
4. Barnet McElroy b. 1832 in Tennessee
5. Minter McElroy b. 1836
6. Thomas G. McElroy b. 1841
Married Nancy _____
    1. John H. McElroy
    2. Trina McElroy
    3. Mildred McElroy
    4. George H. McElroy b. 1873
        1. Mandel McElroy
        2. Loretta McElroy
7. Amos McElroy b. 1845

# Record of John McElroy

If this next group was related, it would have to date back to northern Ireland, but this is an amazing article—I would think that any genealogist would appreciate this. It is just too good to leave out.

(McELROY)

- GENEALOGY -


History of McElroy Family.     Written by
John McElroy, of Warrentown, Jefferson Co., Ohio.
A. D. 1828.     Copied by O.L.A.     Transcribed by F.W.M.


"Some account of the family of John McElroy,
of Warrentown, Ohio.

"Adam McElroy and Rachel McClure, His Wife,
My Grandfather and Grandmother, were born near Glasgow,
in Scotland. The time of their removal to Ireland,
or the time of their death, I know Not.

They had One Son Adam, who lived at Drummore,
in County Down. And one daughter, Rachel, Wife of
George McDonald, And John my Father, who was born in
1716. This is all I know about my Fathers Family.

Grandfather Francis Newell and Jennett, his
Wife, were full Cousins, born in Lancashire, near
Liverpool in England.

Grandmother, born 1674, lived in our family
in her Widowhood, until she died in 1770. Aged 96
years. Her children; William and Elizabeth Erwin.

(2)

His Wife, Francis, and Archibald and Nancy Gordon,
His Wife;  Fanny, wife of John Bran; and Nancy, my
Mother, born in 1718. She and Father married in 1737.
Their offspring; Jean, wife of John Stitt, born in 1737,
Died near St. Clairsville, Belmont Co., Ohio. in 1825.
Aged 88 years.

(2) Francis died in infancy.

(3) Alexander born on 1740 married Mary Donnelson,
Both dead. He in 1817, aged 77 years.

(4) Adam and (5) William, Twins, died young.

(6) Isabella, never emigrated from Ireland. She was
wife of James Chambers, of Kirkeel.

(7) Nancy, wife of Mathew Taylor, born in 1747, died
in 1834, in Huntingdon Co. Pennsylvania. aged 87

Brother Alexander died in the same place, and
Mathew Taylor, Nancy's Husband died 3 yrs. afterwards.

(8) John died in infancy.

(9) Elizabeth, wife of Matthew Anderson, born in 1751,
and died at Gilpin Paper Mills on Brandywine,
Delaware, in 1831. aged 80 years.

(10) & (11) Archibald (1st. & 2nd.) both died young.

(12) John, myself, born May 22, 1758. Our family em-
igrated to America in 1772. My Mother died at Sea,
on May 10th. same year we landed at Marenshook,
May 22nd, my Birthday.   1772 & 1773 lived in
Newcastle, Co. Delaware. 1774 lived with Robert
Finney, of Newport Delaware. Learning Painting
and Glazing. Part of 1775 no employment.
Lived some time with Alexander and with Samuel
Mears in the Path Valley, Pennsylvania.

(3)

The 1st. of January 1776, I enlisted in the
Pennsylvania Battalion, Commanded by Col. Wm. Irvin,
of Carlisle No. 6. 1st. of April got Battalion,
raised and marched two companies at a time to Lancaster,
and then on to Philadelphia, then getting Knapsacks &
Blankets, went by water to Trenton. Then to Elizabeth
townpoint, then by water to New York. Then by water
to Albany, where we received Tents and camp equipage,
about the 1st. of May. Then to Lancingburg, then to
Half Moon. Next to Saratoga, crossed the Hudson River,
at Fort Edwards, then to Fort Wm. Henry. Then crossed
the lake George to Ticonderoga. Then to Crown Point,
and crossed Lake Champlain, to St. John's. Then to
Fort Chamblee, then over the River Sorrell to St.
Lawrence. Then down St. Lawrence and crossed Lake
St. Peter and on to the Three Rivers, where we went
to attack the British advance Guard. But the previous
night the whole army had come up , and the river was
full of Ships and Transports. However we attacked
them, and of course got handsomely beaten, Losings
about 100 men. Mostly Prisoners. When our men spied
the British, they made their escape, with all our
provisions. So we traveled 80 odd miles on good brown
pine swamp water.

(4)

This was the first time I ever knew what real
hunger was. When to Barkee our boats met us with a 3
pound loaf of bread, each man. We tried to purhase
some onions from an Old Scotch Woman, who was churning,
but would not take paper money. We contrived to run
away with her churn, however, and took it into some
bushes in the meadow. This bread and half churned
buttermilk was the greatest feast, The Old Lady
missing her churn, Damed our Yankee Souls to all
intents and purposes. Then we crossed the St. Lawrence, 9 miles wide, to the camp at Sorrell.

Next day we retreated up Sorrell to Chamblee.
Burned four Schooners & a Gun Boat, the Fort and
everything. We could not get up the Falls. Hauled
our Boats up. Burned St. John's, and on to Island
Nour, where we rested a week.

Here the Indians gave us the first salute,
Killing two Officers and two Privates. Two officers,
One Sergent and myself being down at a spring, about
100 yards below the house, providentially escaped.
We being like fools all unarmed. The Indians were
off in less than three minutes, with four Scalps."

(5)

- - - - - - - - - - - - - - - - - - - - - - - - - -

John McElroy, writer of the above, died
February 17th. 1841. Aged 82 years.

- - - - - - - - - - - - - - - - - - - - - - - - - -

(Coleman Cruson, was born November 19, 1816.
(
(Elizabeth A. McElroy, " March 24, 1820.

C. Cruson and E. A. McElroy were married,
January 5, 1842. By the Rev. M.Stevens. Their Children-

1. Margarette Louisa Cruson, Born April 1st. 1843.

2. John Coleman " " Sept.25th. 1844.

3. Albert William " " Febr.28th. 1846.

4. Mary Elizabeth " " Sept.23rd. 1848.

Elizabeth A. " Baptised May 1845.
M. L. " " " 1845.
J. C. " " " 1845.

A. W. " Died Jan. 7th. 1847.

5. Lewis Mc. " Born Febr. 9th. 1853.


John McElroy, Born May 22, 1758. in Drummore
County, Down, Ireland. Married Mary Bohman in 1782.

Their Children-

1. Catherine McElroy, Born February 13, 1783.
2. Ann " " September 4, 1784.
3. John " " July 11, 1786.
4. Mary " " October 13, 1788.
5. Elizabeth " " March 25, 1791.
6. Sarah " " June 27, 1793.

(6)

```
7.  Jacob McElroy,    Born May    10, 1795.
8.  Mary    "         "   August 25, 1797.
9.  One Un-Named    Died July   30, 1799.
```

Mary, His Wife, Died July 30, 1799.

He (John McElroy) was married to Miss Margaret

(Slade) Hughes. March 27, 1800. She was born August

16, 1780, in Baltimore Co.,    Their Children:-

```
10.  Thomas      Born Jan.  3, 1801. (Lived 7 weeks)
11.  Silas       "    Jan. 27, 1802. (Died in Warren-
                                     (town, 1/7/1830.
12.  Alexander   "    Jan. 20, 1805.
13.  Jane        "    March 17, 1807. (Died 1 day old)
14.  Thomas Hughes "  June 21, 1808.
15.  Fenas C.    "    Sept. 18, 1810. (Killed Aug. 10,
                                     (1829. By a tree
16.  One Unnamed, "          1812.
17.  Jane        "    Febr. 27, 1817. (Died 2/15/18.
                                     (with Whooping Cough.
18.  Elizabeth Anderson Born March 24, 1820. Died 3/2/1853.
19.  Wm. H. Harrison,  "  Jan. 20, 1823. " Sept.1823.
                                     at Warrentown.
```

John McElroy Died February 17, 1841.
Aged 82 years 9 months and 5 days.

4th. GENERATION.

Thomas Hughes McElroy, the direct Ancestor in

this Line, Was born June 21, 1808. In Jefferson Co.,

Ohio. And there he married at Warrentown, His Wife.

A Daughter of John and Elizabeth (McKee) Humphrey.

(7)

John Humphrey was a Captain in the Revolution.
Serving as an Officer 7 years under Washington's
Command. He died in Ohio at the venerable age of
90 years. His Wife Elizabeth (McKee) was born in Ireland

Elizabeth Humphrey, Daughter of Captain John
Humphrey and Elizabeth (McKee) Humphrey, (Wife of
Thomas Hughes McElroy) was born in Jefferson County
Ohio, February 15th. 1811.

5th. GENERATION.

The following were the Children of Thomas H.
and Elizabeth H. McElroy: -

1st. John Conner McElroy,        Born Jan.   15. 1836.
     "      "      "              Died Aug.    9. 1836

2nd. Margaret Elizabeth          Born June   7. 1837.
     in Warrentown, Ohio.        Died May   20. 1853.

3rd. William Allen McElroy       Born Sept. 27. 1839.
     in Warrentown, Ohio.

4th. James A. McElroy,               "      Febr. 13. 1842.

5th. John H. McElroy,                "      Aug. 15. 1844.
     in Wapello, Louisa Co. Iowa.    Died in  1917.

6th. Thomas J. McElroy.          Born Aug. 23. 1847.
     in Marrietta, Fulton Co., Ill.

7th. Mary Virginia McElroy.      Born Febr. 6. 1852.
     in Marrietta, Illinois.

Elizabeth Humphrey, Wife of Thomas H. McElroy,

Died April 26. 1876. Aged 65 yrs. 1 month and 7 days.

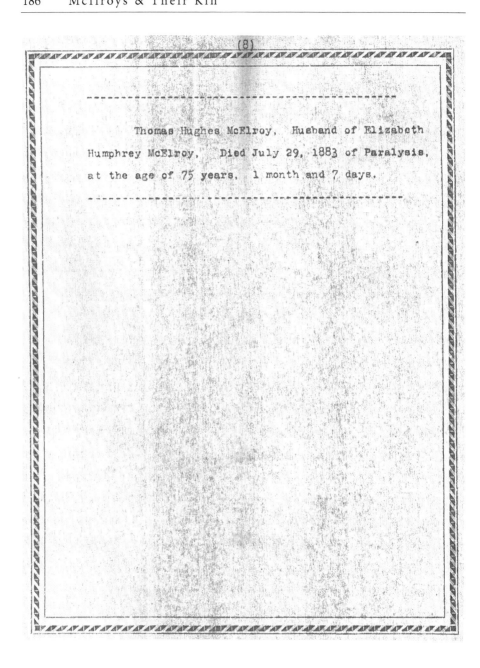

(8)

Thomas Hughes McElroy, Husband of Elizabeth Humphrey McElroy, Died July 29, 1883 of Paralysis, at the age of 75 years, 1 month and 7 days.

(9)

William A. McElroy, Served in the
Civil War. Enlisting in the Union Army, on
the 18th. day of June 1862, at Ellisville,
Illinois, And was mustered into Service of
the United States, as a Private, in Company
"D" 70th. Regiment, Illinois Volunteer Infantry,
at Camp Butler, near Springfield Illinois, July
4th. 1862, for a period of three months.

He was mustered out of Service on the
23rd. day of October 1862, as a Private, with
His Company and Regiment, at Alton Illinois.
By reason of expiration of service.

Father has told his children, of several
of his Thrilling Adventures and narrow escapes,
but will not undertake to relate any of them,
more, than I might mention, while sitting around
the fire place one winter evening, Father was
telling us children some of his war experiences,
and one of them was very exciting indeed.
When He had finished, one of the younger
children says, "Father did you get killed?,

(10)

William A. McElroy, was married, August 30, 1866
at Bushnell, Illinois, to Sarah Jane Drum of that place.

Sarah Jane Drum, was a Daughter of James Drum,
(Whose Mother's maiden name was Ingersoll).

James Drum was born in Ohio in 1825.  His Wife,
Susanna Andrews, was born in Ohio in 1827.

James Drum and Susanna Andrews, was married,
when they were but 17 and 15 years of age.

There was Four Children born to this Union.

Sarah Jane.    Born May 23, 1844  at Woodfield,
                                  Belmont Co. Ohio.

Rachel, David and Daniel,         All are dead.

James Drum, made a trip to Illinois, in 1853,
where he purchased a farm, where they intended to
locate. He returned to Ohio, and with his family,
started for their new home in Illinois,

They stopped on the border line between Ohio
and Illinois, and rented a farm, where he put in a
crop on the Illinois side, along the Ohio river.

Some stock broke in his crop one night, he goes
out in the rain to run them out, and contracted a very
severe cold.  A Doctor was called, who happened to be
drunk, and gave him a large dose of calomel, which
Salivated him, the doctor then placed him in an ice

(11)

pack, and he soon died. and was buried at that place, being 28 years of age.

Thus leaving his wife, with Four small children, (Sarah Jane) the direct ancestor in this line, was only 9 years old at the time of her Father's death.

His wife (Susanna) with the Four children goes on to Marietta Illinois, where her Husband had purchased their home, and raised their four children.

Later she married, Eli Melvin, of that place, to this union four children was born, their names: Josephine, Caroline, Mary and Carrie.

Susanna (Drum) Melvin, was visiting with her daughter Rachel Ford, at Plattsmouth, Nebraska, where she died, February 11, 1877, at the age of 49 years 10 months. Galdstone being the cause of her death.

Sarah Jane, went to live with Doctor and Mrs. Clark, at Bushnell, Illinois, when 13 years old, and remained in their home, until her marriage to William A. McElroy, on August 30, 1866.

To the Union of William A. and Sarah J. McElroy, (Living in Illinois) a Daughter, Mary C. was born on August 24, 1867.

(12)

William A. McElroy, Wife and Baby, emigrated to
Missouri in 1869, and settled in Charlotte Township,
Bates County.

They came by railroad to Pleasanton Kansas, on
the first passenger train to that place, their fare
was 7¢ per mile. $50.00 charges to have their goods
shipped from Kansas City, to Pleasanton. Finding no
Hotel accomodations, they slept in their emigrant car.

Next morning they loaded their goods on wagons,
and started for their home in Missouri, arriving there
on October 13, 1869, on their 80 acre farm 2½ miles
South East of the villiage of Virginia, and 8 miles
West of Butler. By their frugality and industry,
they increased their posessions to 520 acres.

The pine lumber of which their house was built,
they hauled from Pleasant Hill Missouri. The dimension
lumber, was sawed at a mill known as the Old Haymaker
Ford Saw Mill. The carpenters enployed, was Billy
Daniels and Tice Charles. The plasturing was done
by Bob Hurt.

They remained on this farm until the Fall of
1902, when they retired, moving to Butler, having
them a nice home on Mill Street.

(13)

SIXTH GENERATION.

The following were the children of WILLIAM A. and SARAH J. McELROY.

1st. Mary Catharine,  Born Aug. 24, 1867.
at Marietta, Ill.

2nd. Ida Leona,    "  Dec. 5, 1870.

3rd. Minnie Elizabeth,  "  Jan. 6, 1874.

4th. Frank William,  "  Nov. 10, 1876. *Died 8/30/1948.*

5th. Nellie Belle,  "  Dec. 2, 1878.

6th. Clarence James,  "  Sept. 12, 1882. *Died 4/29 Los Angeles Calif form 1966*

7th. Blanche Louisa,  "  April 5, 1884.

The last 6 children was born on the Old Home Place, 8 miles West of Butler, Missouri.

MARY CATHARINE, was married to Everett Drysdale, of Butler Missouri, on December 24, 1885, at the Old Home Place. No children born to this Union.

Everett Drysdale, was a Son of John Newton, and Mary Jane (Allendar) Drysdale.

IDA LEONA, was married to Willie M. Hardinger, of Butler Missouri, on May 24, 1888, at the Old Home Place.

(14)

Willie M. Hardinger, was the only child of,
William Nathaniel, and Mary Ellen (Barryhill) Hardinger

To the Union of Willie M. and Ida L. Hardinger,
was born 5 children.

1st.   Burney M.    Born Aug. 10, 1889. (By accident,
       Burney M.    Died Jan. 10, 1892. (falling into a
                                        (tub of scalding
2nd.   Lee M.       Born Dec. 24, 1892. (water.

3rd.   Elmer H.      "    Apr. 10, 1900.

4th.   Arthur L.     "    Mar. 11, 1902.

5th.   Ruth M.       "    June 15, 1914.


MINNIE E. was married to John T. Hendrickson,
of Butler, Missouri, on December 14, 1892. at the
Old Home Place. To this Union 3 children was born.

1st.   Rena L.       Born June 3, 1894.

2nd.   William Roy.   "    Oct.13, 1897.

3rd.   Jennie E.      "    Dec.21, 1901.


FRANK W. was married to Phila M. Harper, of
Butler, Missouri, on December 15, 1897, at the Home
of her Mothers in Butler, Missouri.

(15)

Phila M. Harper, was a Daughter of Richard Elliot, and Phila Caroline (Hill) Harper

To the Union of Frank W. and Phila M. McElroy, was born 9 children.

| 1st. | Lois Marie, | Born | Jan. | 15, 1899. |
| 2nd. | Nellie May, | " | May | 5, 1901. |
| 3rd. | Joe William, | " | Jan. | 4, 1905. |
| 4th. | Fae Allen, | " | Aug. | 19, 1908. |
| 5th. | William Franklin, | " | May | 12, 1911. |
| | | Died | July | 4, 1913. |
| 6th. | Richard Harper, | Born | April | 6, 1913. |
| | | Died | May | 10, 1913. |
| 7th. | Rex Edgar, | Born | July | 14, 1914. |
| 8th. | Phila Jane, | " | Feb. | 24, 1917. |
| 9th. | James Deo, | " | April | 28, 1919. |

NELLIE BELLE, married Emmett F. Burk, of Butler, Missouri, on February 22, 1899, at the Old Home Place.

Emmett F. was a Son of Monroe and Nanny Belle (Evans) Burk, of Butler, Missouri.

(16)

To the Union of Emmett F. and Nellie B. Burk, there was born 8 children.

1st. Chester A.       Born May 15, 1901.
                            Died Jan.  8, 1903.

2nd. Virgil F.        Born Jan.  3, 1904.

3rd. Mary Jane,        "  May 24, 1905.

4th. Hazel L.         "  June  4, 1907.

5th. Mildred,         "  Feb. 14, 1910

6th. Glen E.          "  Aug. 26, 1912.

7th. Gertrude L.      "  Feb.  3, 1916.

8th. Doris B.         "  Feb. 11, 1919.

CLARENCE JAMES, was married to Agnes Mack, at Riverside, California. Nov. 25. 1909

To this Union 3 children was born.

1st. Charles William Born April 6, 1911.

2nd. Dortha Mildred " Dec. 24, 1914.

3rd. Richard Donald Oct. 16. 1921

BLANCHE L. was married to Fred B. Brayton, of Henry Co. Missouri, on February    1901, at the Old Home Place. To this Union was born 3 children.

1st. Edgar W.        Born Sept. 30, 1901.

2nd. George T.       "  Dec. 25, 1906.

3rd. Wesley D.       "  April 13, 1911.

# Will of James McLroy

In the name of God amen I James McLroy of Prince Edward County calling to mind the uncertainty of this transitory life hear on Earth and that all flesh must yield to Death do make this my last will and Testament in manner and form as followeth my will and desire is that my dear & loving wife may populate the plantation where on I now live and be maintained during her life. Then I give and bequeath to my son Archibald McLroy one shilling sterling, then I give and bequeath to my son John McLroy one shilling sterling, then I give and bequeath to my son Hugh McLroy one shilling sterling, then I give and bequeath to my son Samuel McIlroy one shilling sterling, then I give and bequeath to my daughter Mary McLroy one shilling sterling, then I give and bequeath to my daughter Elizabeth McIlroy one shilling sterling, then I give and bequeath to my son James McLroy one Negro wench named Luce to him and heirs for ever and ... wife give to my son James my land whereon I now live & all my whole estate both real and personal after my wife's death to him and his heirs for ever my will and desire to that their may be no appraisement on my estate. I constitute and appoint my dear and loving wife and my son James McLroy my whole and ... executors of this my last will and Testament as writing my hand this fifteenth day of March one thousand seven hundred & seventy

Sign'd and Delivered, James McLroy

For presents of James Thackston, Samuel Johnson

The inventory of the estate of James McLroy Senior deceased taken this 19th day of October 1742 as followeth 169 aces of land three horses beast 12 head of cattle 17 head of hogs young and old 10 head of sheep two feather beads & two chests & half dozen of chairs one table & one cubbard & two pots half a dozen of plaits two dishes & three porringers & one bole & one quart pot 4 suits of cloths & two plow two axes & two mattix & three hoes & two emity of hogsides & two emity casks & one small trunk & five pounds cash & one cart

James McLroy, Junior

Executor

At a court held for Prince Edward County November 1772. This inventory of the estate of James McLroy deceased was returned and ordered to be rendered.

Watkins

**Mcilroy Will**

In the name God amen I James McIlroy of Prince Edward County Calling to mind the uncertainty of this Transitory life here on Earth & that all flesh must yeald to Death Do make this my last will and Testament In manner and form as followeth Vizt my will and Desire is that my Dear & loving wife may Pofsefs the Plantation whereon I now live and be maintained During her life. Item I give and Bequeath to my son Archable McIlroy one Shilling sterling Item I give and Bequeath to my son John McIlroy one shilling sterling Item I give and Bequeath to my son Hugh McIlroy one Shilling Sterling Item I give and bequeath to my son Samuel McIlroy one Shilling Sterling Item I give and Bequeath to my Daughter Mary McIlroy one Shilling Sterling Item I give and Bequeath to my Daughter Elizebeth McIlroy one Shilling Sterling Item I give and Bequeath to my son James McIlroy one Negro Wench Named Luce to him and his heirs for ever and I like wife give to my son James My land whereon I now live & all my Whole Estate Booth Real and Pursonall after my wifes Death to him and his heirs for ever my will and Desire Is that their may be no appraisement on my estate I Constitue & appoint my Dear & loving wife and my son James McIlroy my whole and sole Executors of this my Last will and Testament as witnefs my hand this Xfteenth Day of March one Thousand seven hundred & Seventy

Sign'd & Deliverd                                 James McIlroy (seal)
In Presents of
James Thackston   Samuel Johson

**McIlroys Invent.** The Inventory of the Estate of James McIlroy Senior Deceasd Taken this 19th day of October 1772 as followeth vigt 169 acres of Land three Horse Beast Twelve head of Cattle Twelve Head of Hoogs yong & ould and Ten Head of sheep two feather Beads & two Chests & half Dozen of Chears one Table & one Cubbard & two Pot Half a Dozen of Plaits Two Dishes & three porringers & one Bole & one Quart Potte four Suits of Cloths & two Plow Tacklin Two Axes & two Mattix Three Hoes & two Emty Hogsheds & two Emty Casks & one small Trunk & five Pounds Cash & one Cart &c

                                 James McIlroy Junior
                                 Executor

At a Court held for Prince Edward County November 1772. This Inventory of the Estate of James McIlroy deceasd was returned and ordered to be recorded.

                                 Test
                                 Watkins D66

# Possible Proof that John McElroy was a son of James and Sarah McCue

**Also a statement from J.M. Bishop, grandson of Archibald McIlroy, and a statement from Matt McIlroy in response to this proof**
(Note: Some of this may replicate previous information)

## The Scotch-Irish McElroys in America

The Scotch-Irish McElroys in America, by Reverend **John M. McElroy**, D.D., of Ottuwa, Iowa, was published in 1901, by the Port Orange Press, Brandow Printing Company, Albany, N.Y.

Following is an extract from a letter by the author, Reverend **John M. McElroy**, of Ottuwa, Iowa, about 1903, to **Charles F. McElroy**, then at Indianapolis, Indiana. The book, "Scotch-Irish McElroys in America," did not include Charles F. and several preceding ancestors. The purpose of the letter was to show where these McElroys fitted into the book. The author said he intended to get out another revised issue in which these names would appear, but he died without doing so.

John **McElroy**, of Scotch-Irish stock, supposed to have been born in Ireland about 1730 or later, lived in the Waxhaw settlement in South Carolina (on the North Carolina Line) with his wife, Martha, and was a soldier in the Revolutionary War. Andrew Jackson and his brother Robert lived with their widowed mother in the same settlement. Both of them were soldiers (very young) and both came home from Camden, South Carolina, where they had been prisoners with smallpox. Robert died of the disease. (The foregoing in regard to the Jacksons I get from history.)

According to the old family record John McElroy came home from the army at the close of the war with smallpox. He took up his abode in the pigpen and stayed there until he got well. I have no doubt he is the John registered on page

22 of "Scotch-American McElroys." He was probably a prisoner along with the Jacksons at Camden, and these prisoners were released, according to history, in April 1781.

**John** and **Martha McElroy** had ten sons—John, George, Nimrod, David, Archibald, James, William, Samuel, and two more, probably Wilkinson and Absalom. They had two daughters—Bettie, who married a Calhoun and died young, leaving one son who was probably John Ewing Calhoun, a cousin to the Senator, John C. Calhoun. The other daughter, Martha, perhaps married a Davis or a Russell. Of the ten sons, two settled somewhere in Kentucky— John and one other. The other eight went southwest, settling in Georgia and Alabama.

Archibald, son of John, born in Waxhaw January 25, 1772, married Elizabeth Smith and died April 6, 1826. They were married at Cave Creek, Ashe County, North Carolina, September 22, 1787. His wife died December 20, 1863, at 93 (or 90) (?) years of age, and must have been born about 1770 or 1773.

**Archibald and Elizabeth McElroy** had 14 children:
John, born November 4, 1798
George W, born April 1, 1800, died of cholera July 4, 1833
Martha, born April 13, 1802, died October 8, 1808
Sarah (Davis), born December 1, 1803 in Indiana
Amelia (Hackney), born December 1, 1803 in Indiana
Cowan, born November 6, 1805
Archibald, Jr., born November 16, 1807
Elizabeth, born December 14, 1809, and is now in Missouri
Samuel, born February 12, 1812; died March 1, 1847
Jane, stillborn March 1, 1815
Wilkinson Washington, born June 10, 1918; died 1847
Lydia, born August 8, 1820; married Bishop; 11 children; died 1878 in Collin County, Texas at age 58
Patsy, born February 5, 1823
Violet, died March 13, 1848

Of these fourteen, the first eight were born in Cave Creek Settlement, North Carolina; the others nine miles northeast in Lee County, Virginia; near Station Creek Church, Methodist.

**J.M. Bishop** and one brother were soldiers in the Union army. J.M. McElroy of Texas and most others of the connection were in the Confederate army. Bishop wrote me two years ago that his grandmother, **Elizabeth Smith McElroy**, lived to be 93 years of age. She gave him records that she had kept about the Waxhaw McElroys. These are the same records that are reported by her Texas grandsons. This Texas man had seen an old family record and had copied part of it for Bishop's mother who died in 1848, the substance of which is given above. He has a particularly distinct recollection of that smallpox incident. When he came home from service in the Confederate army he was a little afraid of smallpox, as he had been somewhat exposed. Old Grandma told him he'd "better not take the pox; if you do we'll put you in the pigpen like grand-dad."

# A Letter From Reverend John M. McElroy

Your pedigree seems to run about thus:

**James McElroy** from Belfast, Ireland, to Pennsylvania, and thence to Campbell County, Virginia

**John McElroy**, from Pennsylvania to South Carolina. Soldier; born about 1730

**Archibald McElroy**, born January 25, 1772, at Waxhaw, South Carolina; died April 6, 1826, in Lee County, Virginia

**George W. McElroy**, born April 1, 1800, in Lee County, Virginia, died of cholera July 4, 1833, in Washington County, Indiana

Most of these sons went south to Georgia and Alabama, two of them—John and one other—to Crab Orchard, Kentucky. Archibald McElroy born January 25, 1772, died April 6, 1826, married Elizabeth Smith at Cave Creek, Ashe County, North Carolina, September 22, 1797. She died December 20, 1863, at the age of 93. Their home was in Lee County, Virginia, 45 miles from Cumberland Gap.

Archibald and Elizabeth had 14 children:[*]
1. John, born November 4, 1798
2. George W., born April 1, 1800
3. Martha, born April 13, 1803, died October 8, 1808
4. Sarah (Davis) born December 1, 1803
5. Amelia (Hackney), born December 1, 1803
6. Cowan, born November 6, 1805
7. Archie, born November 16, 1807
8. Elizabeth, born December 14, 1809
9. Samuel, born February 12, 1812, died march 1, 1847
10. Jane, born March 1, 1815 (twin)
11. Wilkinson, born June 10, 1818, died 1847
12. Lydia, born August 8, 1820, married Reverend Jonathan Bishop (11 children), died Collin County, Texas, 1878
13. Patsy, born February 5, 1823—Tennessee
14. Violet, died March 13, 1848 (twin)

---

[*] This may seem repetitious, but this is in verbatim from a letter from Reverend John M. McIlroy stating that he intended to place this in his next revised edition, but he died before he had a chance to revise the book.

Lydia McElroy (Archibald, John, and James), born August 8, 1820, married Reverend Jonathan Bishop and became the mother of 11 children and died in Collin County, Texas, in 1878.

James Bishop (Lydia, Archibald, John, and James) was born in Lee County, Virginia, November 7, 1839, private soldier in 4$^{th}$ Tennessee, Union Cavalry, promoted Captain, served

three years. Resides at Norman Oklahoma.

George W. McElroy (Archibald, John, James) born April 1, 1800, settled in Washington County, Indiana, 1833, died of cholera July 4, 1833.

(NOTE—he died on a boat returning from New Orleans and was given seaman's burial in the Mississippi at the mouth of the Ohio as the boat was not allowed to land because of the cholera n board.—CPM)

His children were Nimrod, born 1826, died Whitewater, Kansas 1903, Archie, John, and Emily.

Nimrod McElroy (George W., Archibald, John, and James) was the father of seven sons and six daughters.

George W. McElroy (Nimrod, George W., Archibald, John, and James), born in 1848, educated at Eureka College, Illinois, a minister in the Christian Church, married April 25, 1875, Laura O. Foster.

Nimrod McElroy, born October 26, 1825, in Lee County, Virginia, died April 19, 1903, at Whitewater, Kansas.

George W. McElroy, born April 15, 1848, in Washington County, Indiana; died October 30, 1880, near Kirwin, Smith County, Kansas

Charles F. McElroy, born April 26, 1876, in Red Willow County, Nebraska; now living at 631 South Fourth Street, Springfield, Illinois.

John M. McElroy

As stated, John M. McElroy died before publishing his revised edition of "Scotch-Irish McElroys in America." About 1935 his daughter, Miss Abigail McElroy copied for me certain notes which she found among his papers, and which presumably were to have been incorporated into the revised book, as follows:

### "Scotch-Irish McElroys in America"

"Further information in regard to John McElroy, son of James, of Virginia, and brother of Hugh, Samuel and James, of Kentucky.

John McElroy lived in the Waxhaw settlement, near the South Carolina line in Mecklenburg County, North Carolina. He was born about 1730, or earlier, and probably married in Cumberland County, Pennsylvania. His father settled in Campbell County, Virginia, but John went further south and settled in a

Scotch-Irish community n the Waxhaw. Probably his younger brothers seldom if ever saw him, his home begin 200 miles distant.

John was a soldier in the Revolutionary War, serving probably under General Green and as Militia Man. He with Robert and Andrew Jackson came home from the army with smallpox, probably from military prison at Camden, South Carolina, about 1780.

John McElroy had a family of twelve children—two daughters and ten sons. His daughter Betty married a Calhoun. Their son, John Ewing Calhoun, was born in 1801, a cousin to the distinguished John C. Calhoun.

The sons of John C. McElroy, given from memory by an aged descendant living in Texas, were: John, George, Nimrod, David, Archibald, James, William, Samuel and two more, perhaps Wilkinson and Absalom.

Died at Kirwin Kansas, October 30, 1880. He had two children—Charles F., and a daughter Georgia Pearl, Indianapolis, Indiana. Charles was born in Red Willow Township, Nebraska, April 26, 1876.

Samuel McElroy, a lawyer, son of Nimrod, Judge of the Kansas Court of Appeals, died 1902, at Cripple Creek, Colorado. His children were Frank Roscoe, Carroll B., Mary, Athol, Mildred, Hal.

Adam P. McElroy (Nimrod, George W., Archibald, John, and James) was for some years a teacher in Fort Worth, Texas, but is now a physician in Boyd, Texas. He has one child, Archibald.

Penina J. Van Tuyl (Nimrod, George W., Archibald, John, and James) resides at Plattesmouth, Nebraska."

### Matt McElroy's Family Record Written in 1917

John McElroy was born in Ireland (date unknown). When 2 years old was brought to Burks Co., Penn. by his father, James.

James' wife (from Ireland) was a Mackhune, I think.
John's (his son) was a Marthy Moore, I think. (Signed: J.M. McElroy.)

Archibald McElroy, son of John & Martha McElroy, was born in Waxhaw Settlement in Mecklenburg County North Carolina, Jan. 25, 1772.

Elizabeth Smith was born in Warren County, Virginia, May 26, 1779. She being the second daughter of George and Elizabeth Smith. Her maiden name was Betty Earl.

Archibald & Betsey were marred at her father's house on Cove Creek, Ash County, North Carolina by Ezekial Baird, Esqr. Of Watugariven, September 22, 1797.

## Genealogy Relating to John McElroy
The following information is furnished by Adam Pascal McElroy
(Nimrod, George W., Archibald, John, James)

**Nimrod McElroy** subscribed for a family Bible which was published in 1972. On the outside front cover in gold letters is the name "N. McElroy." Entries in this Bible prior to 1880 were made by George W. McElroy, second son of Nimrod. George W. died October 30, 1880. The Bible apparently remained in the possession of Nimrod McElroy until his death in 1903, when it came into the possession of his daughter, Mary Ann McElroy Boyd, who made certain entries in it. She later gave it to Adam Pascal McElroy, who about March 10, 1935, gave it to Charles F. McElroy, who now has it.

**Adam Pascal McElroy** was informed by Nimrod McElroy (his father), that George W. McElroy (his grandfather) then living in Washington County, Indiana, died of cholera on a boat returning from New Orleans. He was given seaman's burial in the Mississippi River at the mouth of the Ohio River because the boat was not allowed to land by reasons of the cholera on board.

**Mary Gilstrap**, was born near Crab Orchard, Kansas, and was married to George W. McElroy in Lee County, Virginia. After his death she remarried (name of second husband unknown) and moved to Coffee County, Kansas, where she died about 1859 to 1861.

The following information is furnished by Mrs. Blanch Corfman Everett, (Cora Van Tuyl Corfman, Penina J. McElroy Van Tuyl, Nimrod, George W., Archibald, John, James), 411 Heil Avenue, El Centro, California.

In response to her application for membership in the Daughters of the American Revolution, she received a letter saying:

"We notice that the sketch you sent to us, which was copied from the records of Reverend John M. McElroy, states that John McElroy served probably under Gen. Green, and as a militia man. We find no proof of this, however. There was a Jon. McIlroy who served in Col. James Roebuck's Regiment, S.C. during the American Revolution, whom we believe to be your ancestor. This man was probably the same one who was listed in the 1790 Census of S.C., page 71, as a resident of the 96th District, Greenville County. In the Census record his name is spelled McElroy. Will you not make an effort to obtain his date of death!"

Mrs. Blanche Everett has written for this information, but has not informed me of the result.

# Mcllroys of Various Spellings
# in the Revolutionary War

**1. Adam McElroy**
Pennsylvania
Private under Captain Ahenham Marshall in Pennsylvania Musketry Battalion
b. in Ireland
d. in Easton, Pennsylvania
**2. Alexander McElroy**
Adam's son
b. 1752 d. 1818
m. Mary Donaldson in 1770
**3. Alexander McElroy**
Bucks County, Pennsylvania
Nockamixon Township
Private Associate
Underage
**4. Andrew McElroy**
from North Carolina
Private
R 6783
1st m. Johanah Hancock
2nd m. Phoebe _____
**5. Archibald Mcllroy**
Lt. Col. 4th
d. 1806
m. Sarah McClelland
**6. Archibald McLroy**
Union County, South Carolina
Killed at King's Mountain
**7. Avington Muckleroy**
b. 1750 in Johnston County, North Carolina
d. 1797 in Oglethorpe County, Georgia
m. Sarah Dawson

Patriot
Granted land for services
D.A.R.
**8. Michael Muckleroy**
Died while prisoner of war at Halifax, Nova Scotia from starvation around
September 1777
**9. Benjamin McElroy**
Son of William and Isabel
b. 2-20-1743
Salem, Massachusetts
**10. Charles McElroy**
Pennsylvania
**11. Daniel McElroy**
b. 1755
d. 1830
m. Rebecca Wishart
Lancaster County, Pennsylvania
**12. Daniel McElroy**
b. 1735
Chester CO, Pennsylvania
d. in Green County, Tennessee
**13. David McLeroy**
Suffolk County, Massachusetts
Private 1-8-1777
**14. Daniel McIlroy**
d. 1813 in Ohio
Laudoun County, Virginia
Captured at Battle of Long Island
**15. George McAlroy**
Captain of first US Navel Ship
**16. George McIlroy**
Bucks County, Pennsylvania
Private 3rd Battalion
Nockamixon Township (associate under age)
2b Lt. 2nd Co. 3rd Batt.
**17. George McIlroy**
Windsor Township
Middlesex County, New Jersey
**18. Hugh McLroy**
b. 1734

Lt.
Prince Edward County, Virginia
m. Ester Irvine
**19. James McElroy**
b. 9-11-1759 in Cape Fear, North Carolina d. 2-9-1848 in Allen County,
Kentucky
m. Fanny Langston
Prisoner
Courier for General Washington at one time
**20. James McElroy**
Washington County, Pennsylvania
**21. James McElroy**
Mecklebury County, North Carolina
**22. James McElroy**
b. 1764
d. 1850
Lt. NY
**23. James McElroy**
Lancaster County, Pennsylvania
**24. James McElroy**
Pennnsylvania
**25. James McElroy**
Patriot and signer of New Hampshire Declaration of Independence (D.A.R.)
m. Elizabeth Robinson
**26. John McElroy**
d. 1790 in Mecklebury County, North Carolina
m. Martha Moore
Lt. South Carolina
**27. John McElroy Jr.**
son of above
**28. John McElroy**
son of Archibald
killed at Gulliford Courthouse
**29. John McElroy**
Adam's son
**30. John McElroy**
m. Mary
Johnson County, North Carolina
Indian Creek

**31. John McElroy**
North Carolina
**32. John McElroy**
**33. Micajah McElroy**
b. 9-30-1760 d. 10-19-1832
D.A.R.
Hillsbourough Dist. Wake County North Carolina
**34. Patrick McElroy**
Lt. From Virginia
killed on ship down Ohio River
m. Elizabeth Heth
**35. Robert McElroy**
Massachusetts
**36. Ruben McElroy**
**37. Samuel McElroy (Macleroy)**
Salem, Massachusetts
Pvt. in Moses Hart Co.
Muster roll 8-1-1775
88 days
**38. Samuel McElroy**
b. 1745 d. 1806
m. Mary Irving
was at Yorktown when Cornwallis surrendered
D.A.R.
**39. Thomas McElroy**
b. 1751 in Ireland
moved to America (Virginia) in 1773
pension appeal rejected
enlisted 1776
Chester Co., Pennsylvania
From W. Virginians in Revolution
**40. Timothy McElroy**
Alexander Township
Hurterdon County, New Jersey
**41. William McElroy**
from Johnson County, North Carolina
Killed in Revolutionary War
**42. William McElroy**
Pvt. Rhodes County
**43. William McElroy (Mclelory)**

Boston Massachusetts Capt. Banester Co.
enlisted 1-10-1777
**44. William McElroy**
Sergeant in Colonel Mines County, New Jersey
Sons of American Revolution
Married Elizabeth Maxwell

# Photographs

McIlroy School in McIlroy Community; 1817; probably the first school in Arkansas; made about 1870

Early Randolph County School; "Five Mile Spring School;" about 1895; I.V. and Essie McIlroy and Herma Lewis in center

Home of William Martin Lewis and Martha Lewis; Five Mile Spring; Randolph County, Arkansas; about 1880

Home of Samuel Benjamin McIlroy and Amanda Lewis McIlroy; Five Mile Spring (Current picture); built before 1900-logs have been covered

Home of Samuel Benjamin and Amanda in Texas after they moved to Texas; Hill
County, Texas; Five Mile Spring
Pictured are Sam, Amanda, S.B., Lewis, Dallas, Essie, I.V., his wife, and their baby;
baby's name Emma Dee-1906

Home of S.B. McIlroy and Linna Hooker; Hill County, Texas; Vaughn Community;
about 1940

Home of James Roland McIlroy and Virginia McIlroy from 1957 to present; Celina, Texas

Hammet McIlroy; Randolph County, Arkansas; about 1880

William Martin Lewis and 4th Wife Martha Lewis; about 1880

Samuel Benjamin McIlroy; about 1890; Randolph County, Arkansas

Sherman Douglas McIlroy; Raised in Hood County, Texas; about 1935

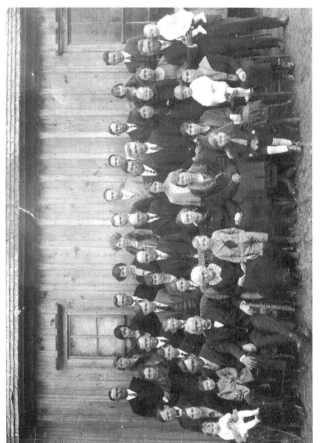

John Carson Hooker and Odelia Hooker's 50th Wedding Anniversary

Back Row: Jack Grant, Hazel Grant, Thelma Hooker, Hooper Sanders, Flonnie Sanders, Lucille Sanders, J.D. Sanders, Harold Hooker, William Hooker, Alex Hooker, Linna Hooker McIlroy, S.B. McIlroy; 2nd Row from Top: Bessie Hooker, Will Hooker, James Johnson, Lorena Johnson, Cooper Johnson, Tom Sanders, Fred Bilby, Neal Crowell, Edna Hooker holding son Raymond, Irmine Hooker, James Otis Hooker holding grandson James Roland McIlroy; 3rd Row From Top: Ralph Hooker, Cliette Hooker, John Hugh Hooker, Leonard Hooker, Marguerite Hooker; Bottom row: Goldie Hooke holding daughter Bernice, Roy Hooker holding daughter Mozelle, John Carson Hooker, Adelia Anderson Hooker, Lewis Hooker, Francis Bilby, Edna Sanders, Garland Crowell, Gladys Crowell, Francis Preston, Sadie Preston

Ellis County Family Reunion

Back Row: Carl West holding James Ray, Myrtle West, 2nd to Back Row: Blanch McElroy holding Kathryn McElroy, Ollie Jones holding Lois, Dee McElroy, Sam Jones, Buck McElroy, Bessie holding Lorene, Agness McElroy, G.P. McElroy, Ruby McElroy, Beryr McElroy, Dover McElroy holding Alyne, Bernice, Gaighter Williams McElroy, Orville McElroy, Eura McLain, George McLain, 3rd to Back Row: Jeff McElroy, Minerva McElroy, J.C. Gililands, Mattie Gilleland, George Gilleland, Grandma Rogers, Grandpa G.W. Rogers, Front Row: Garland McElroy, Vernon Jones, Raymond McElroy, Odell Jones, J.B. McElroy, Cecil McElroy, Otis Earl McElroy

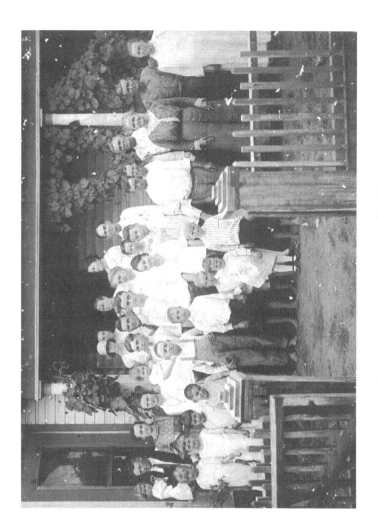

The Lewises, Hill County, Texas, 1919, probably after the funeral of Martha

At far right are Philip and Ella, his wife next to Philip is Amanda McIlroy; behind her are other brothers Philip and Perry; 2nd to Amanda's right is S.B. McIlroy and to his right is Hazel Lewis

978-0-595-46736-5
0-595-46736-9

5350411R0

Made in the USA
Lexington, KY
29 April 2010